DAYDREAMS WALKING

JEREMIAH DINE

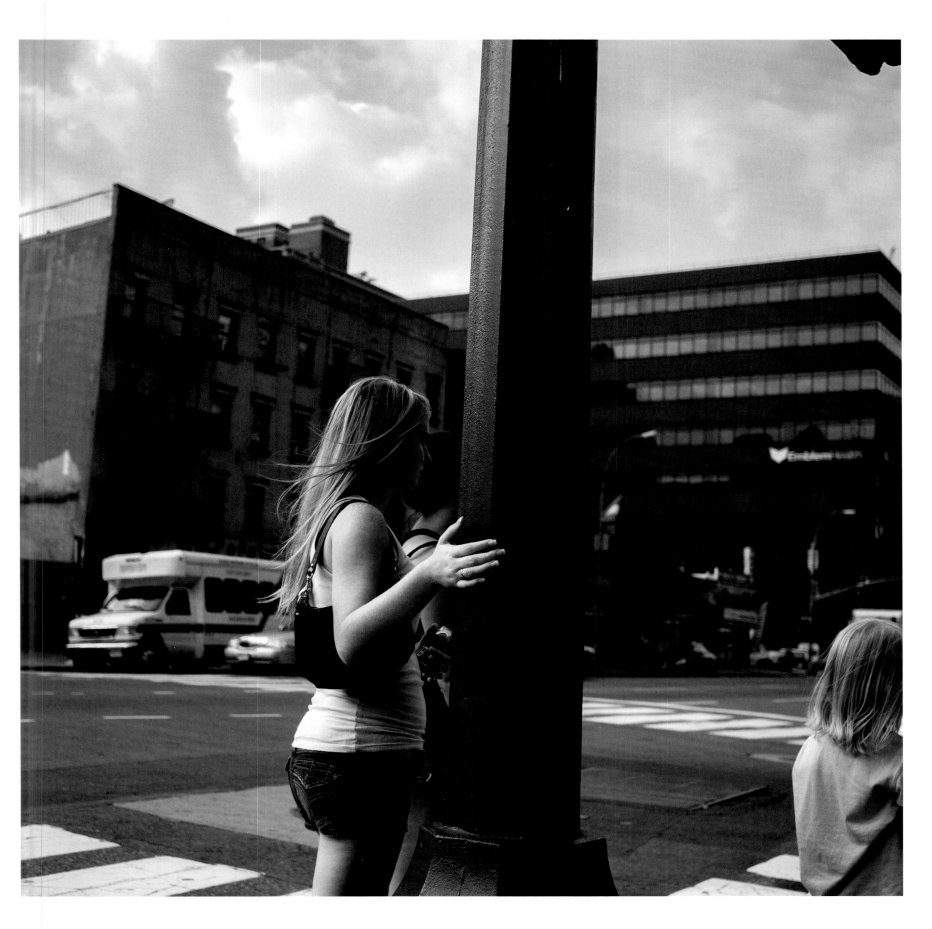

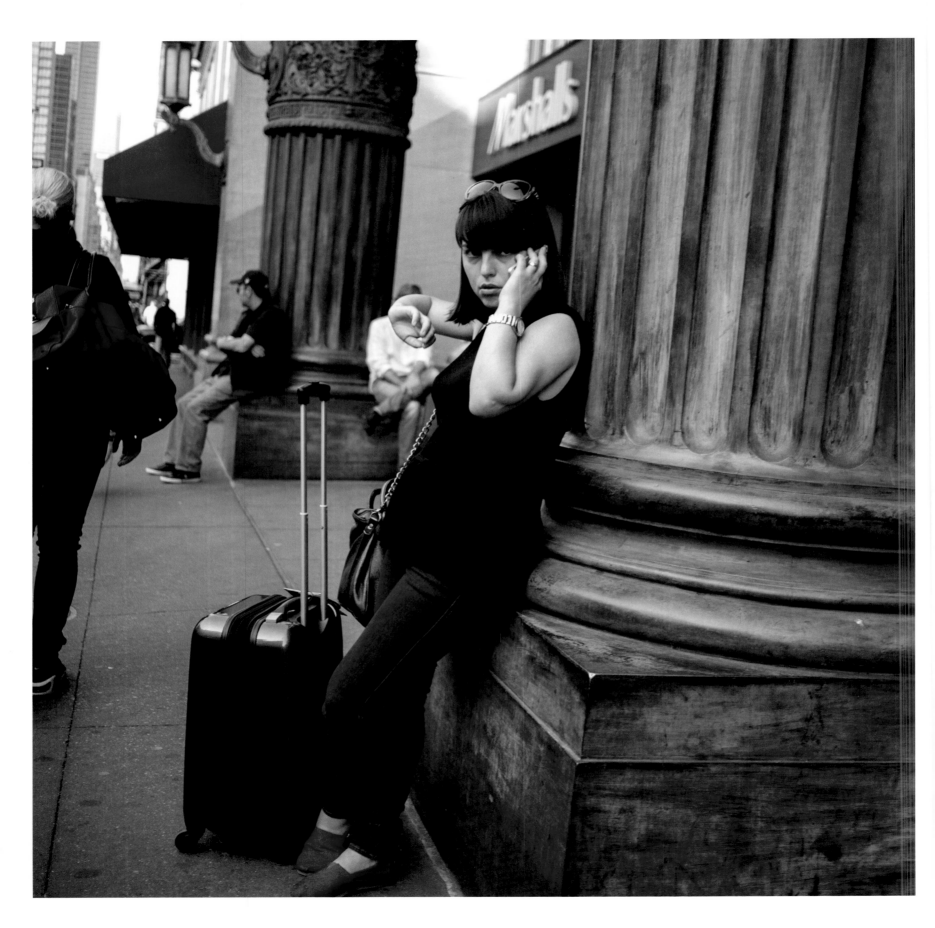

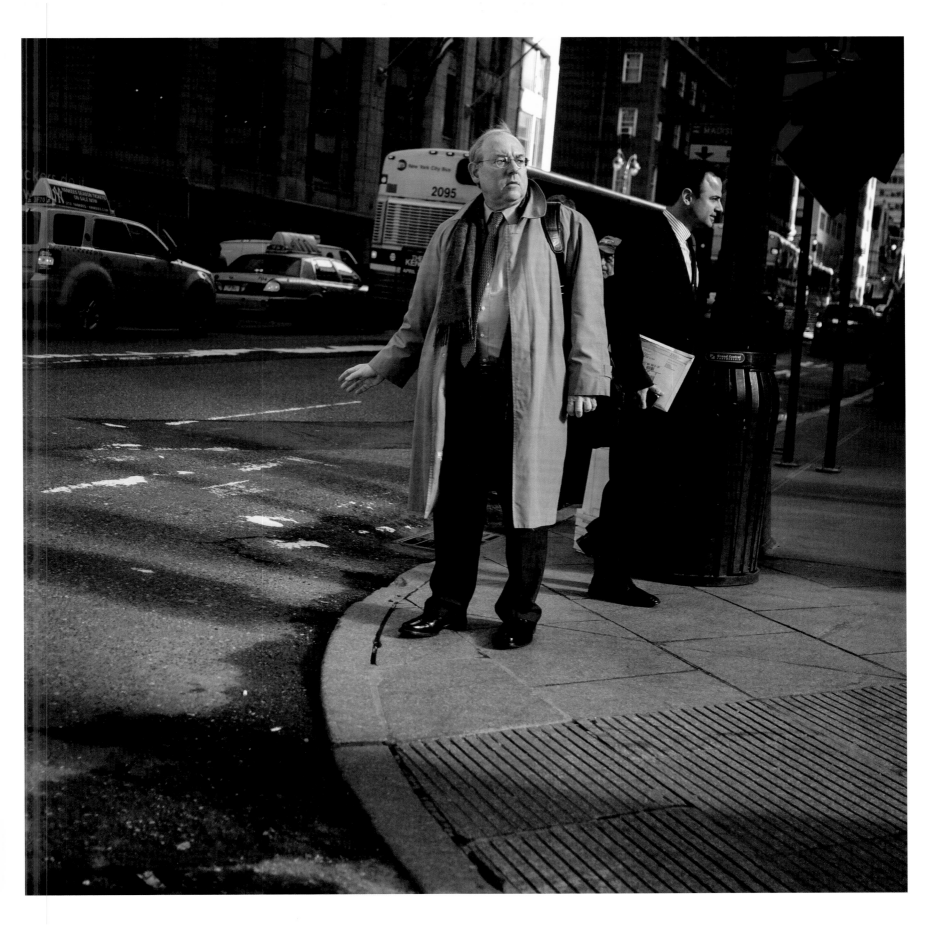

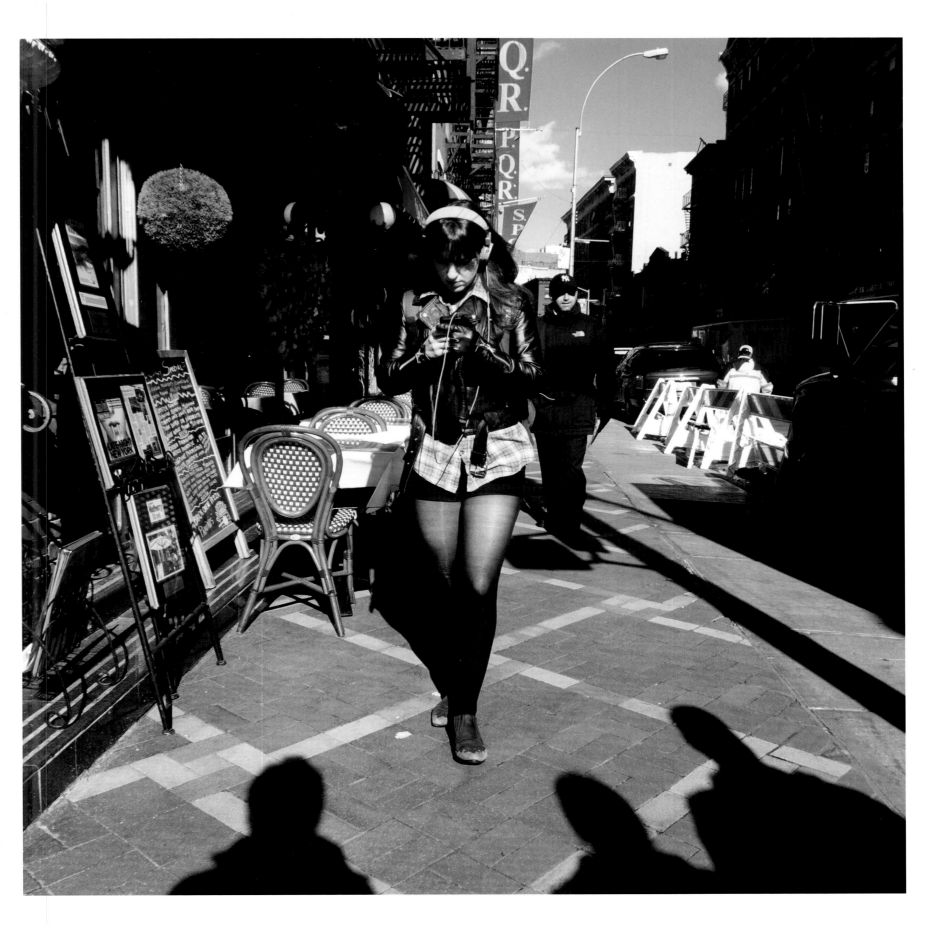

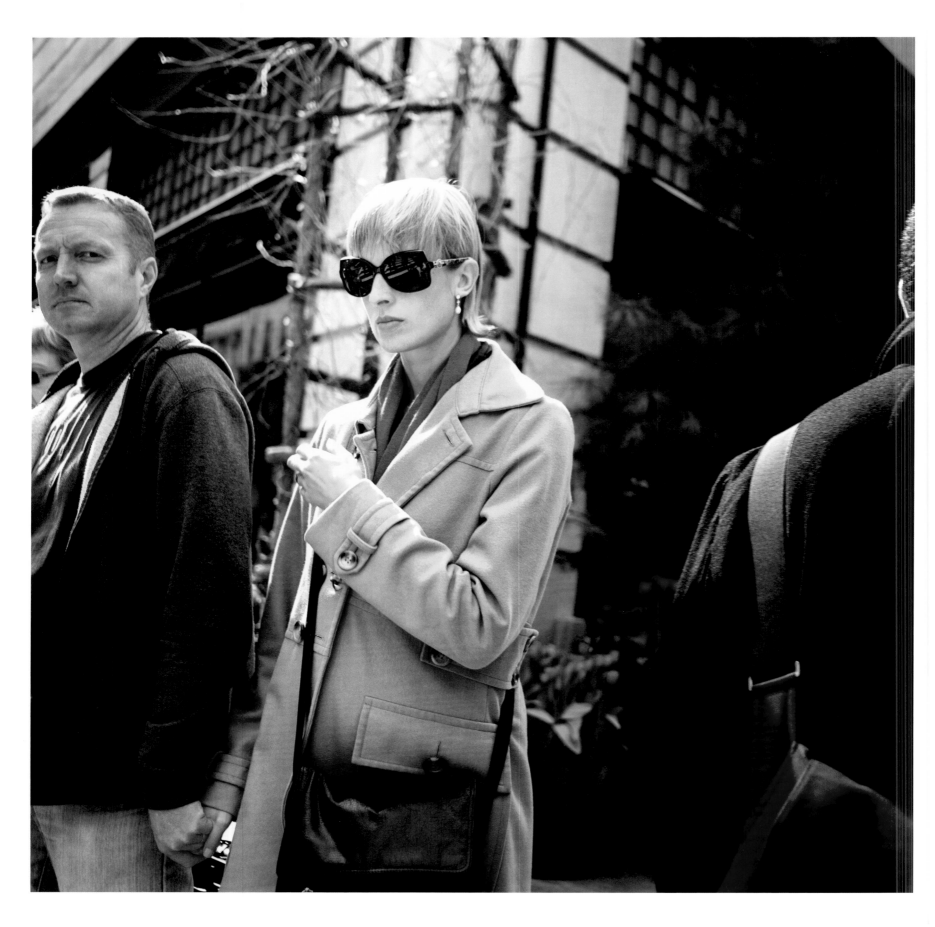

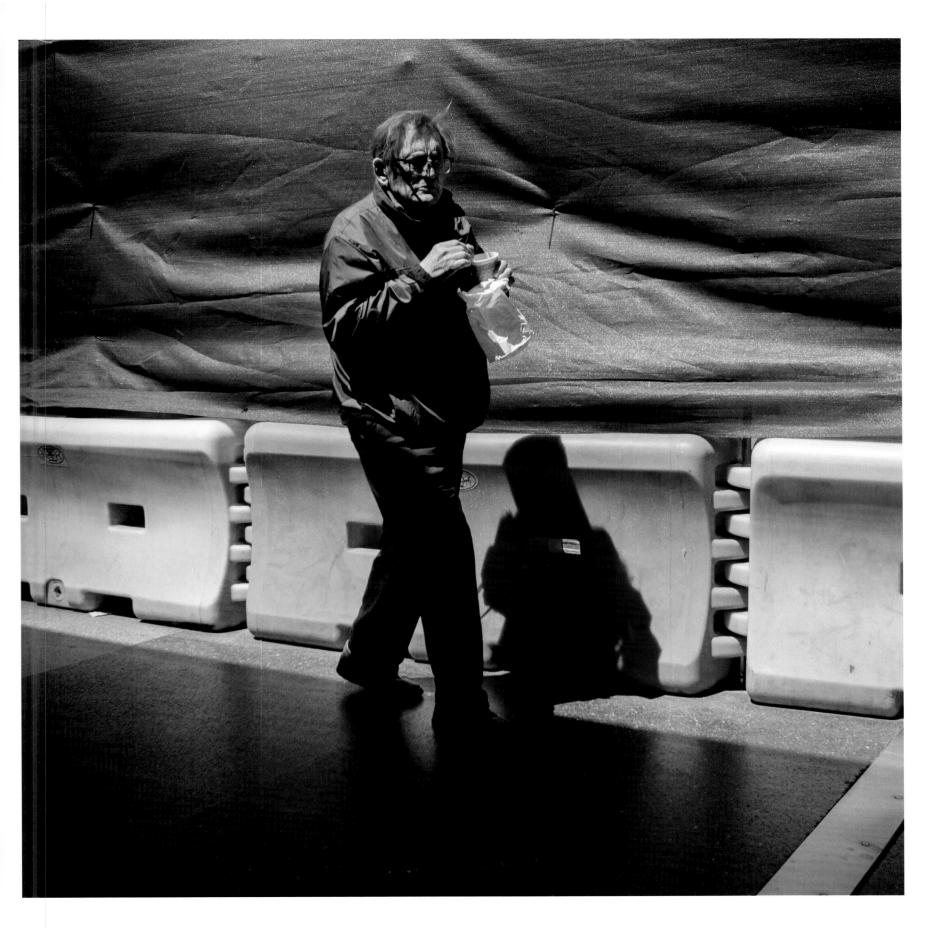

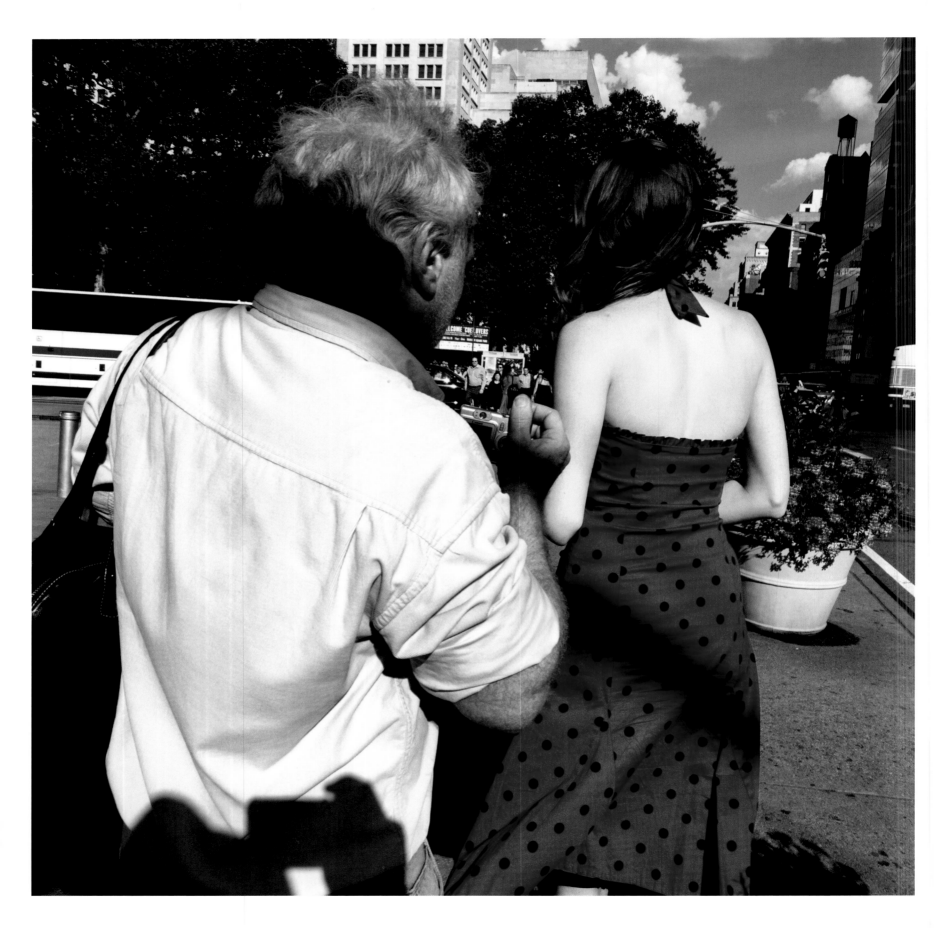

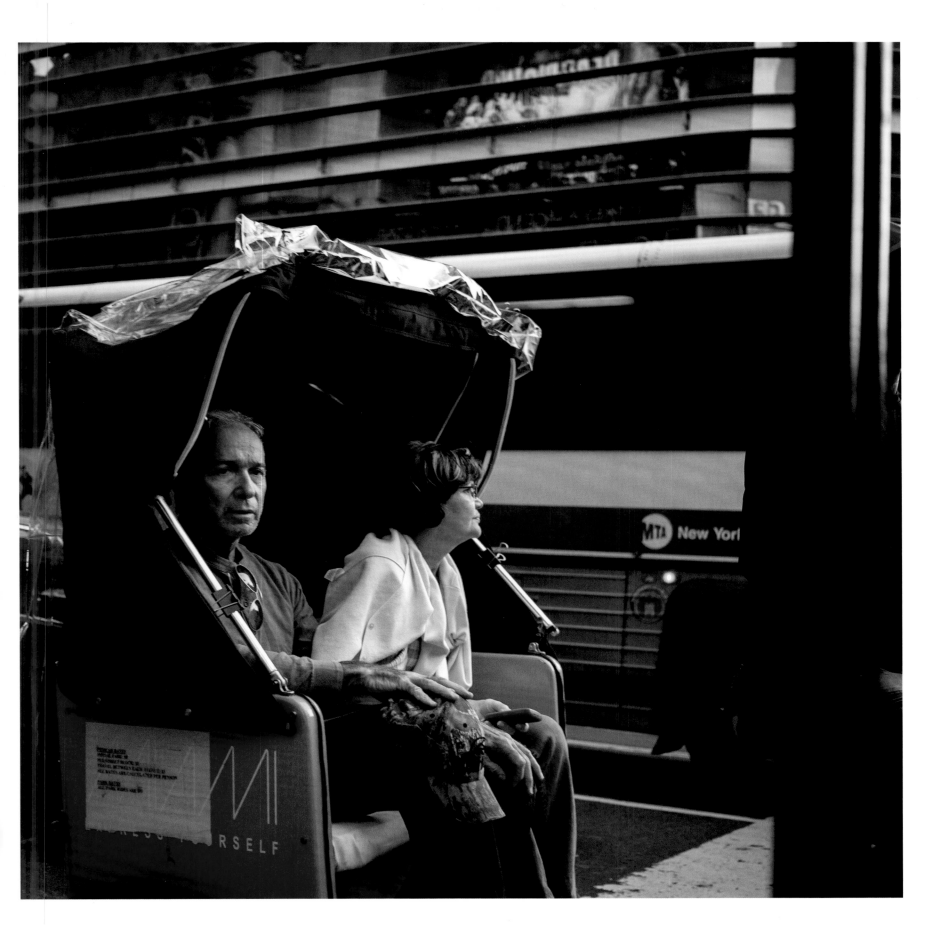

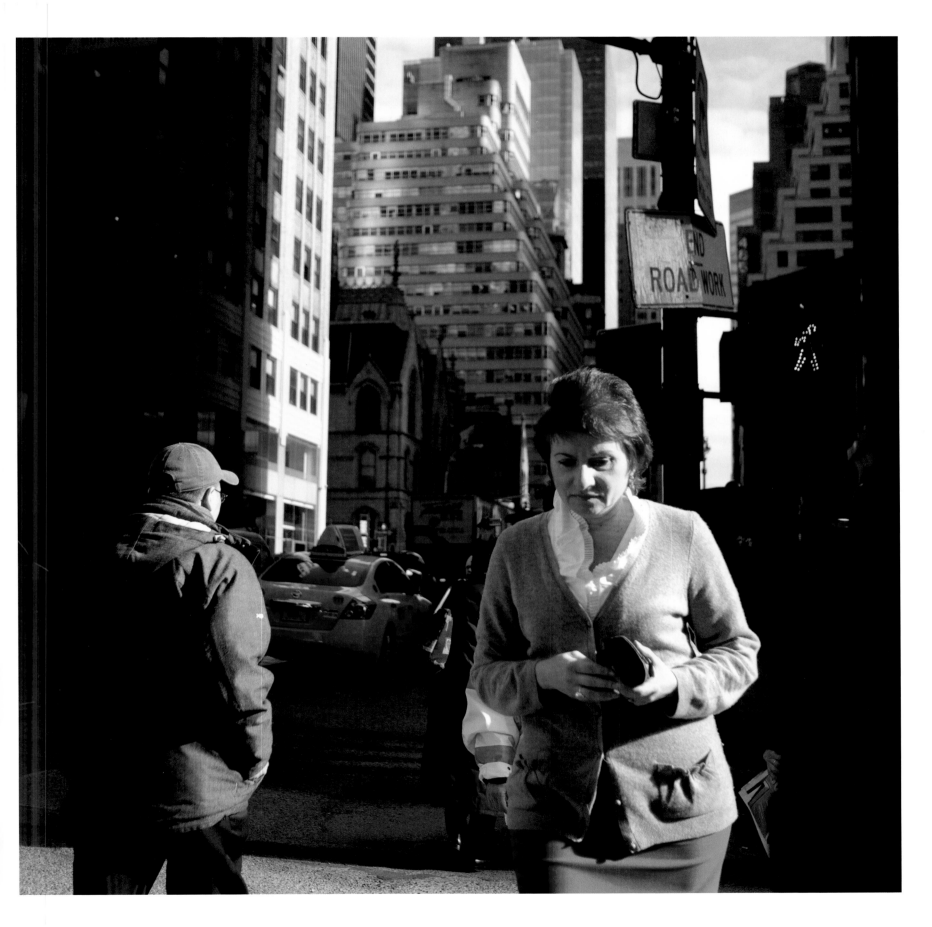

MUSIC

by Frank O'Hara, 1954

    If I rest for a moment near The Equestrian
pausing for a liver sausage sandwich in the Mayflower Shoppe,
that angel seems to be leading the horse into Bergdorf's
and I am naked as a table cloth, my nerves humming.
Close to the fear of war and the stars which have disappeared.
I have in my hands only 35¢, it's so meaningless to eat!
and gusts of water spray over the basins of leaves
like the hammers of a glass pianoforte. If I seem to you
to have lavender lips under the leaves of the world,

    I must tighten my belt.
It's like a locomotive on the march, the season

    of distress and clarity
and my door is open to the evenings of midwinter's
lightly falling snow over the newspapers.
Clasp me in your handkerchief like a tear, trumpet
of early afternoon! in the foggy autumn.
As they're putting, up the Christmas trees on Park Avenue
I shall see my daydreams walking by with dogs in blankets,
put to some use before all those coloured lights come on!

    But no more fountains and no more rain,

    and the stores stay open terribly late.

SOUNDTRACK

- "Pannonica," Thelonious Monk
- "Monkey Suit," Pernice Brothers
- "Walk on The Wild Side," Lou Reed
- "Disconnection Notice," Sonic Youth
- "See No Evil," Television
- "Ashes of American Flags," Wilco
- "Ornithology," Charlie Parker
- "Main Title," *Taxi Driver*, Bernard Herrmann
- "Knives of Summertime," Sparklehorse
- "End of the Line," Roxy Music
- "Can I Kick It?," A Tribe Called Quest
- "Everybody Is a Star," Sly & The Family Stone
- "Feel the Pain," Dinoasaur Jr.
- "The Shakes," Atlas Sound
- "Ain't That Enough," Teenage Fanclub
- "You Can Have It All," Yo La Tengo
- "There is a Balm in Gilead," Archie Shepp and Jeanne Lee

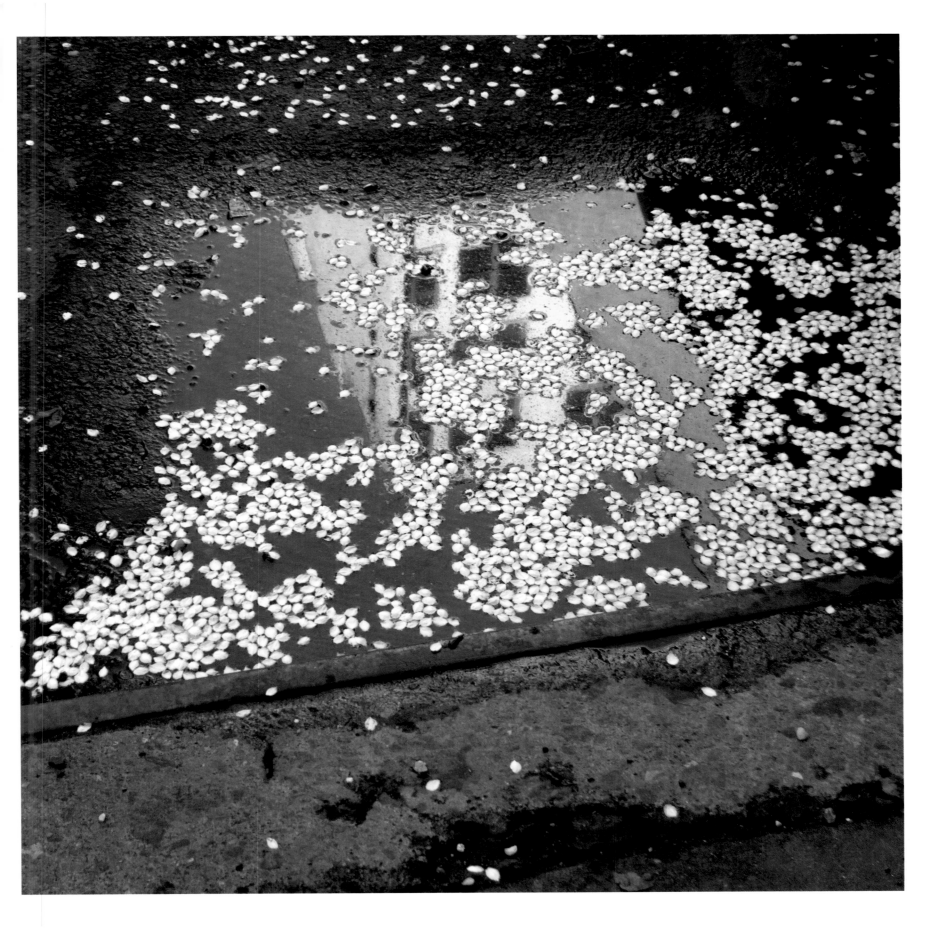

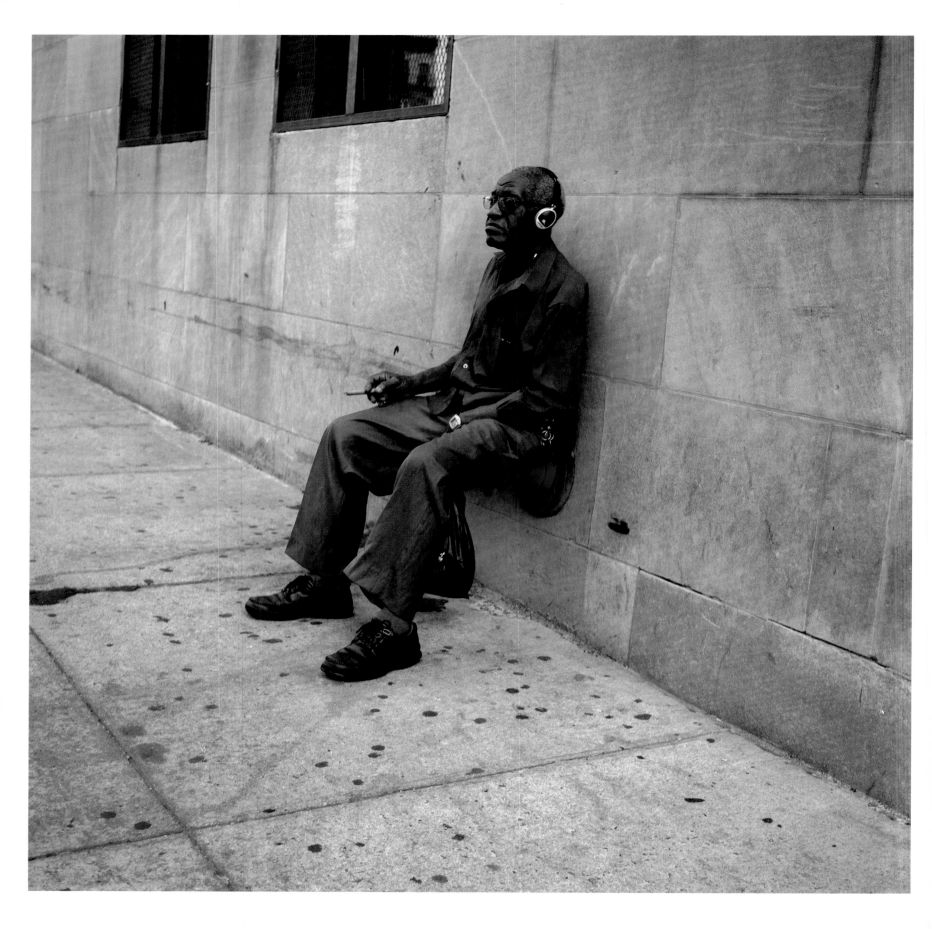

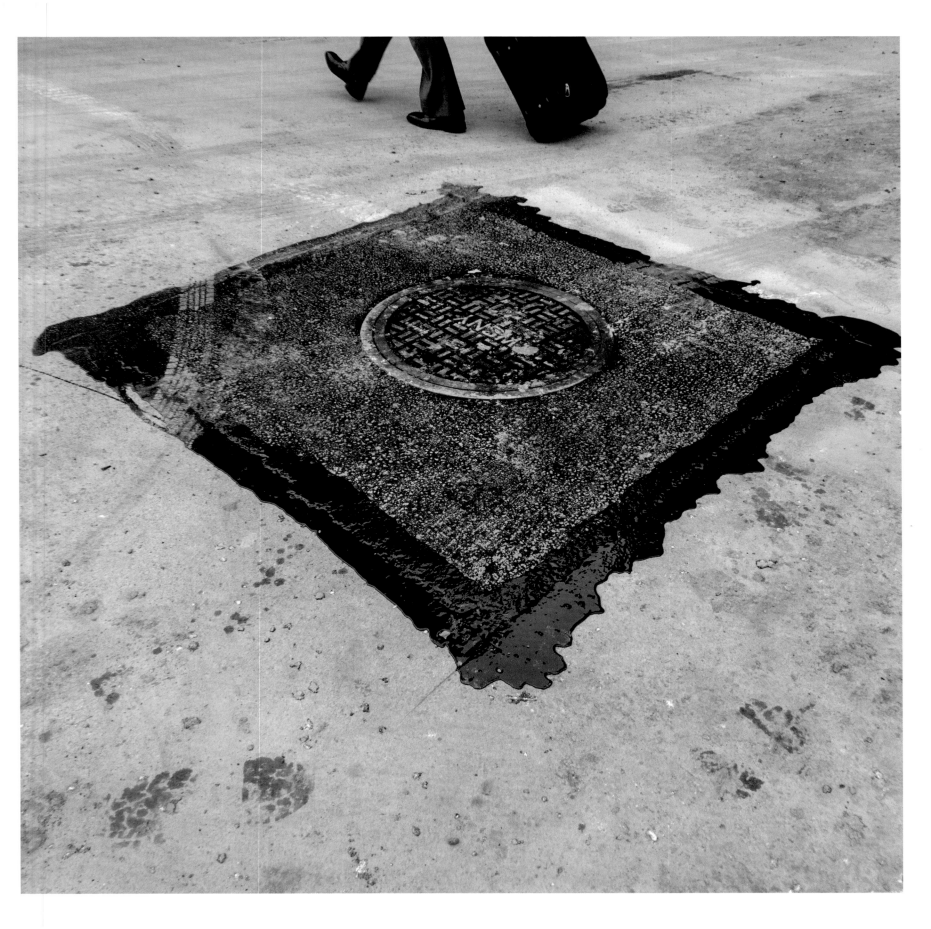

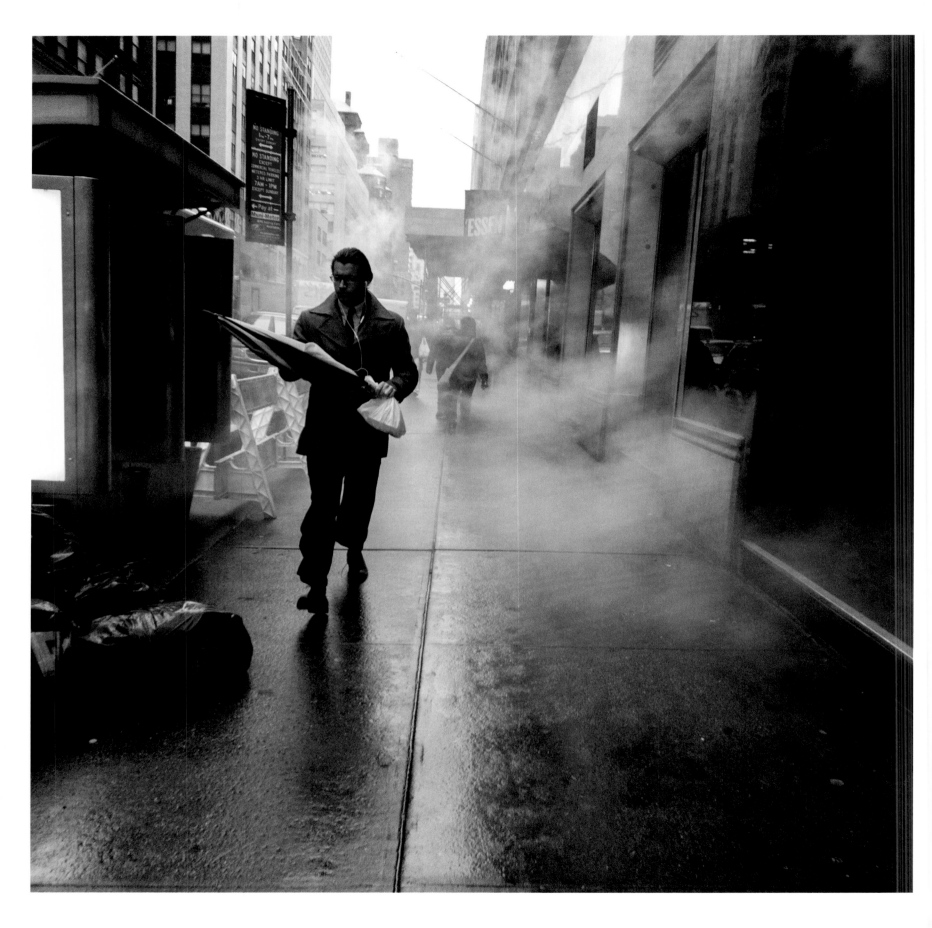

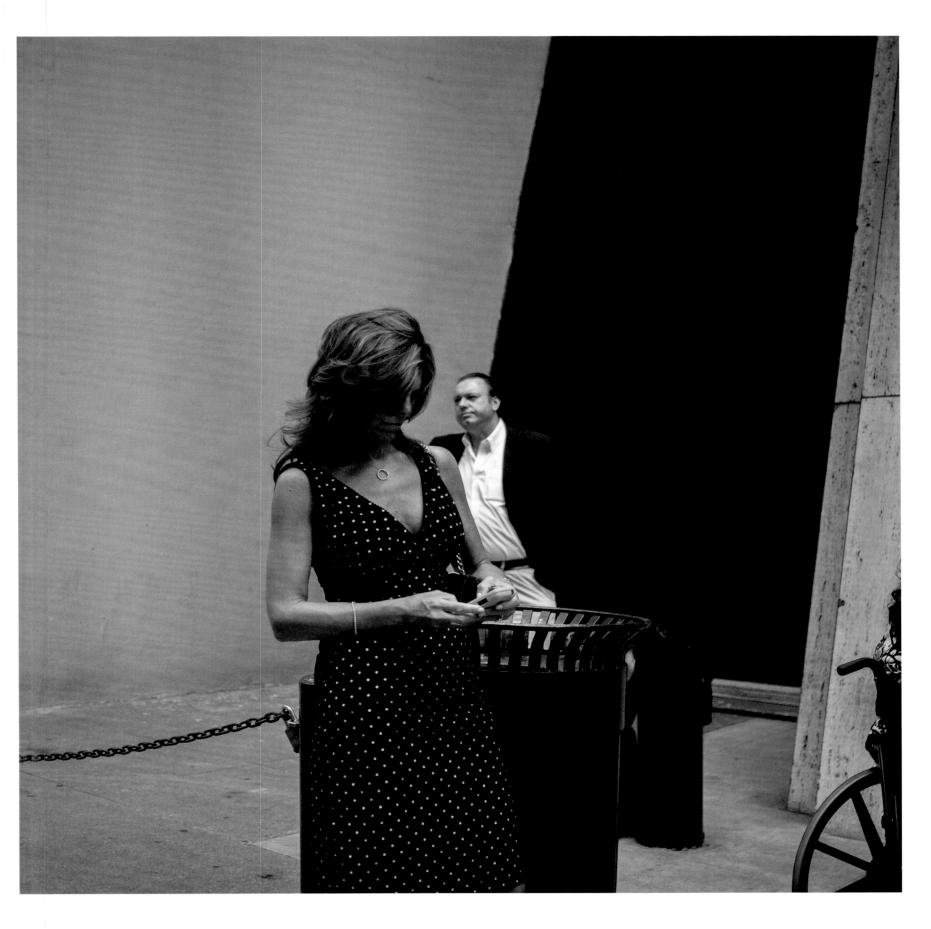

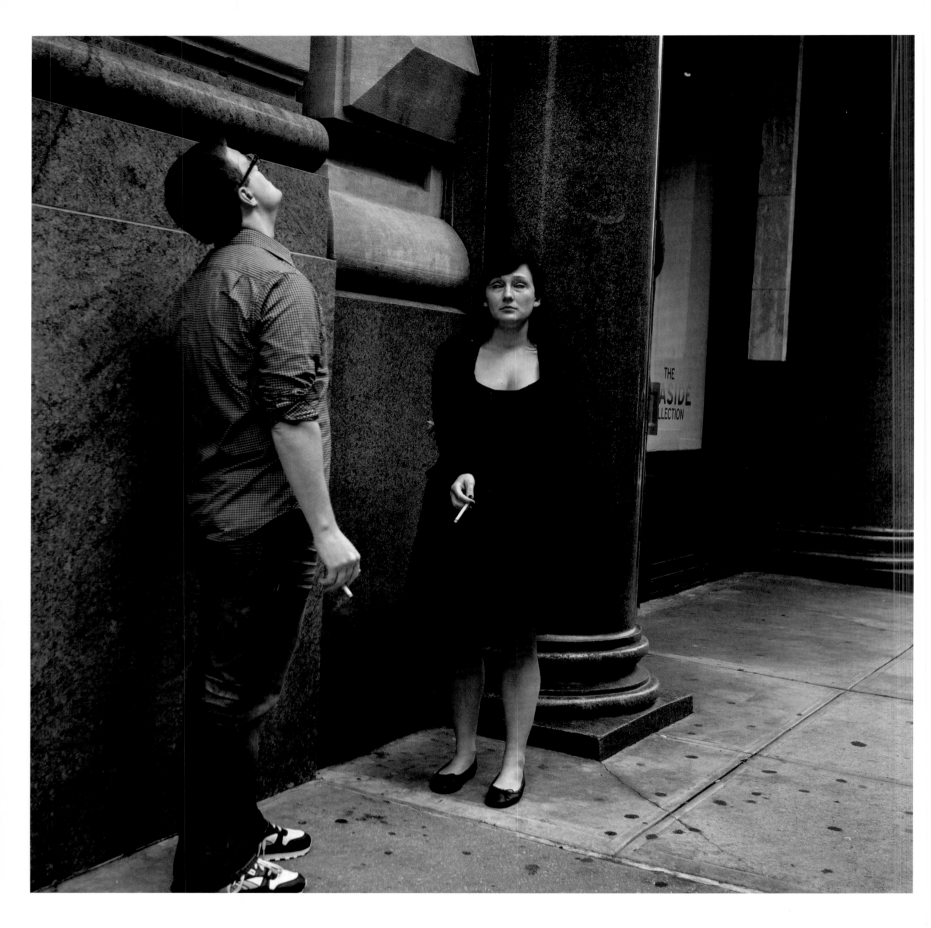

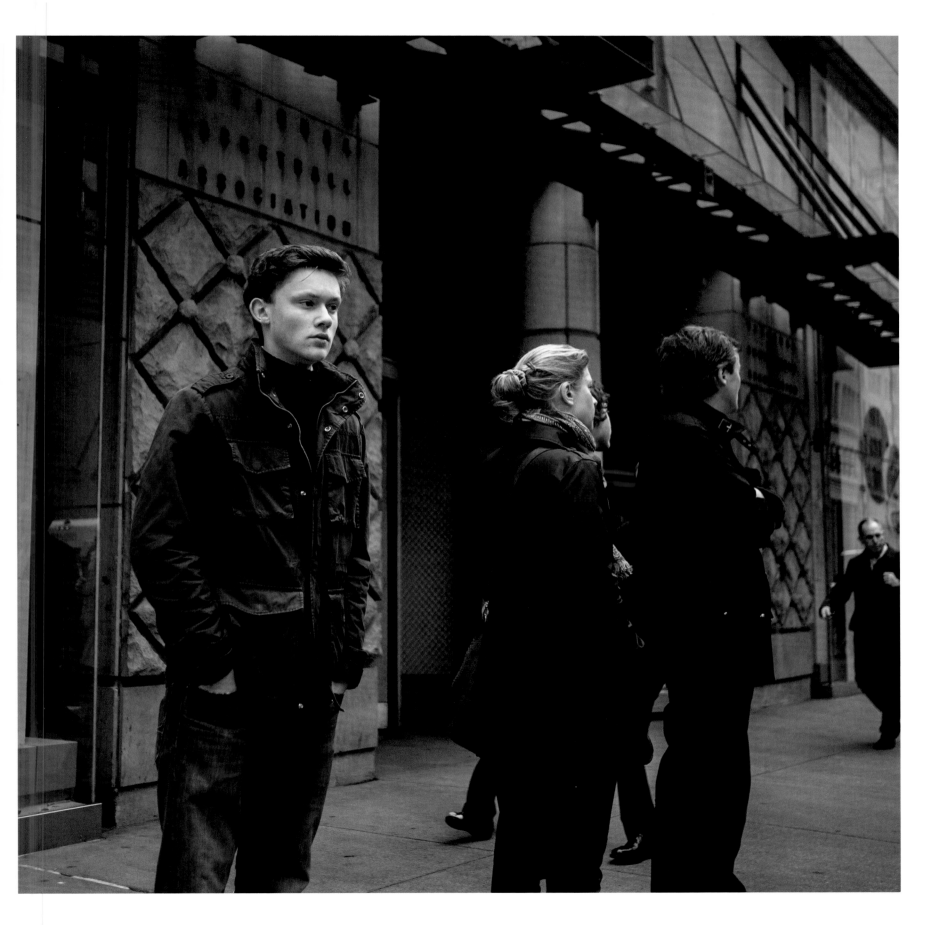

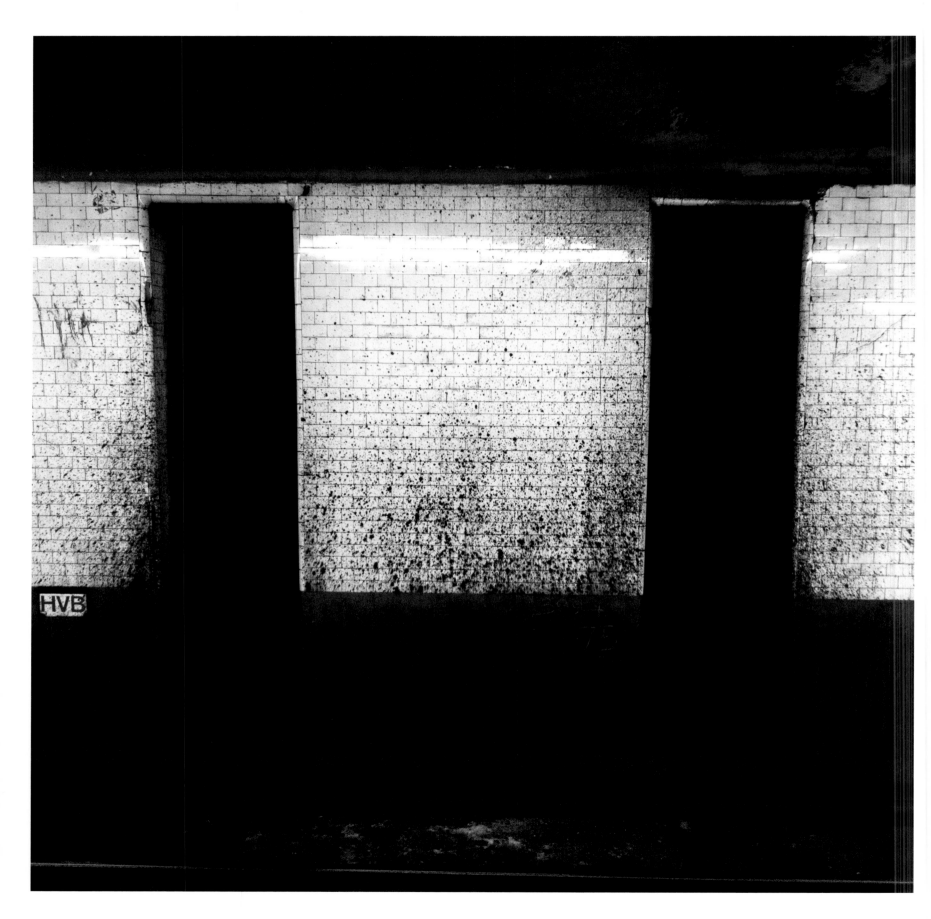

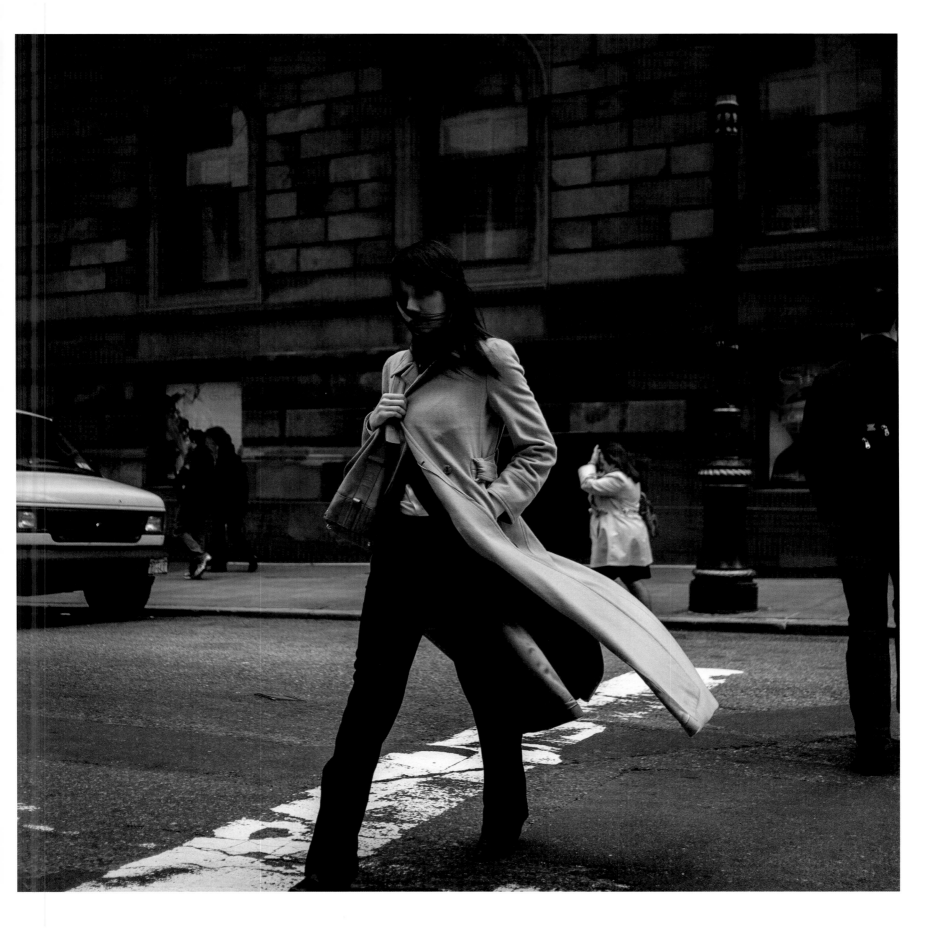

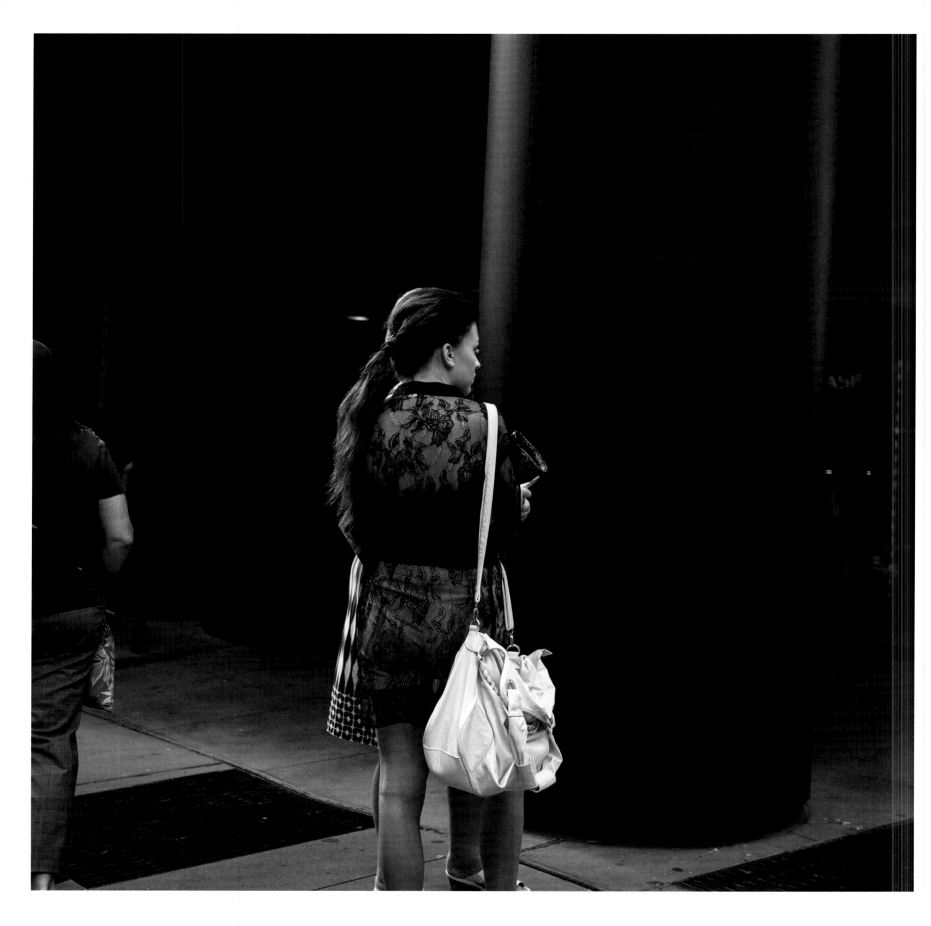

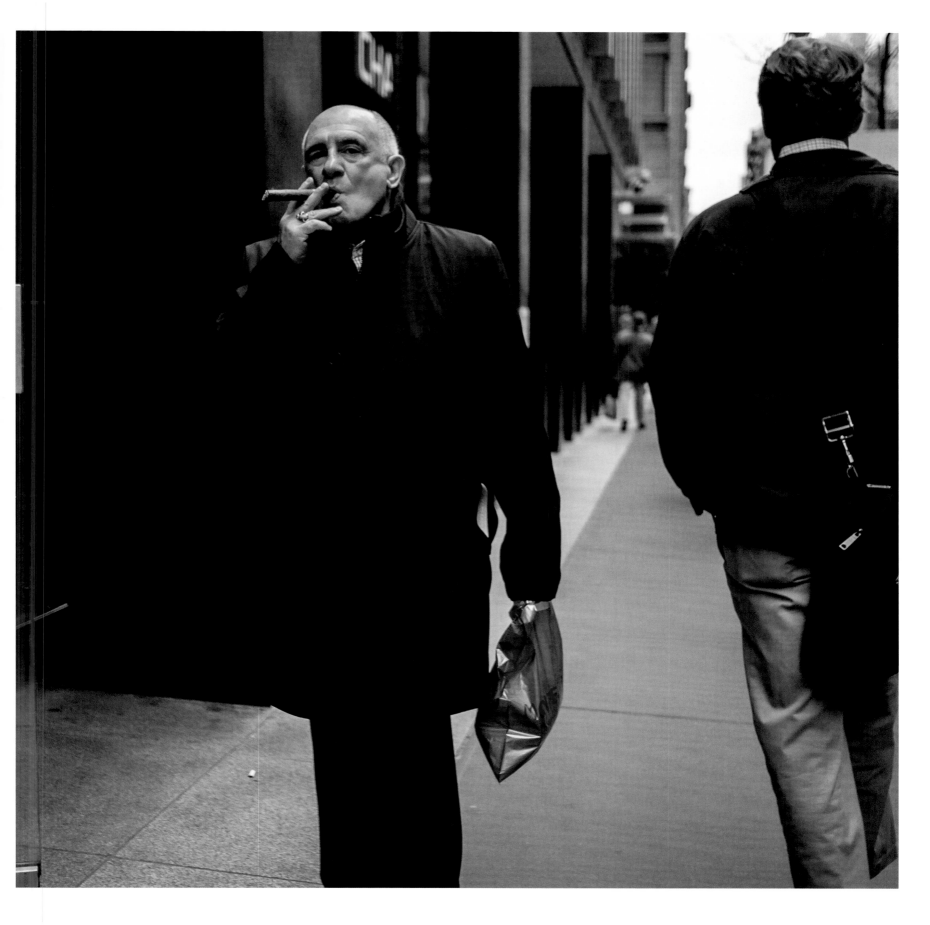

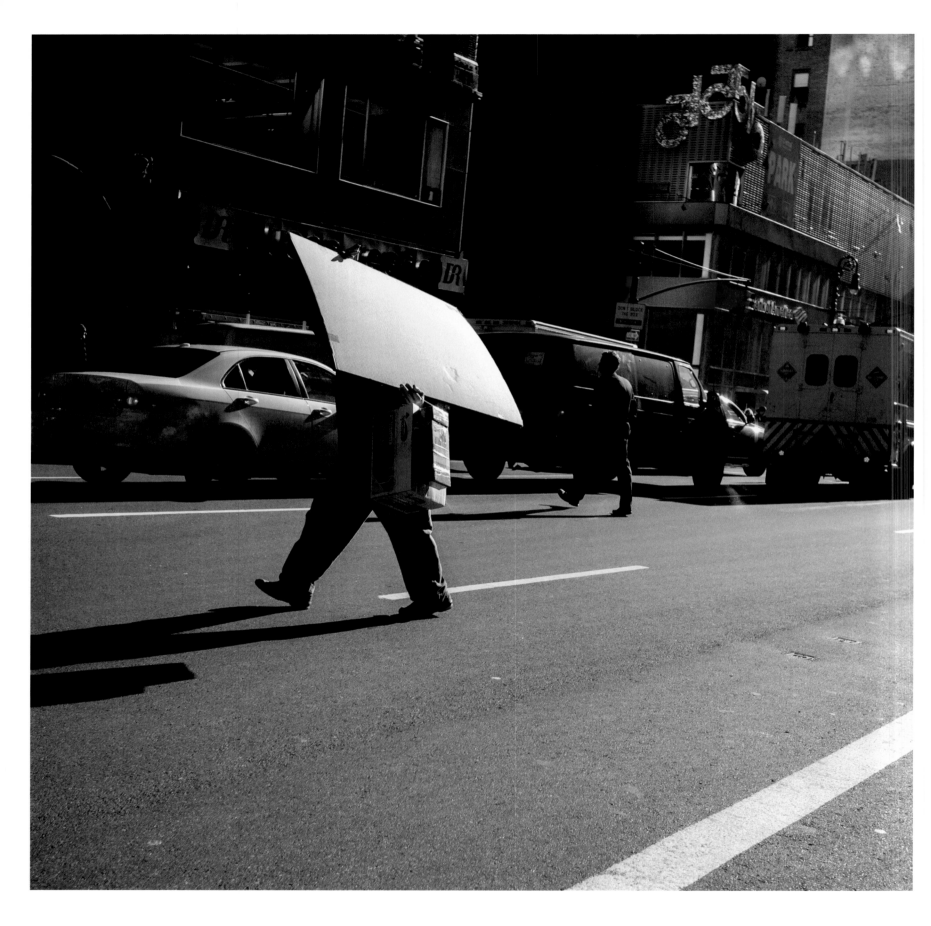

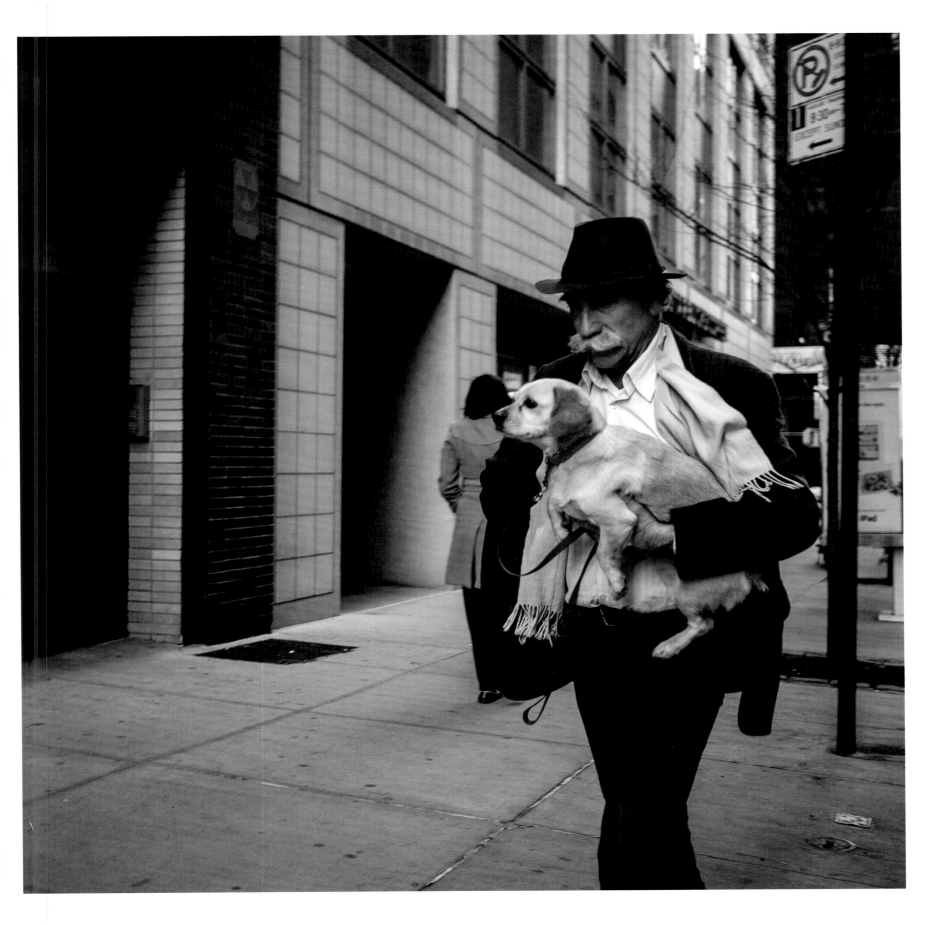

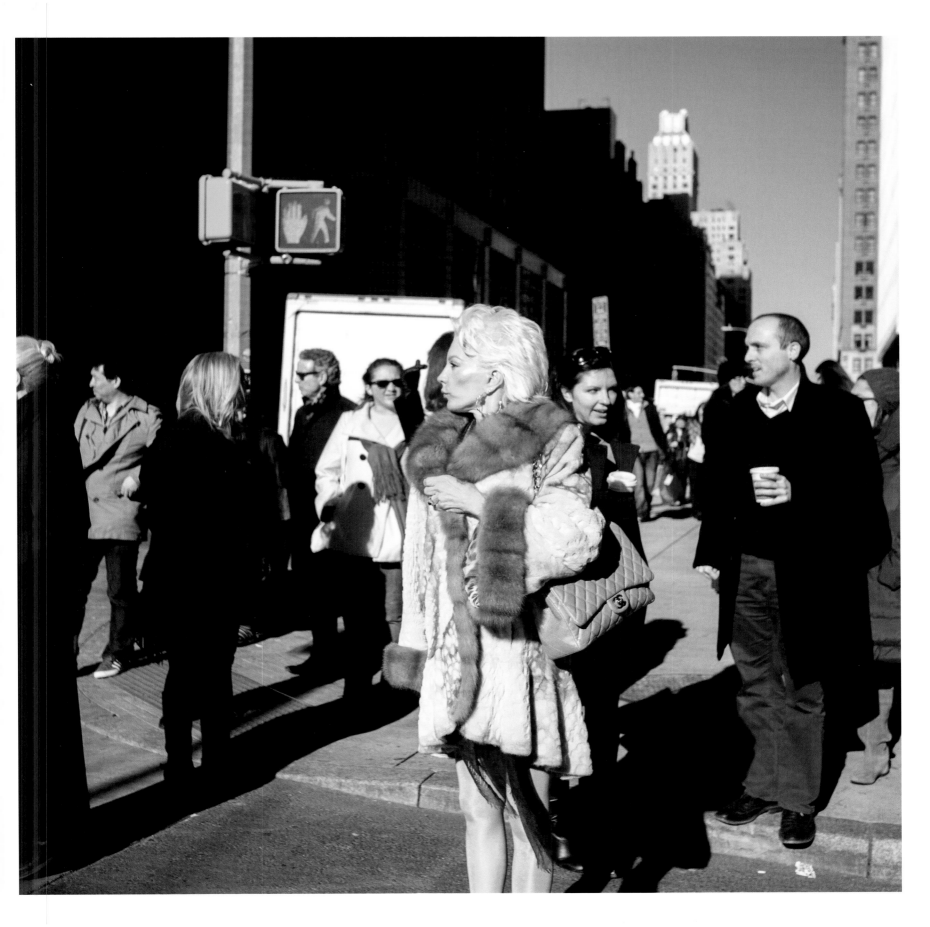

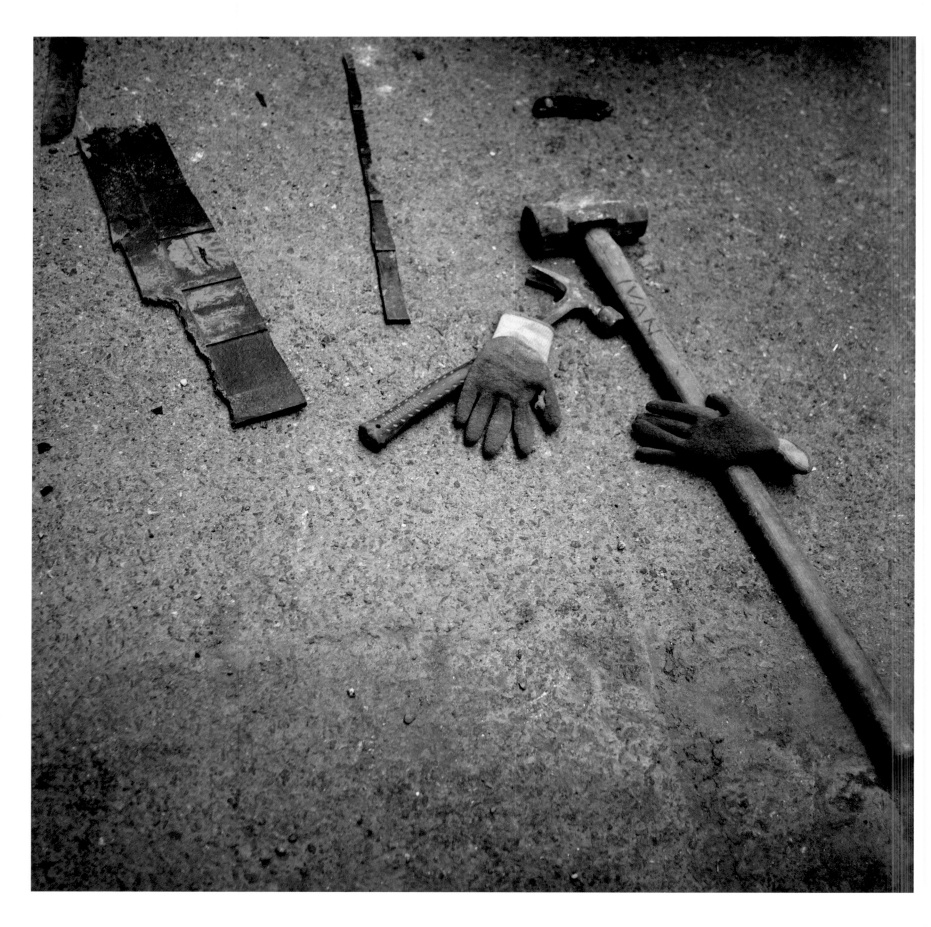

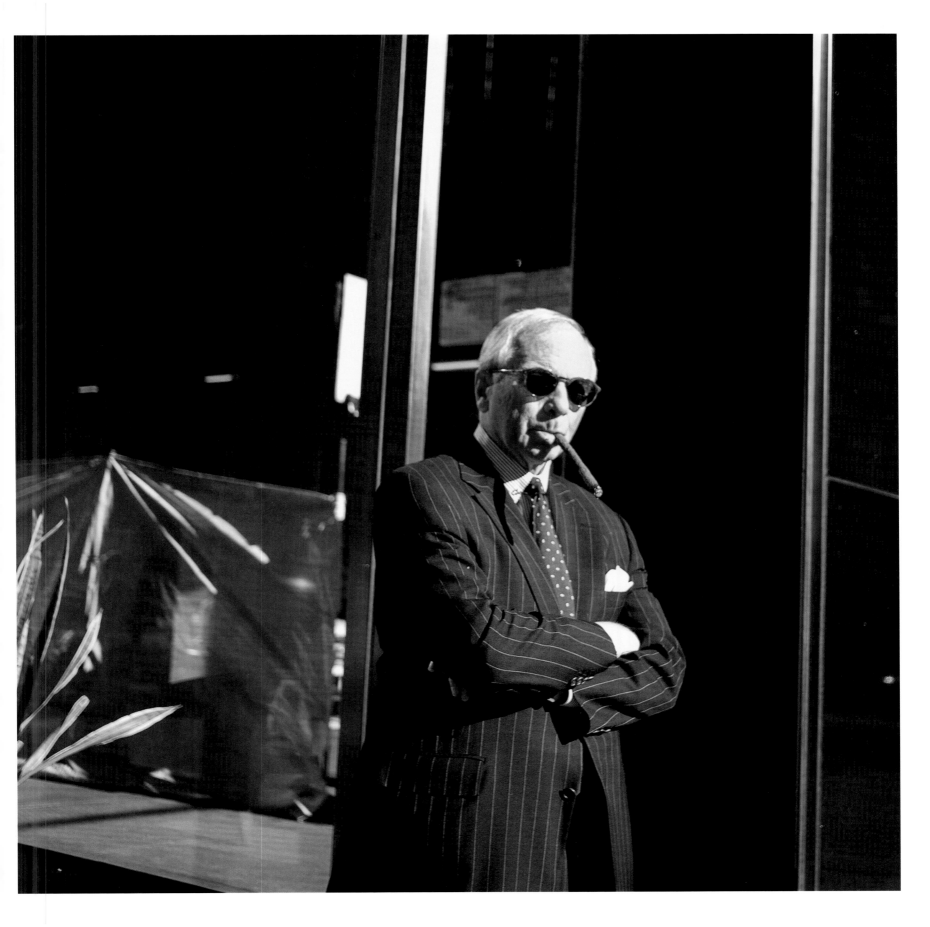

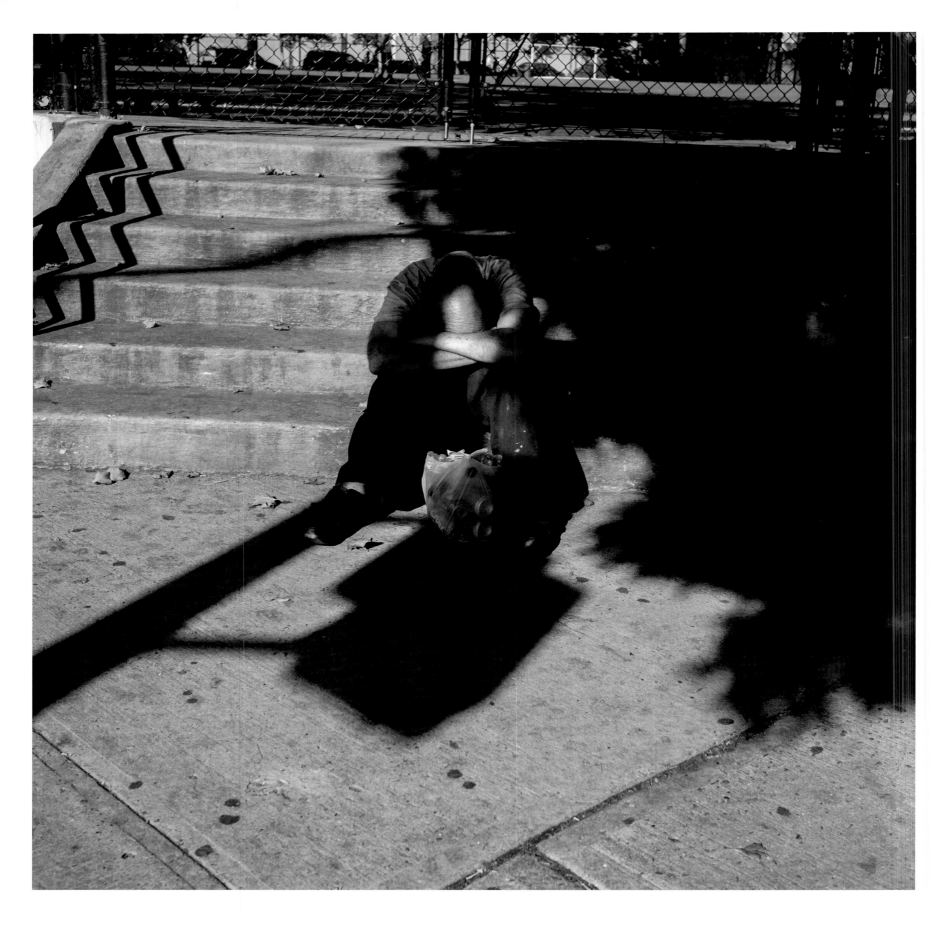

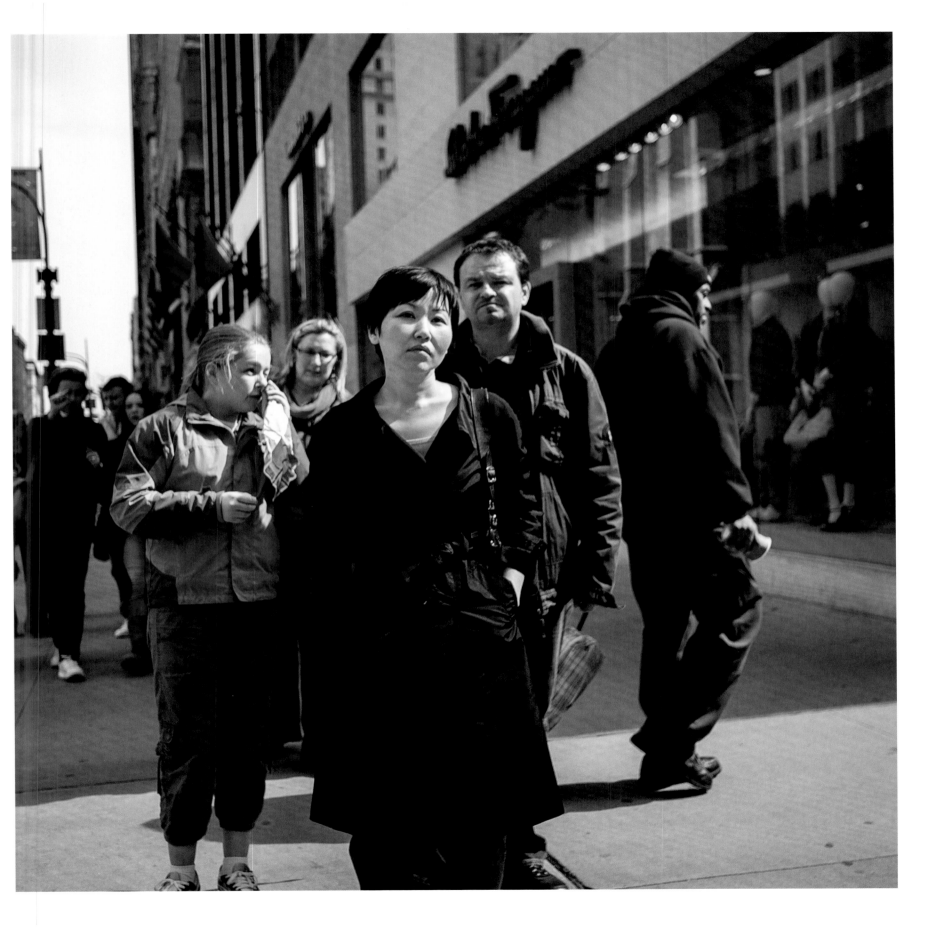

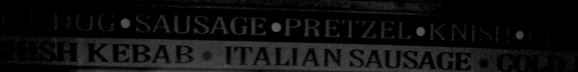

HOT DOG • SAUSAGE • PRETZEL • KNISH •
SHISH KEBAB • ITALIAN SAUSAGE • COLD DRINKS

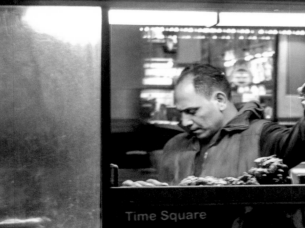

Time Square

HOT DO
BEEF OR CHICKEN
PRETZEL
SAUSGE
KNISH

Time Square

HONEY
ROASTED
CHESTNUTS

Time Square

Time Square

HOT DOG
PRETZEL
SAUSGE
KNISH

BEEF OR CHICKEN

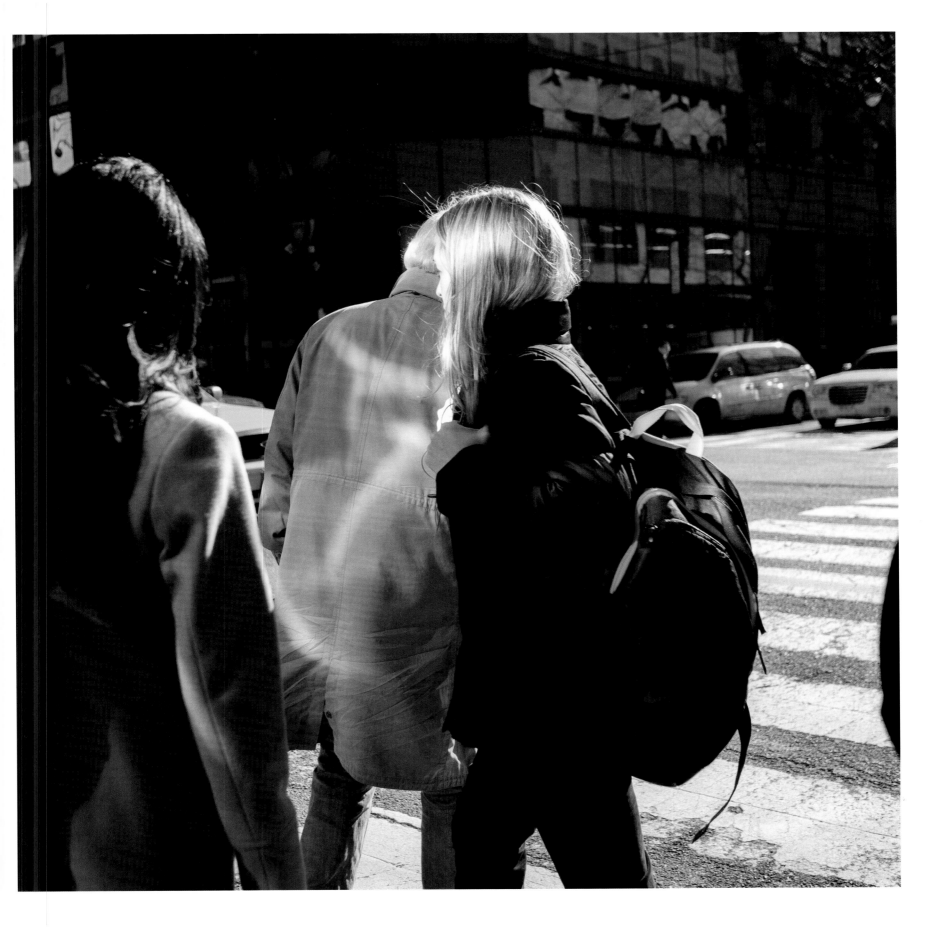

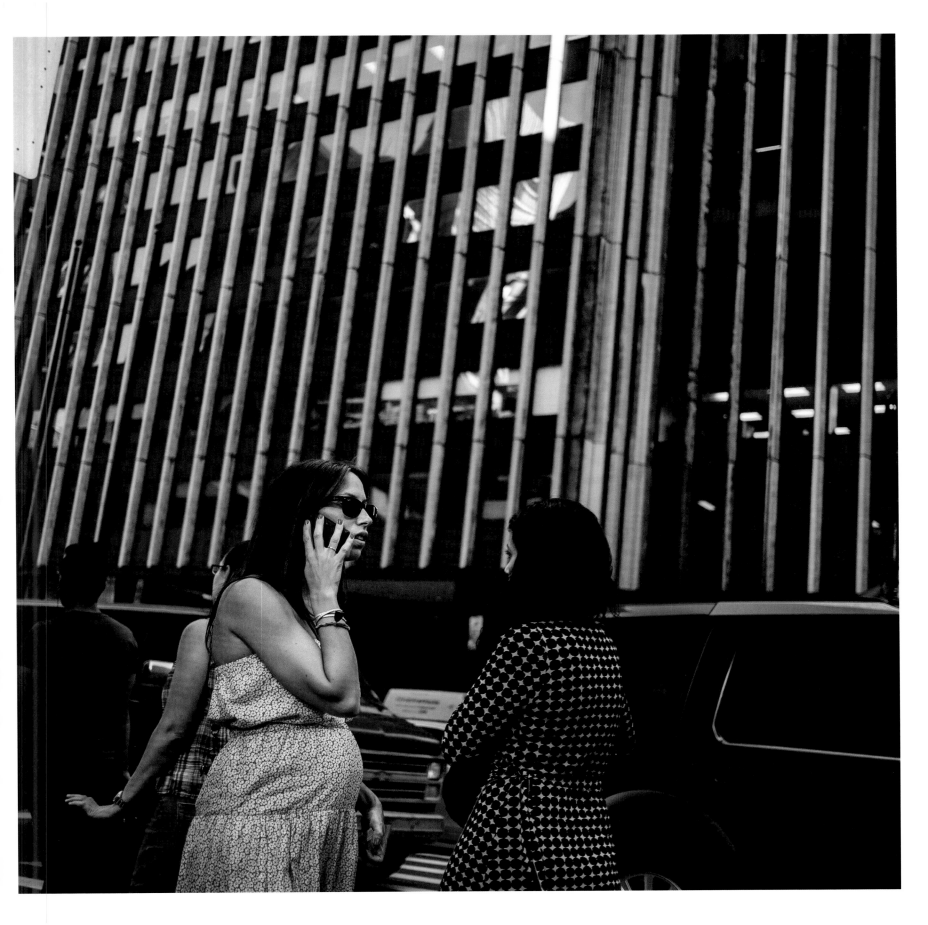

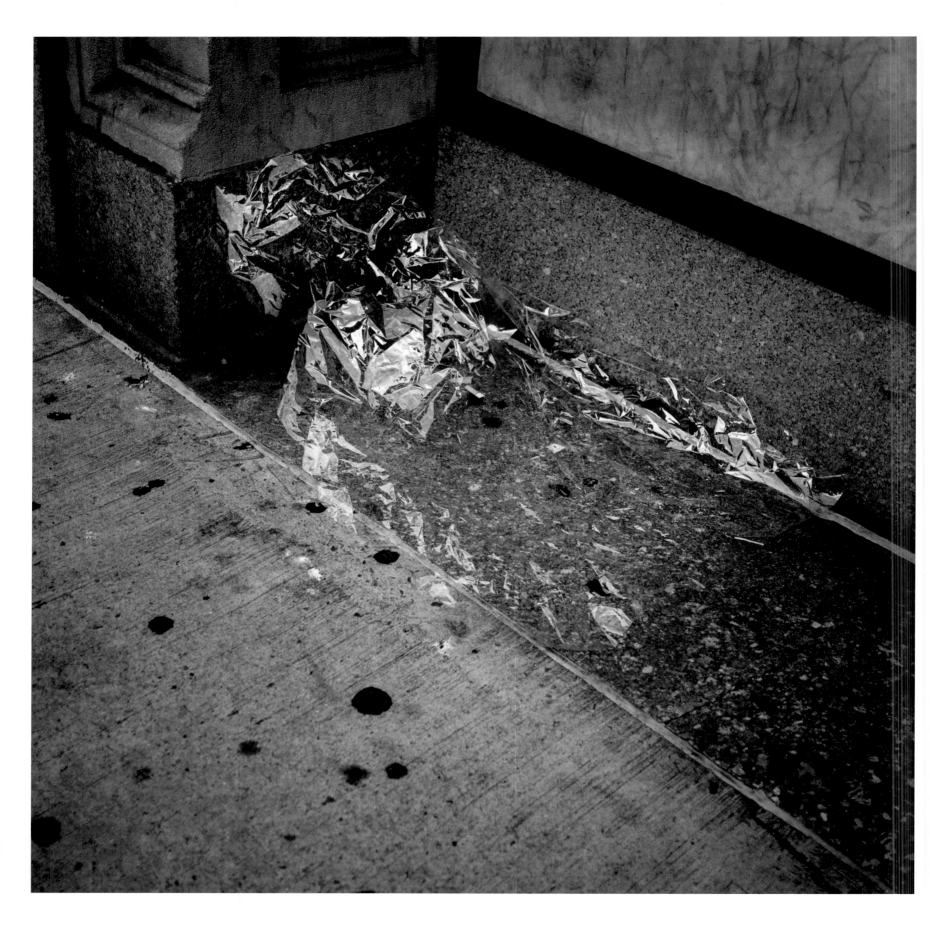

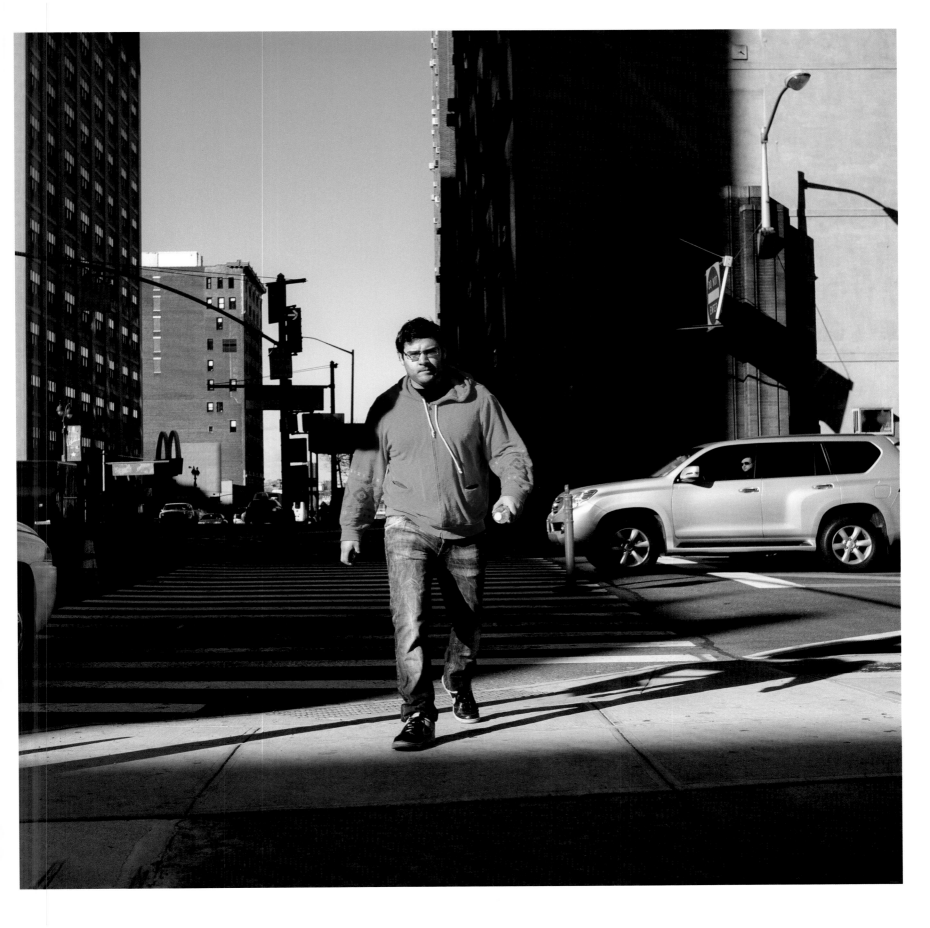

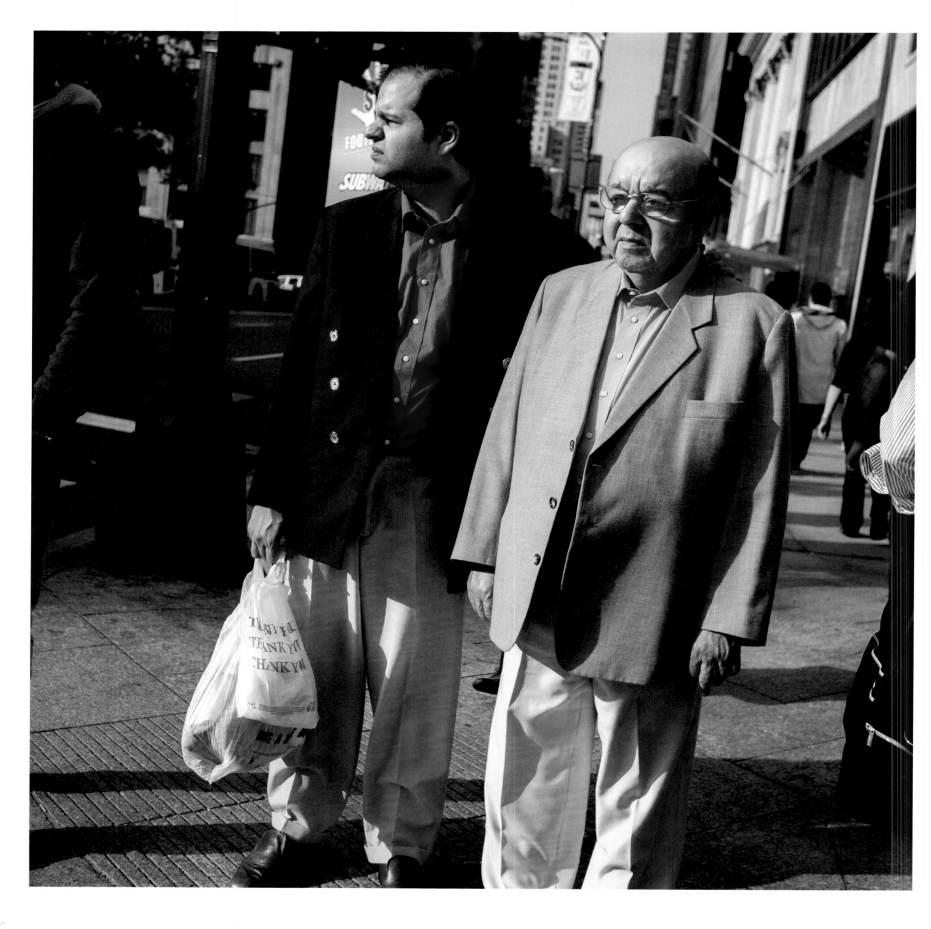

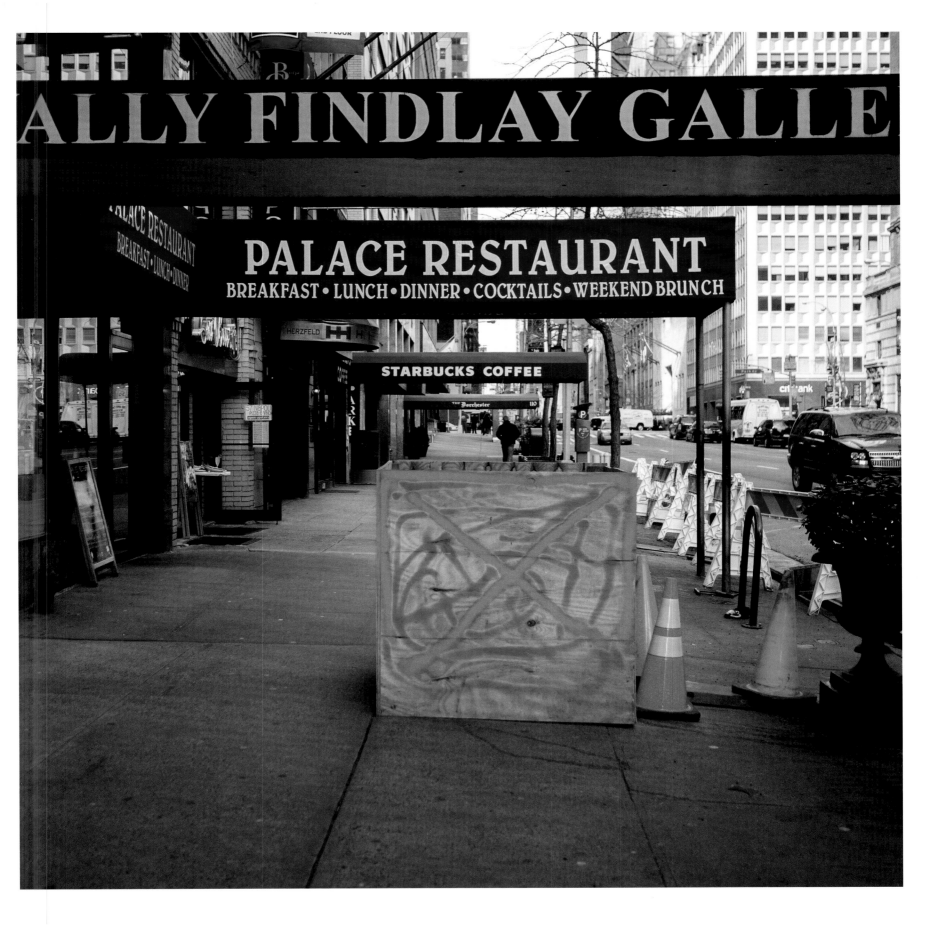

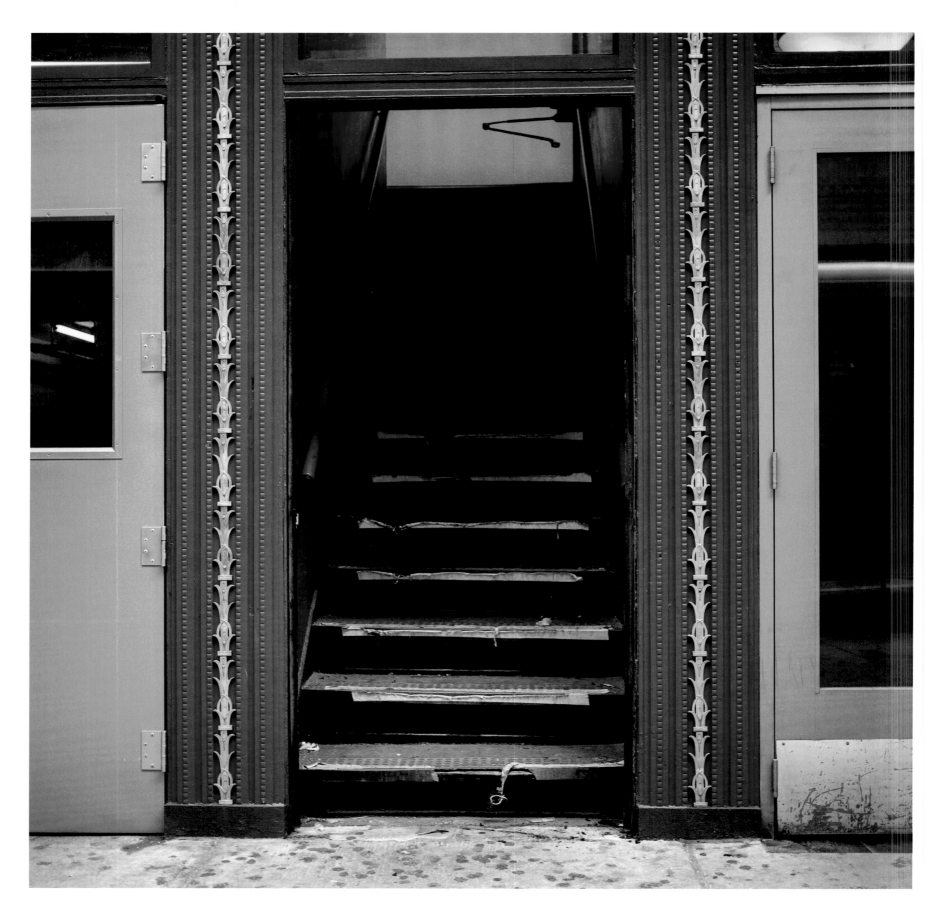

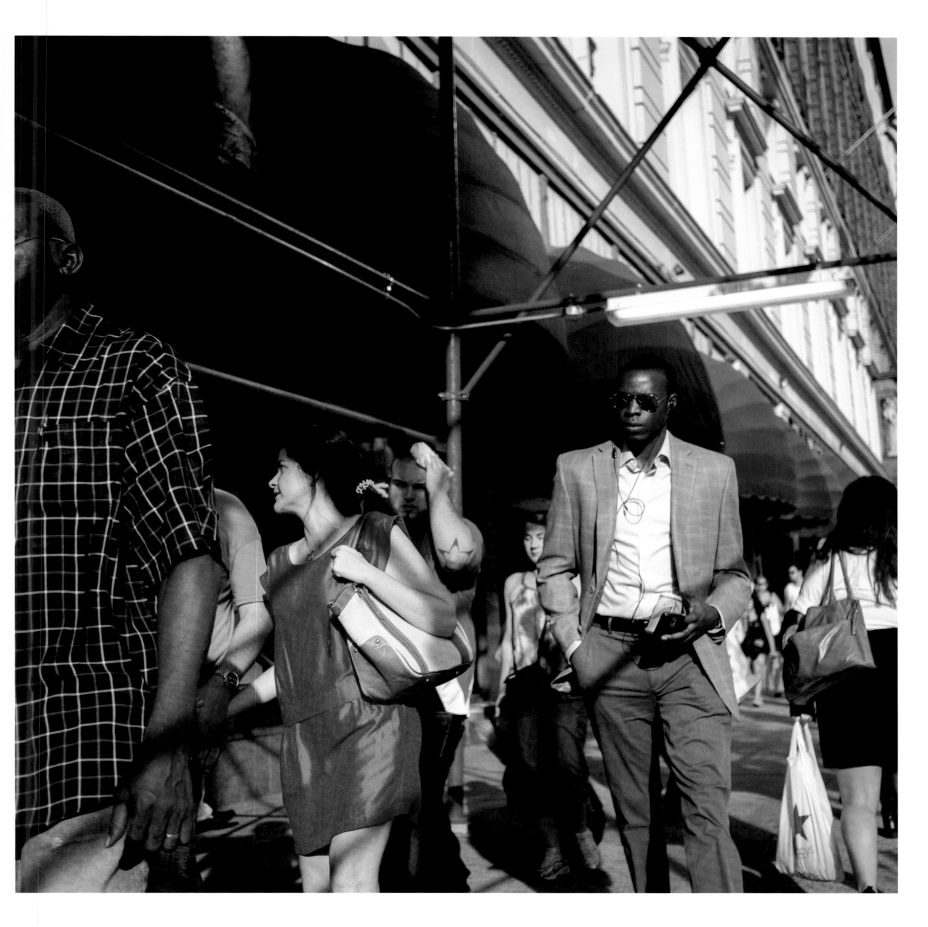

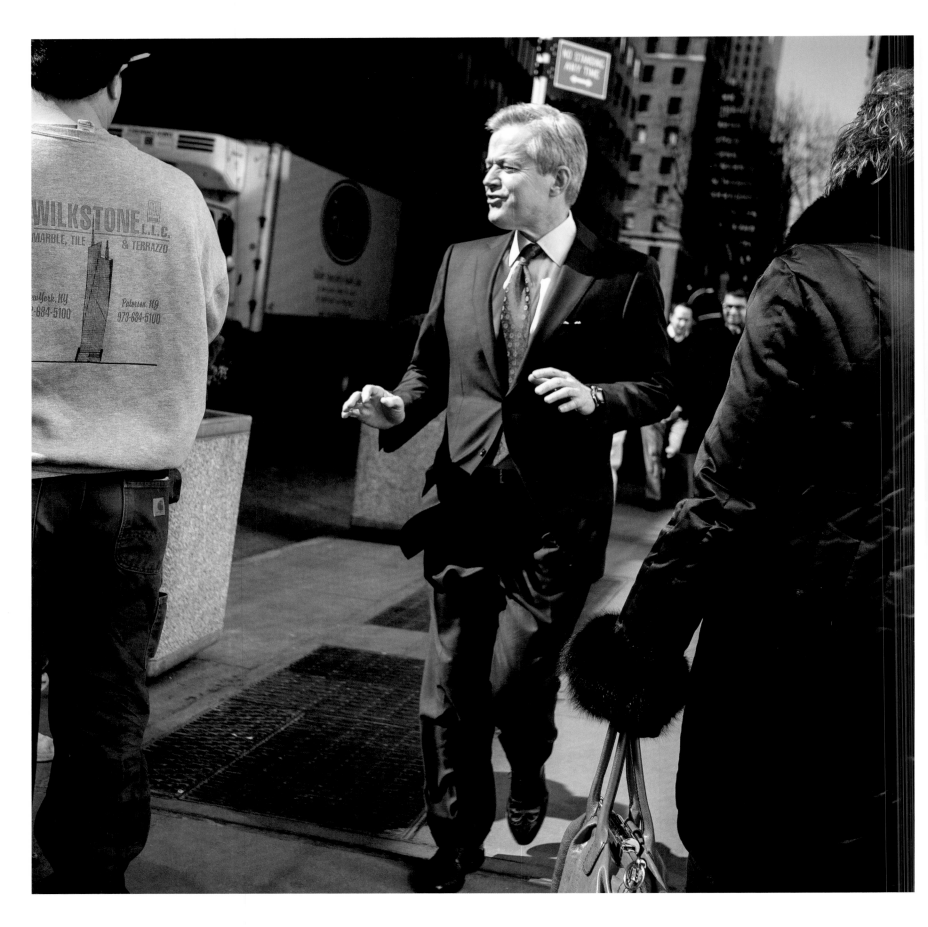

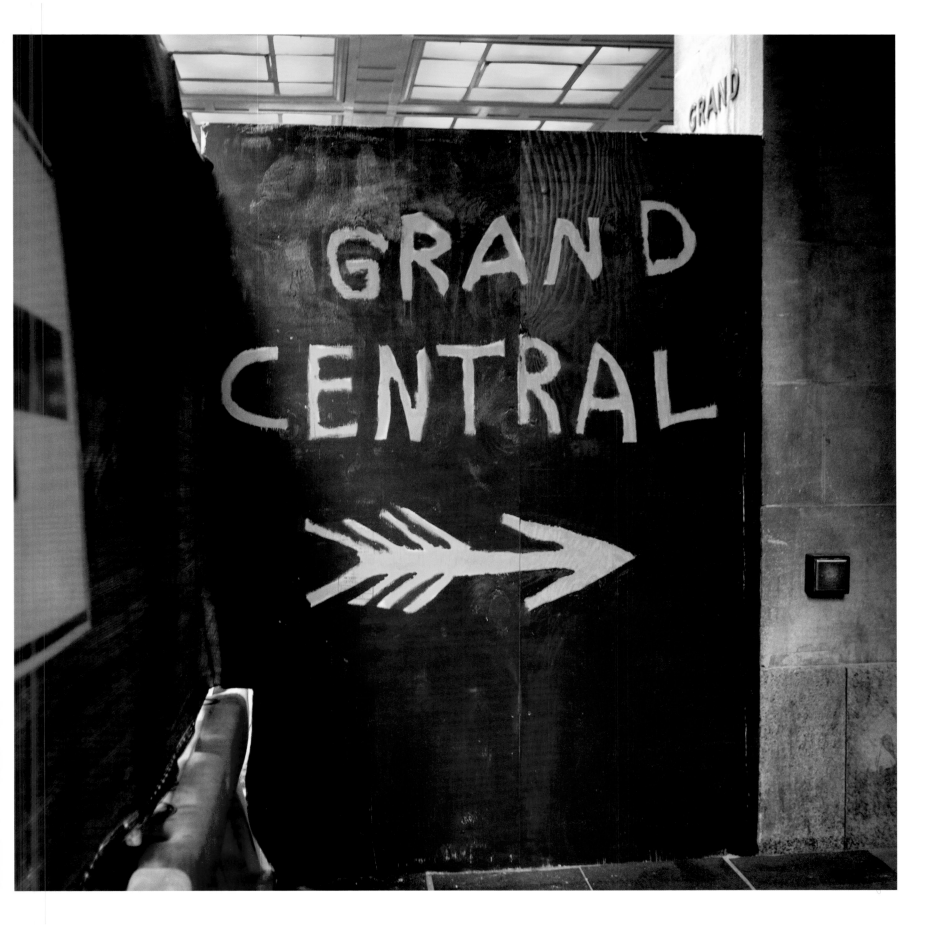

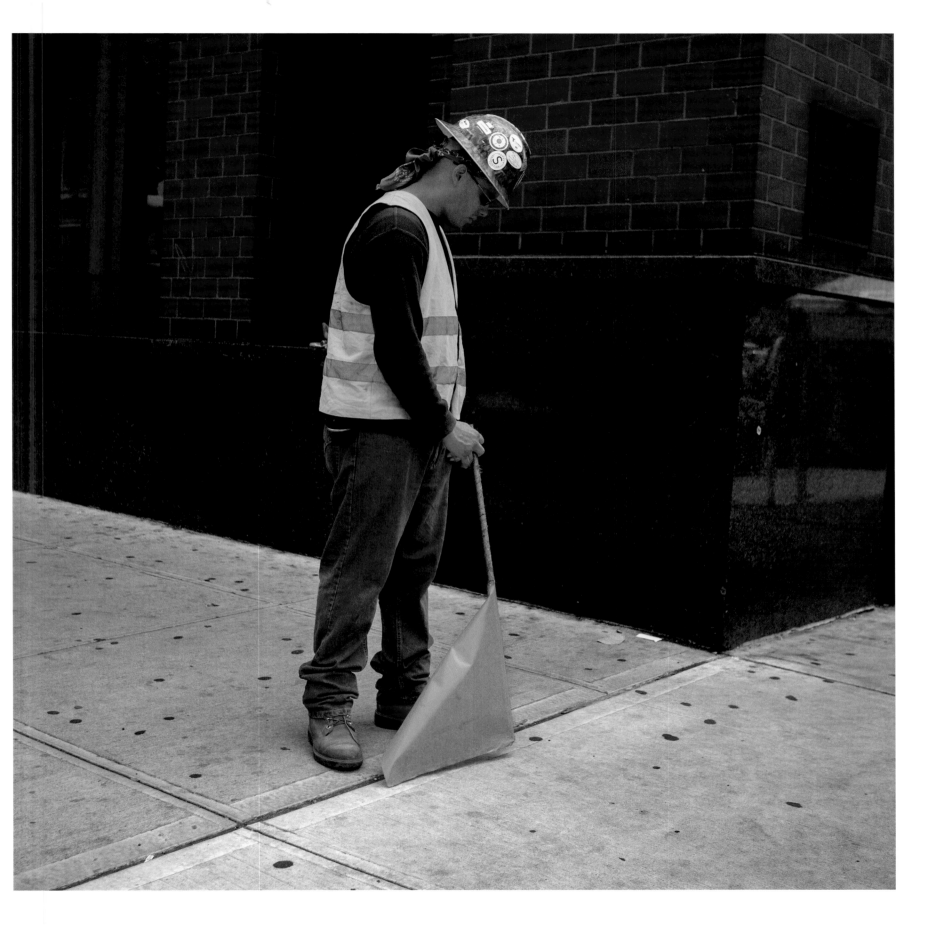

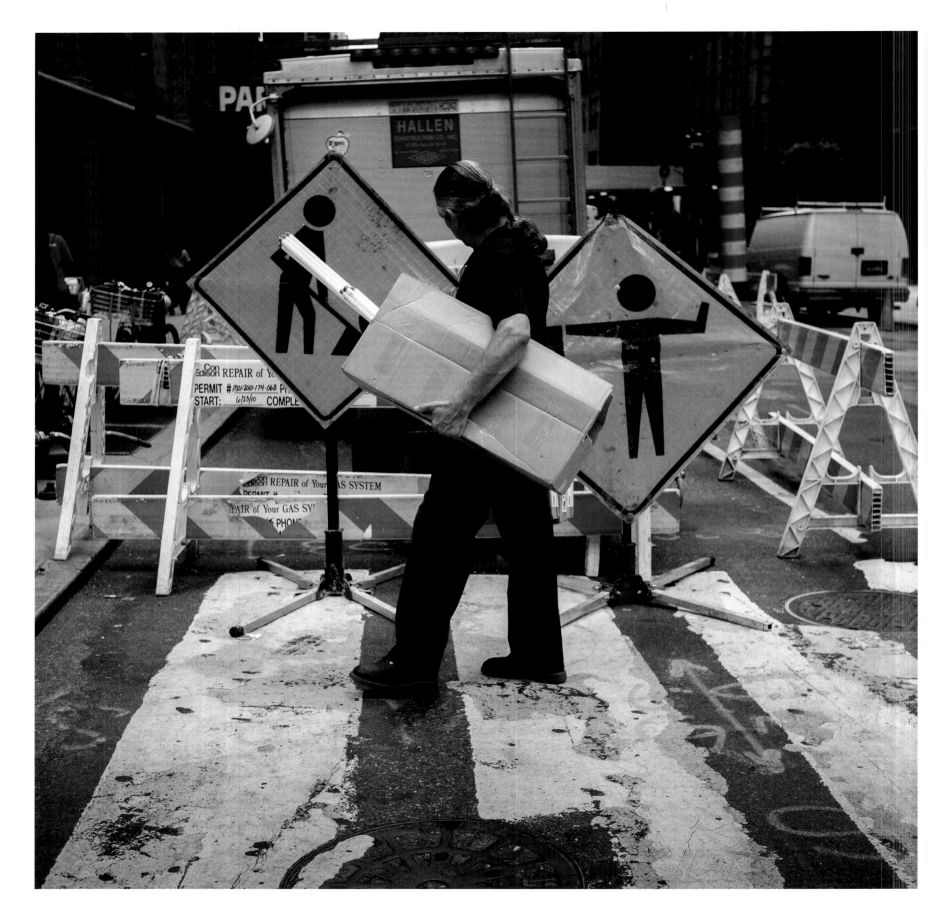

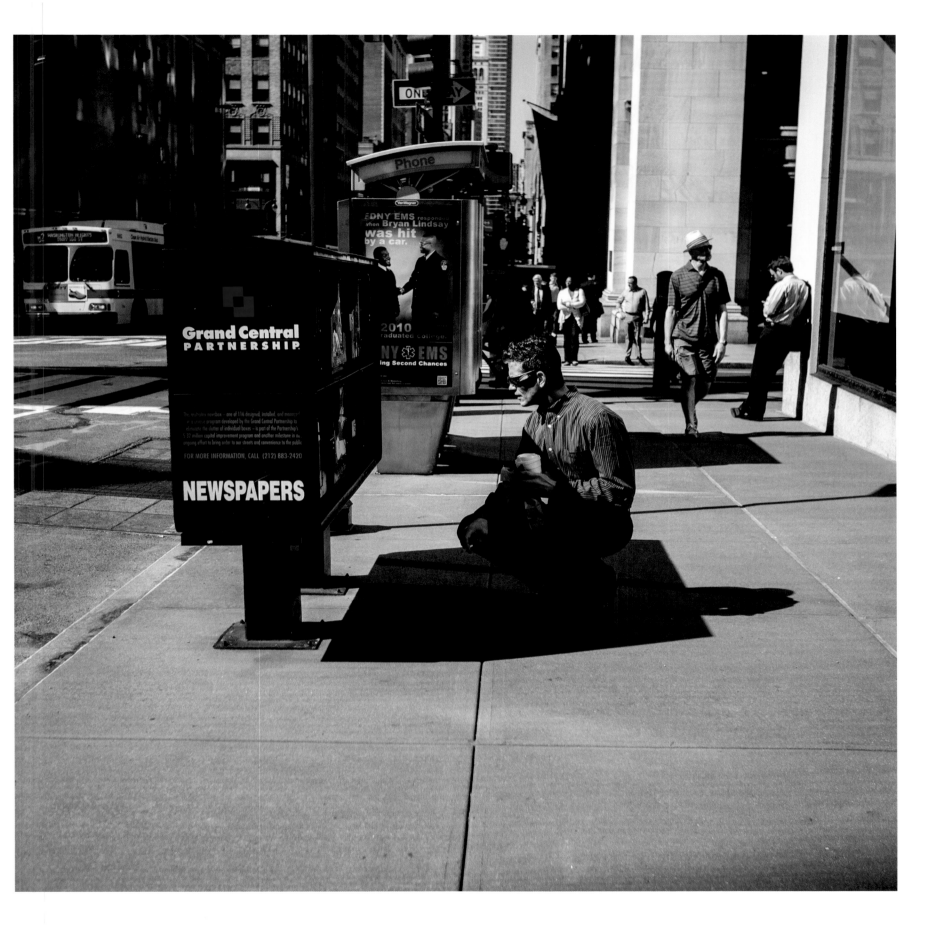

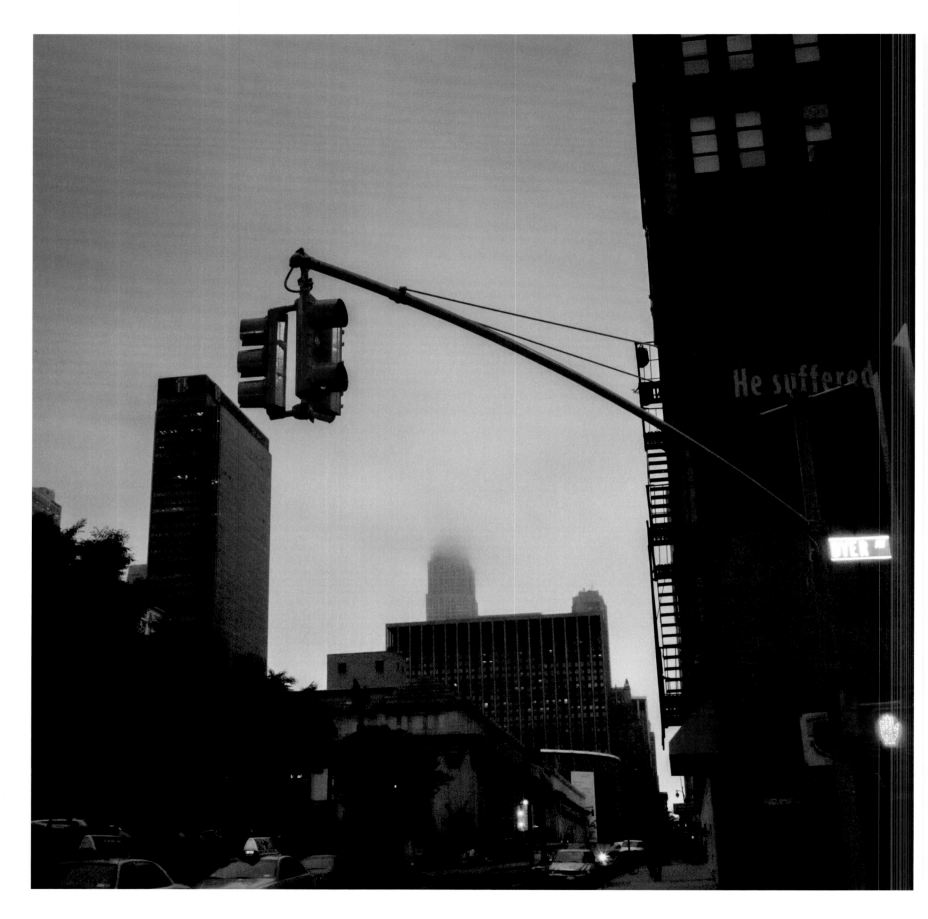

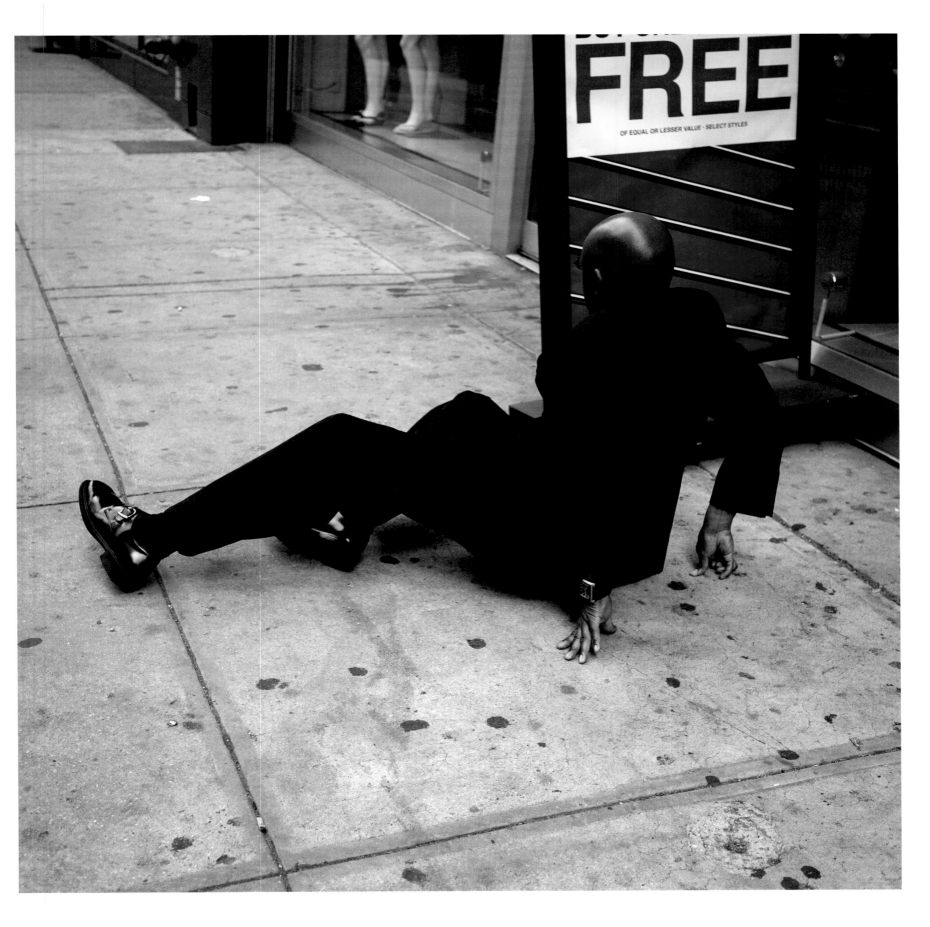

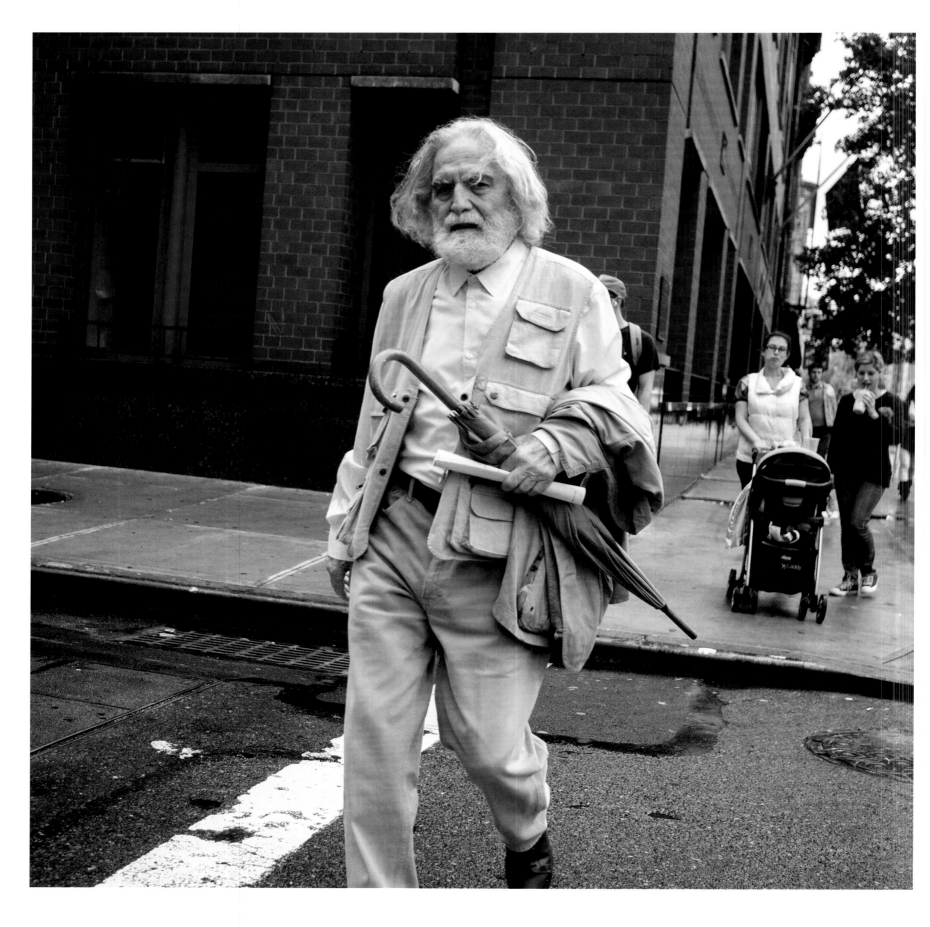

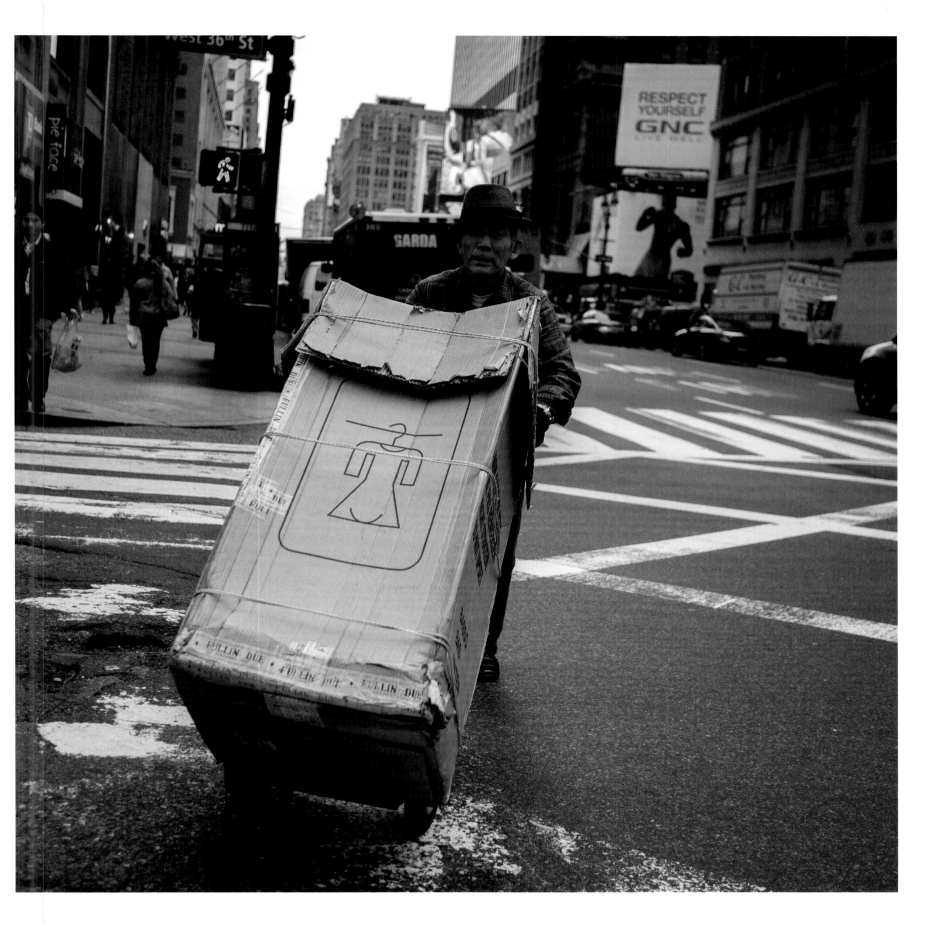

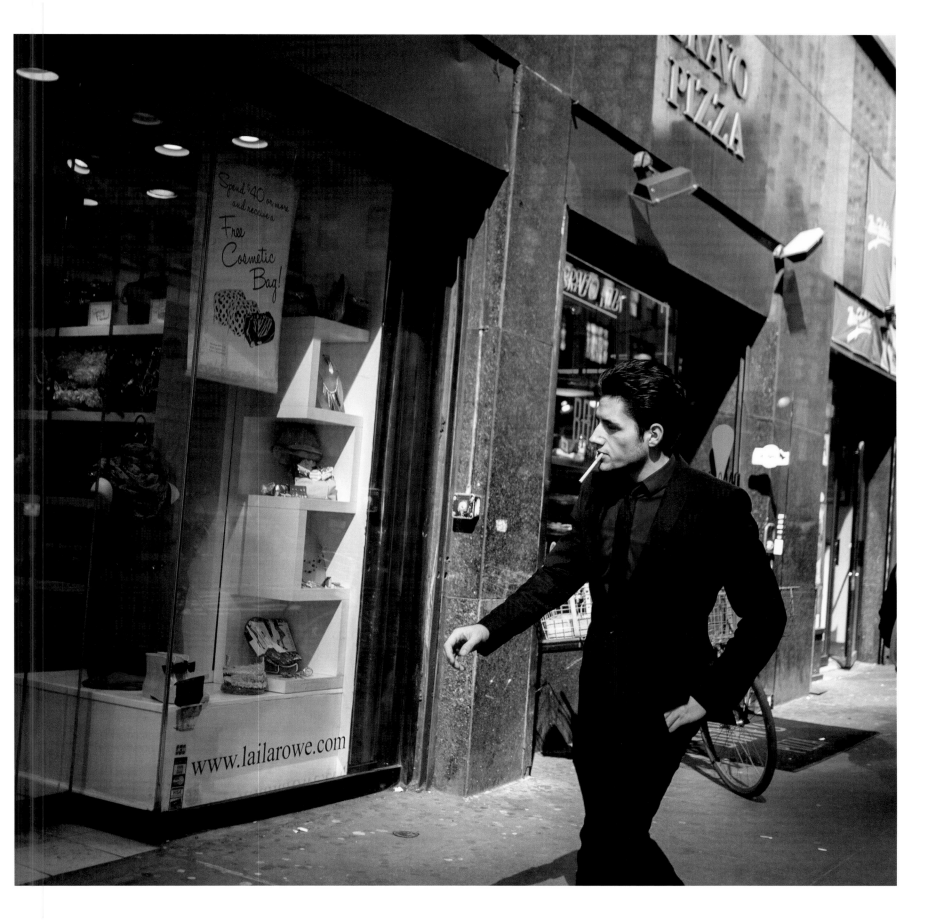

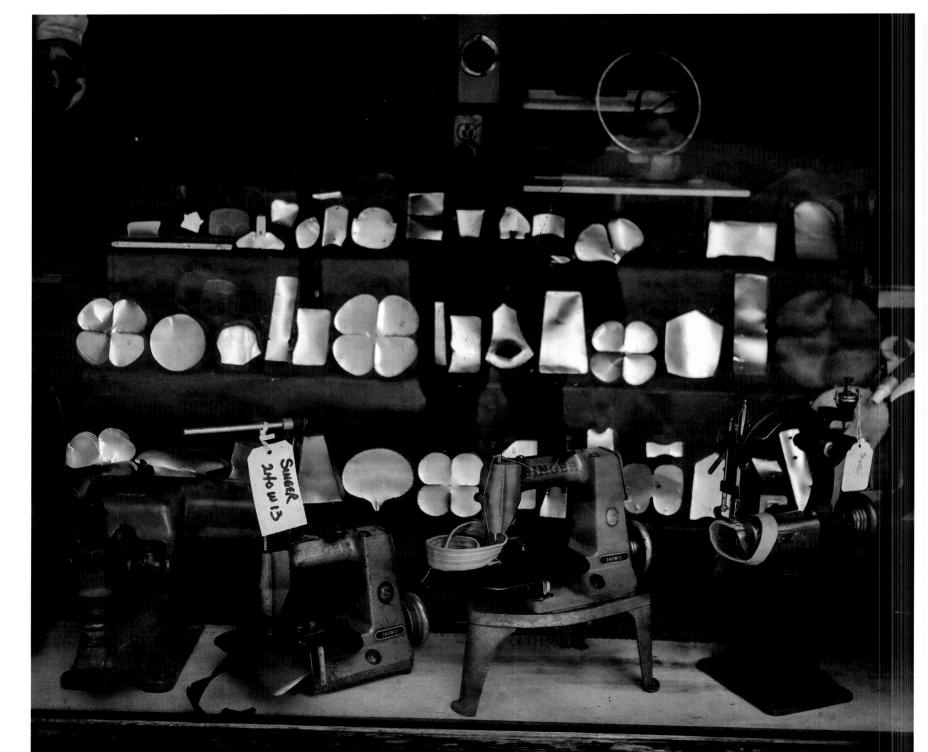

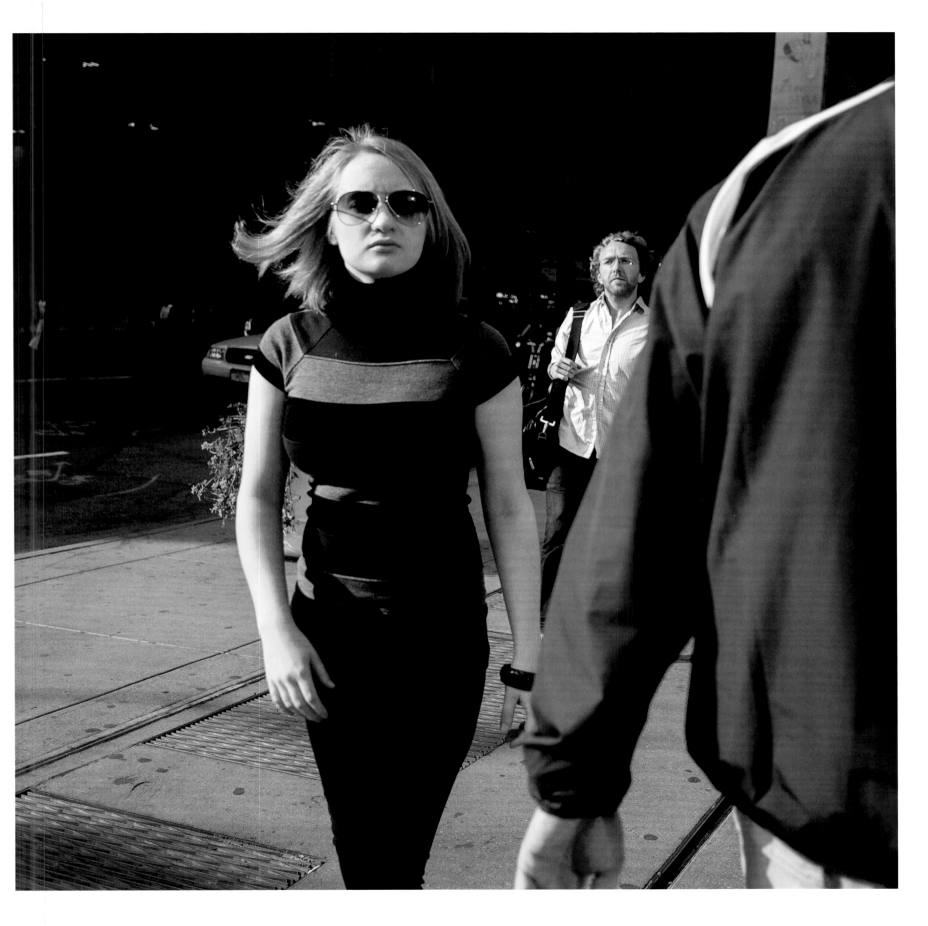

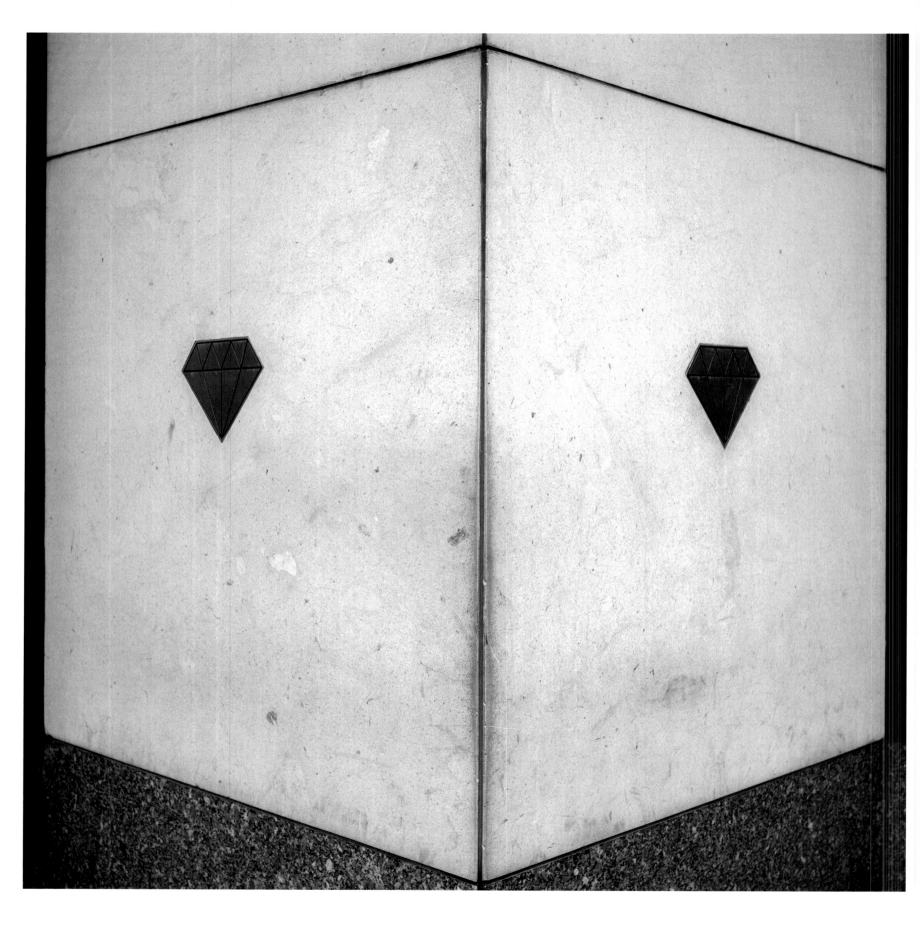

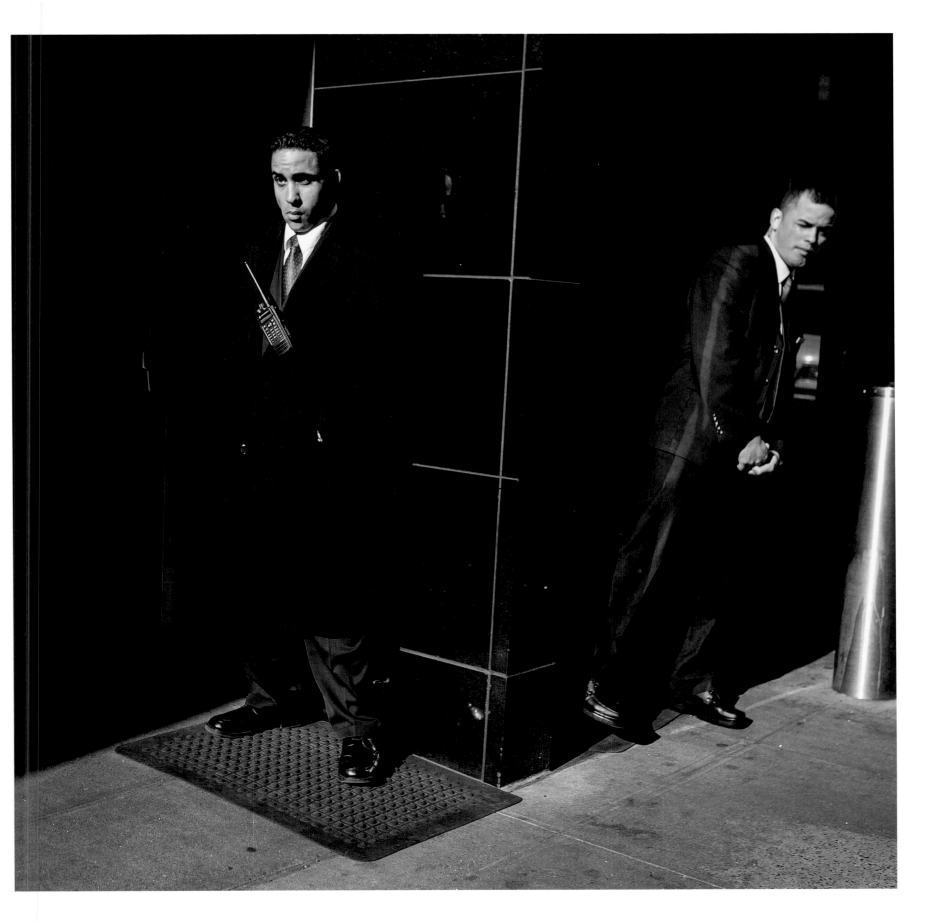

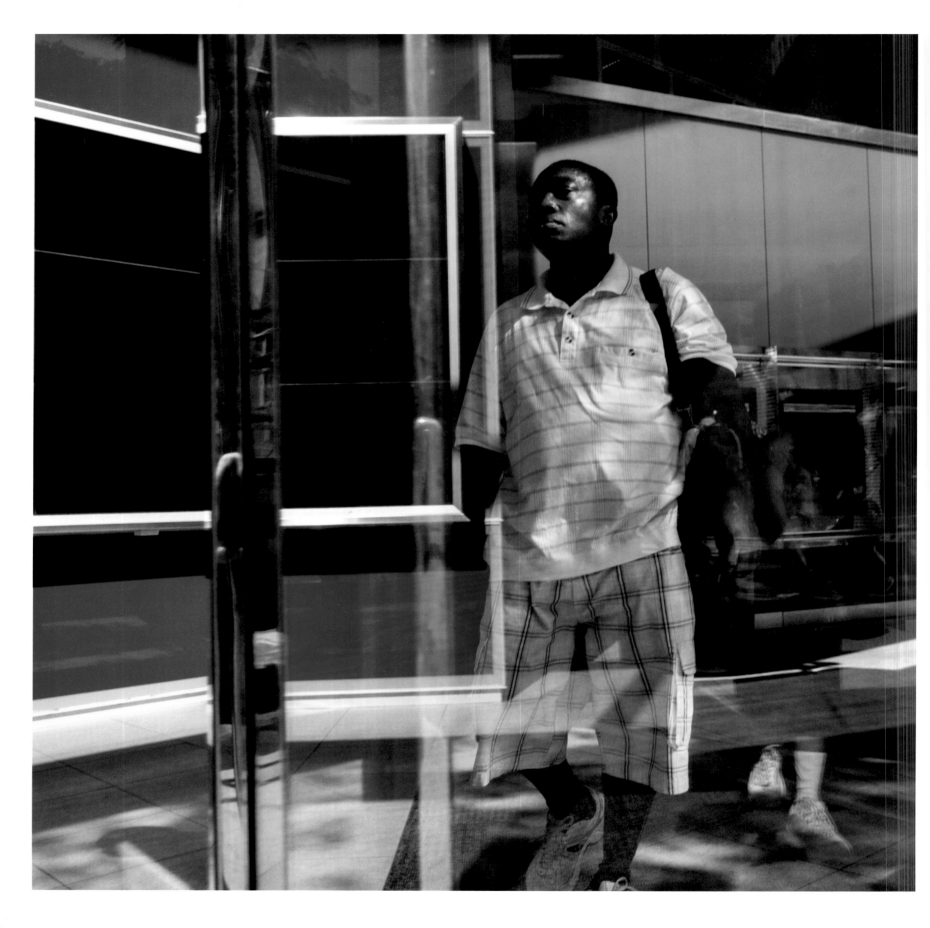

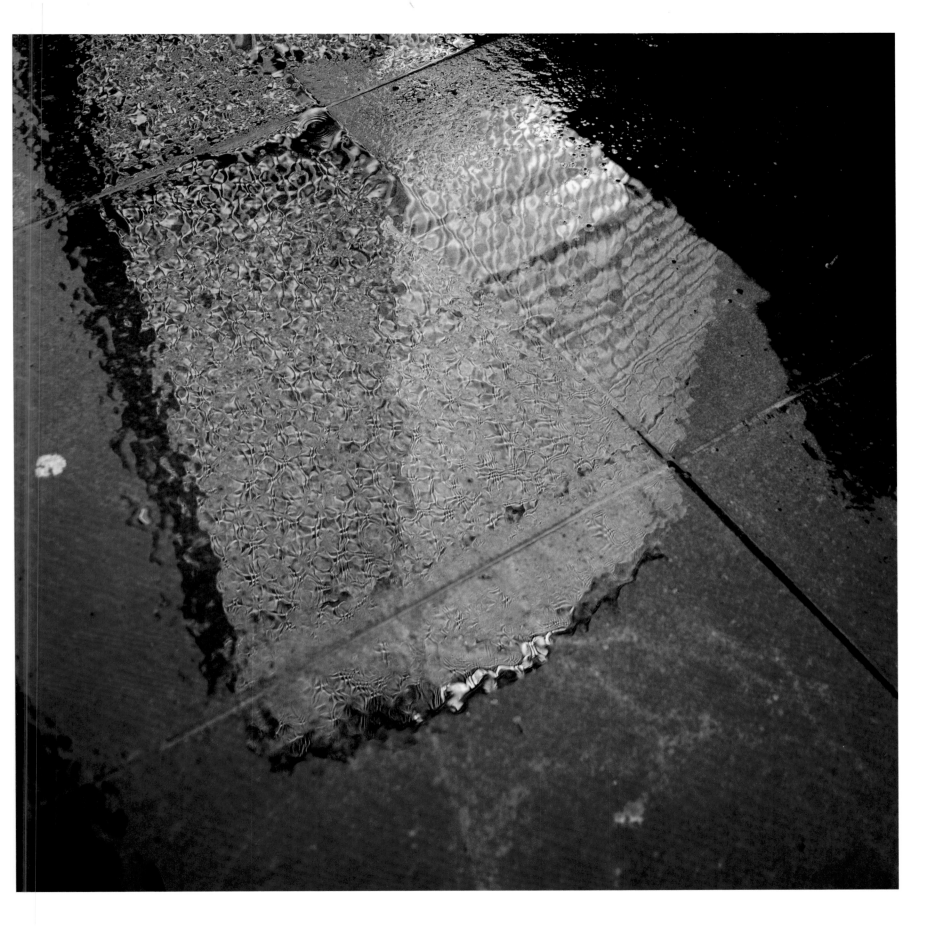

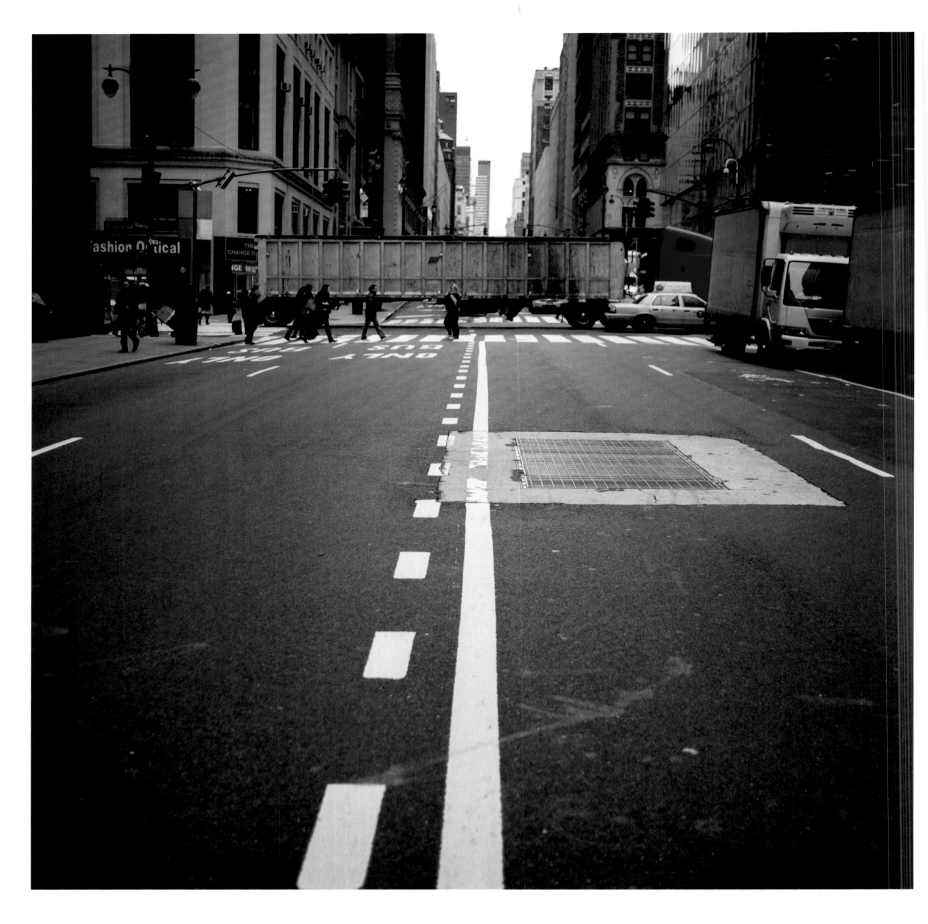

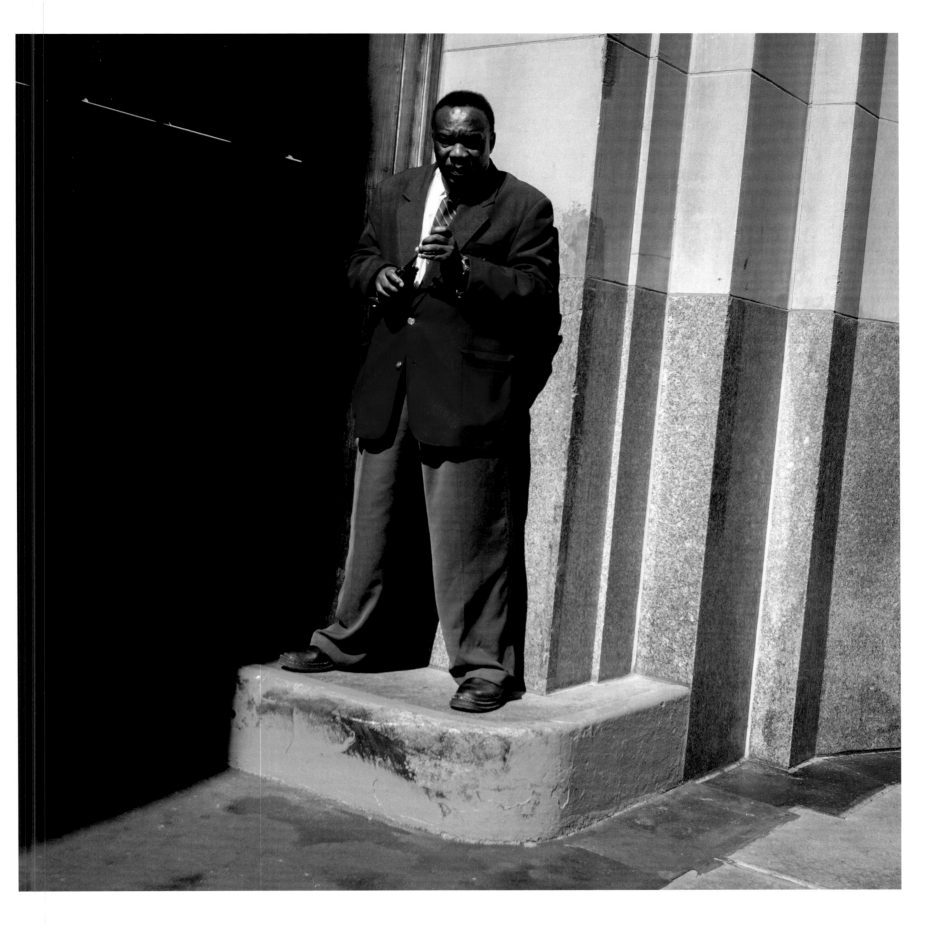

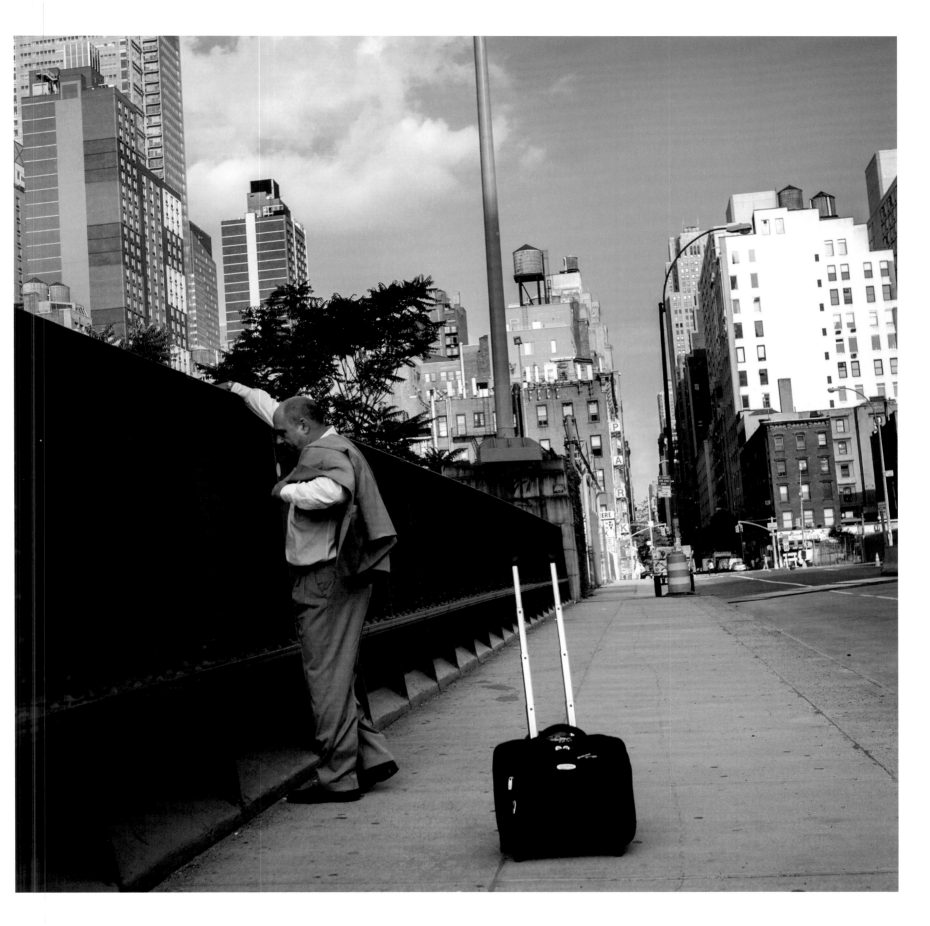

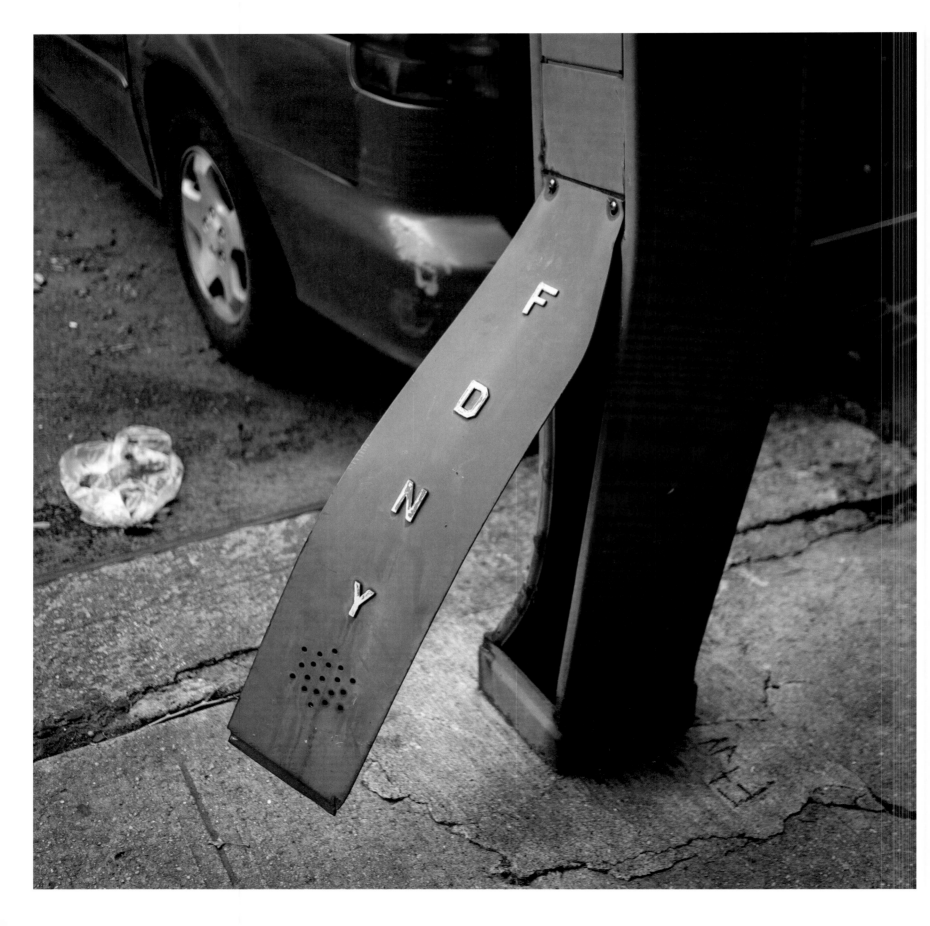

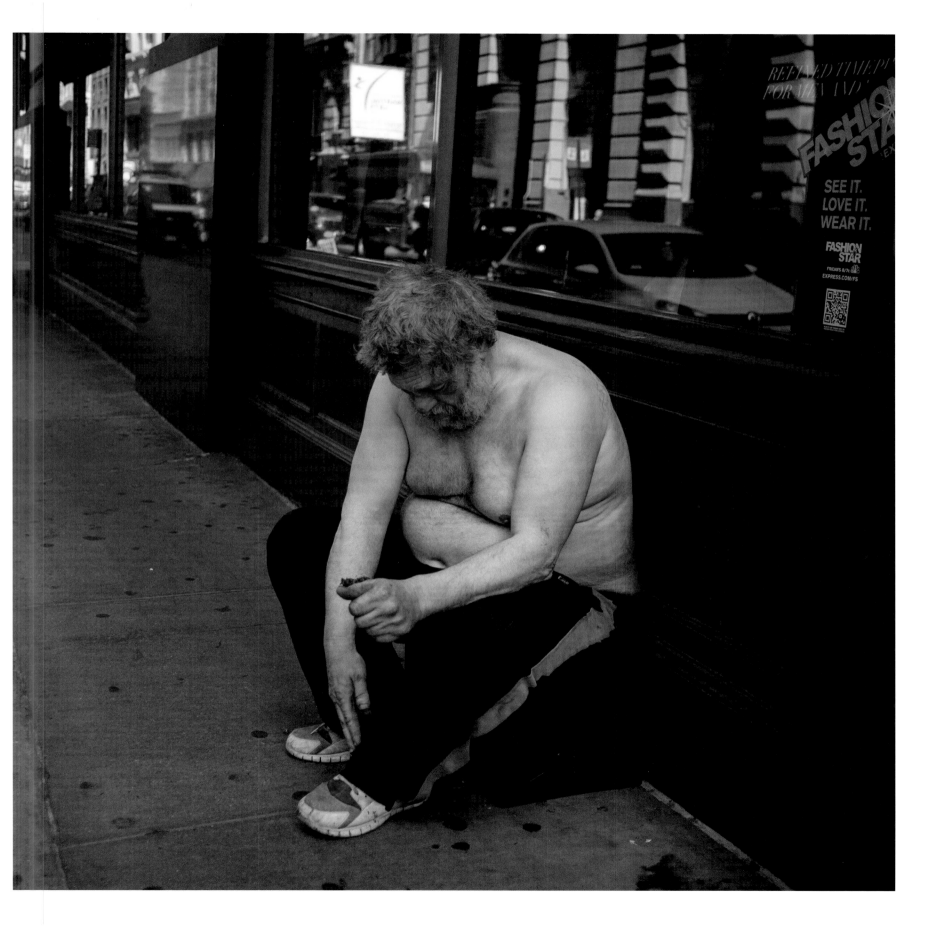

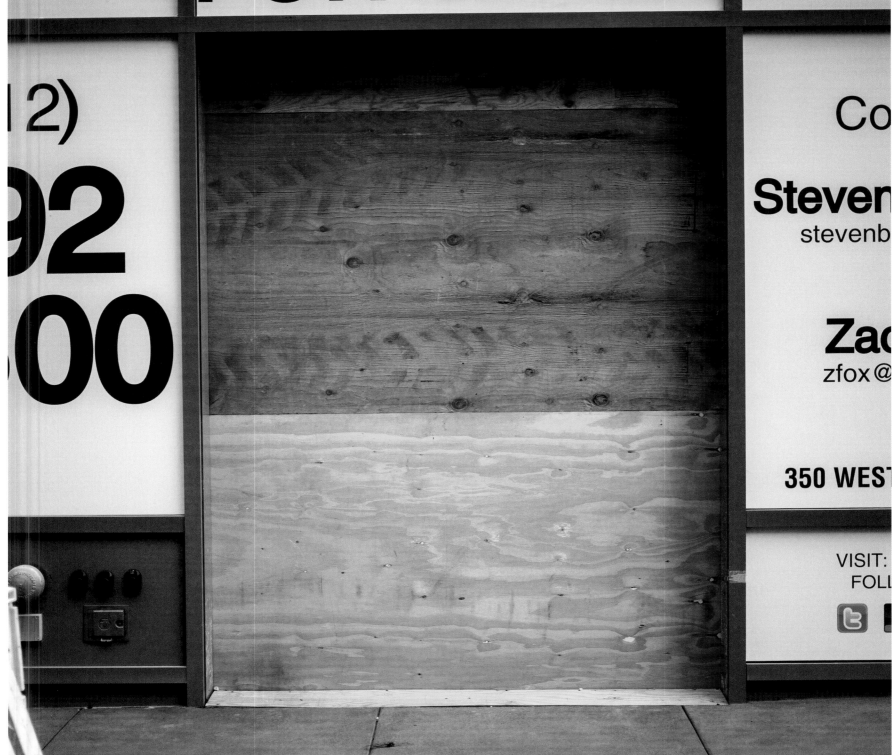

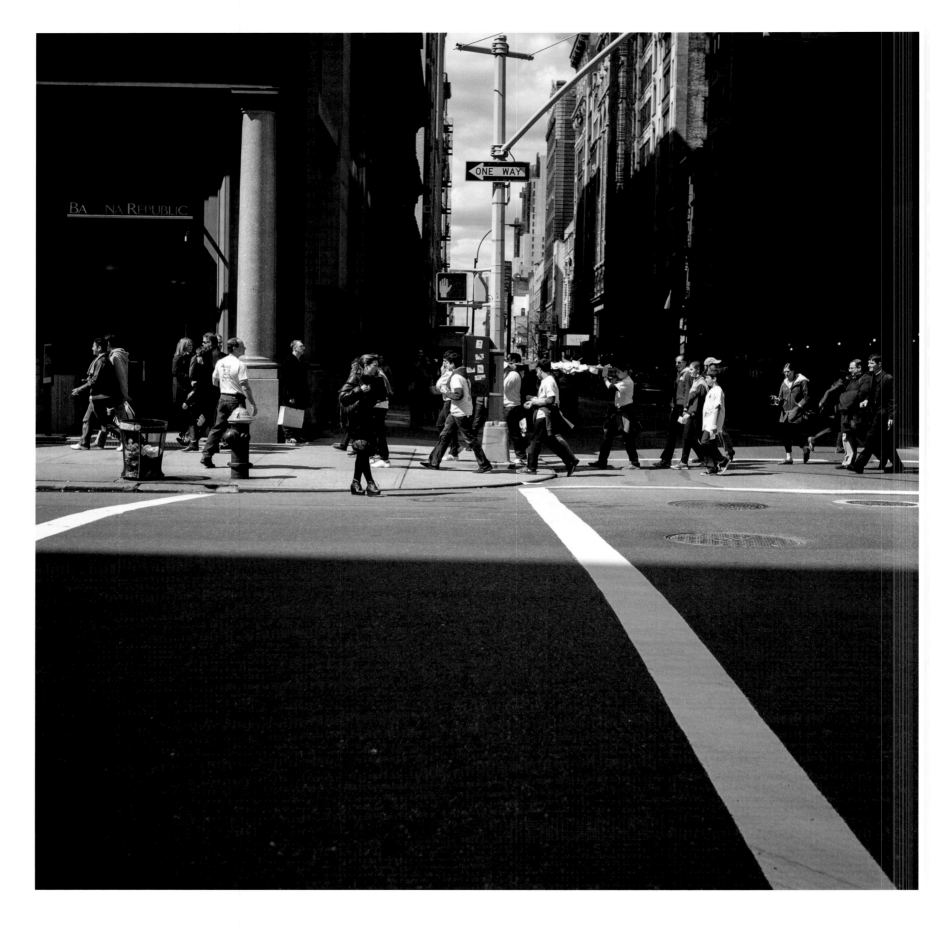

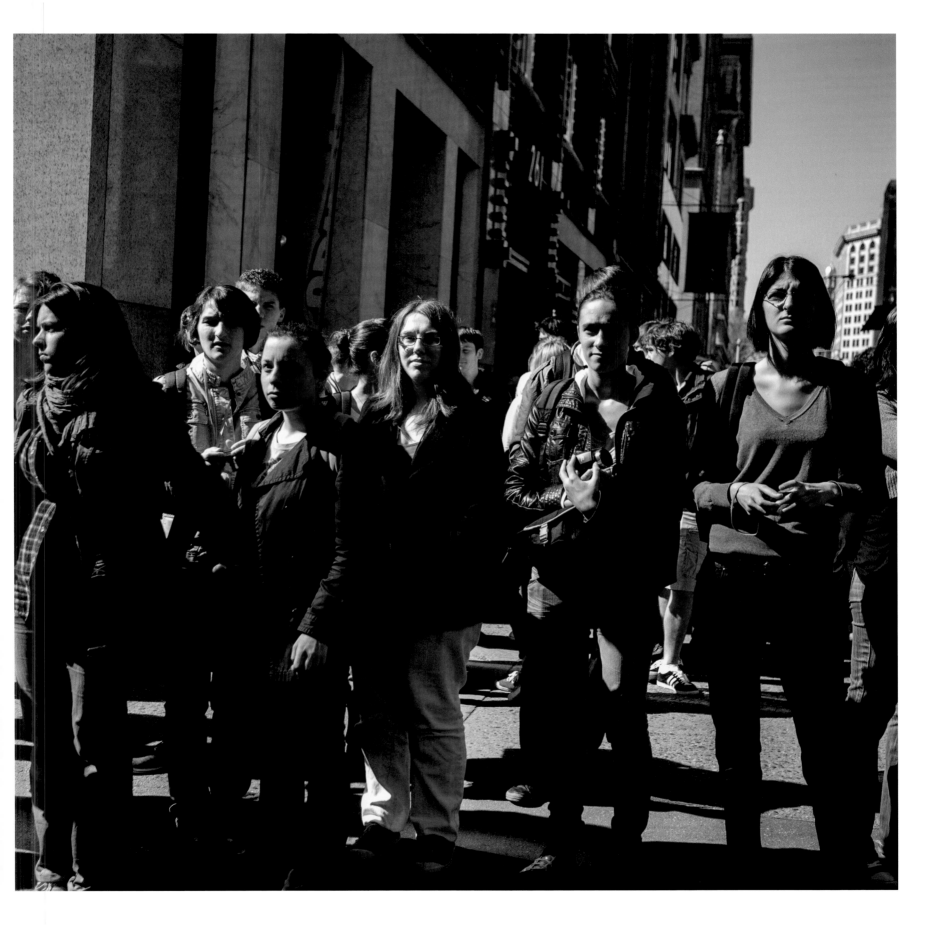

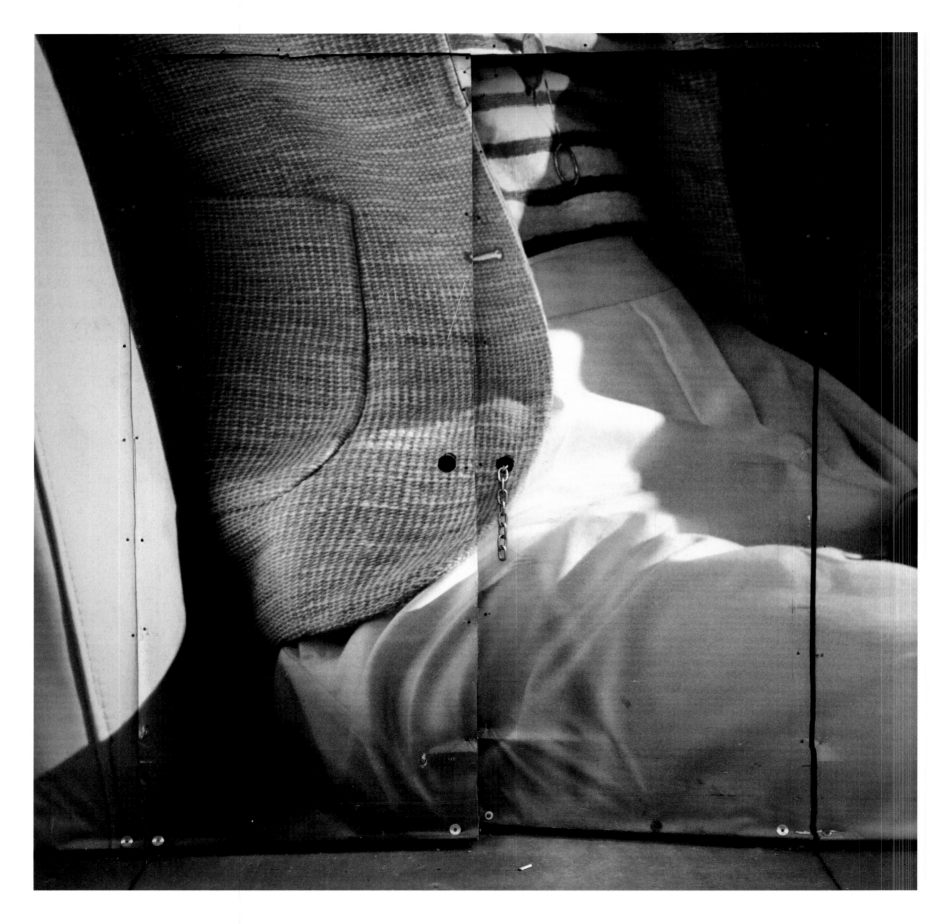

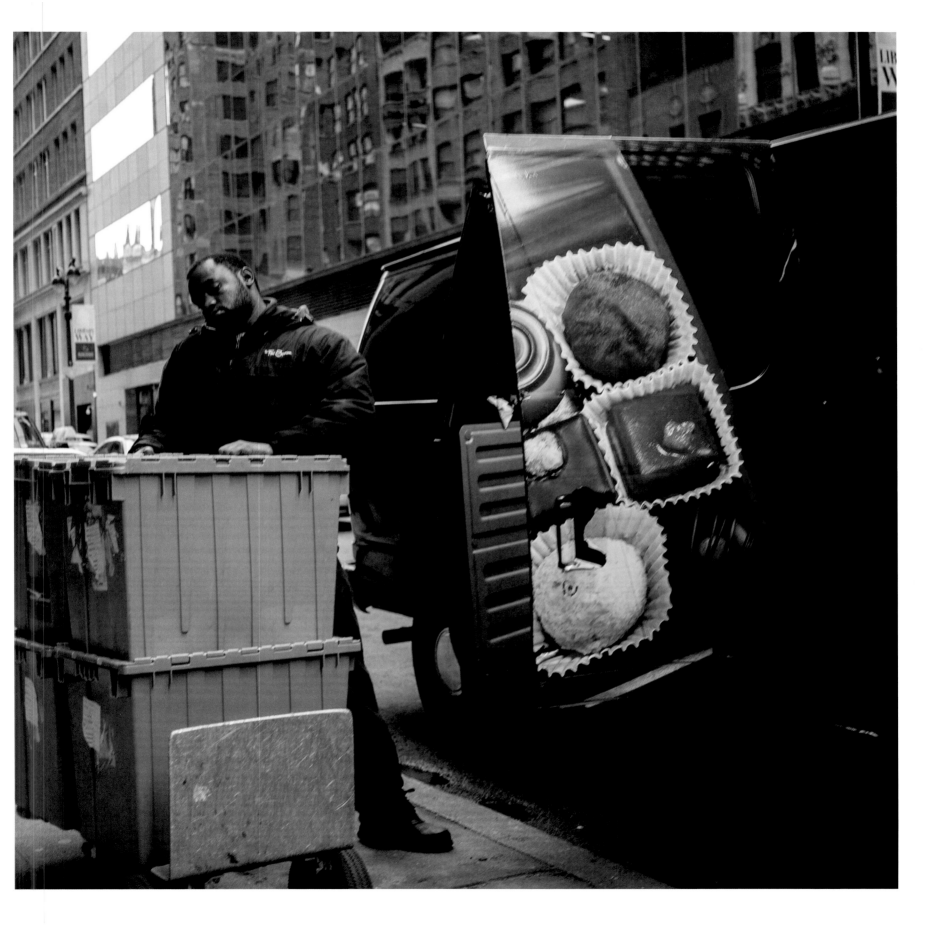

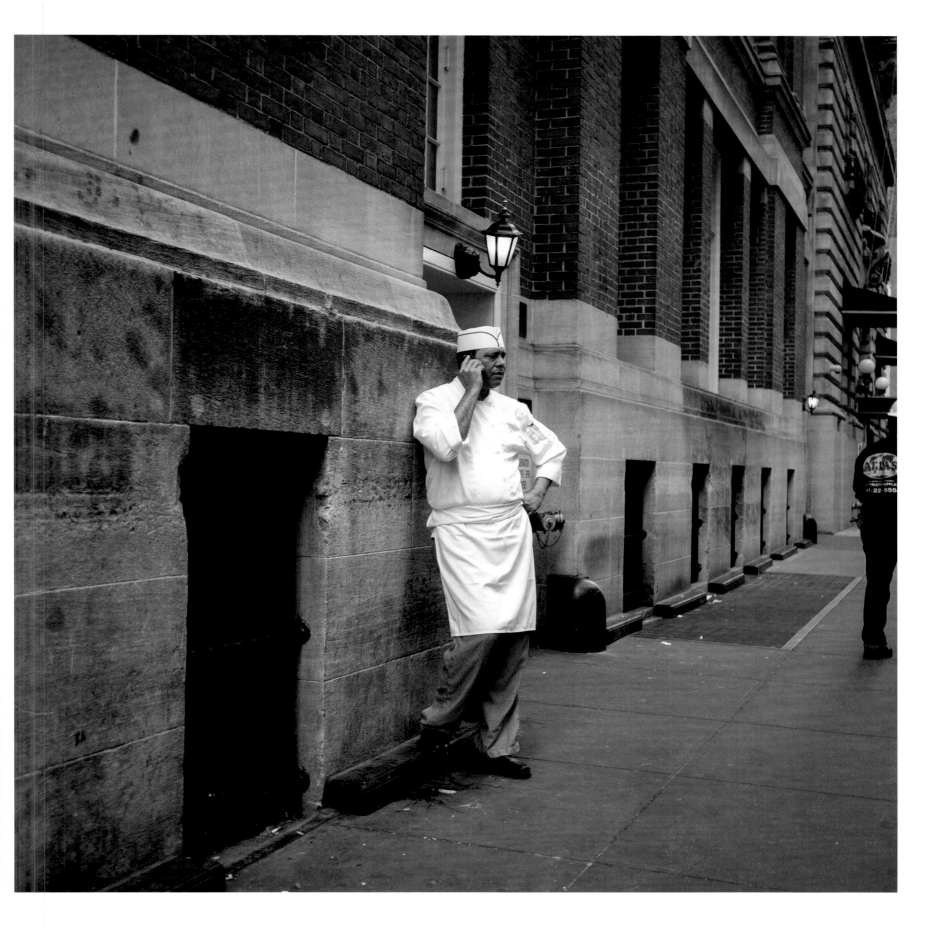

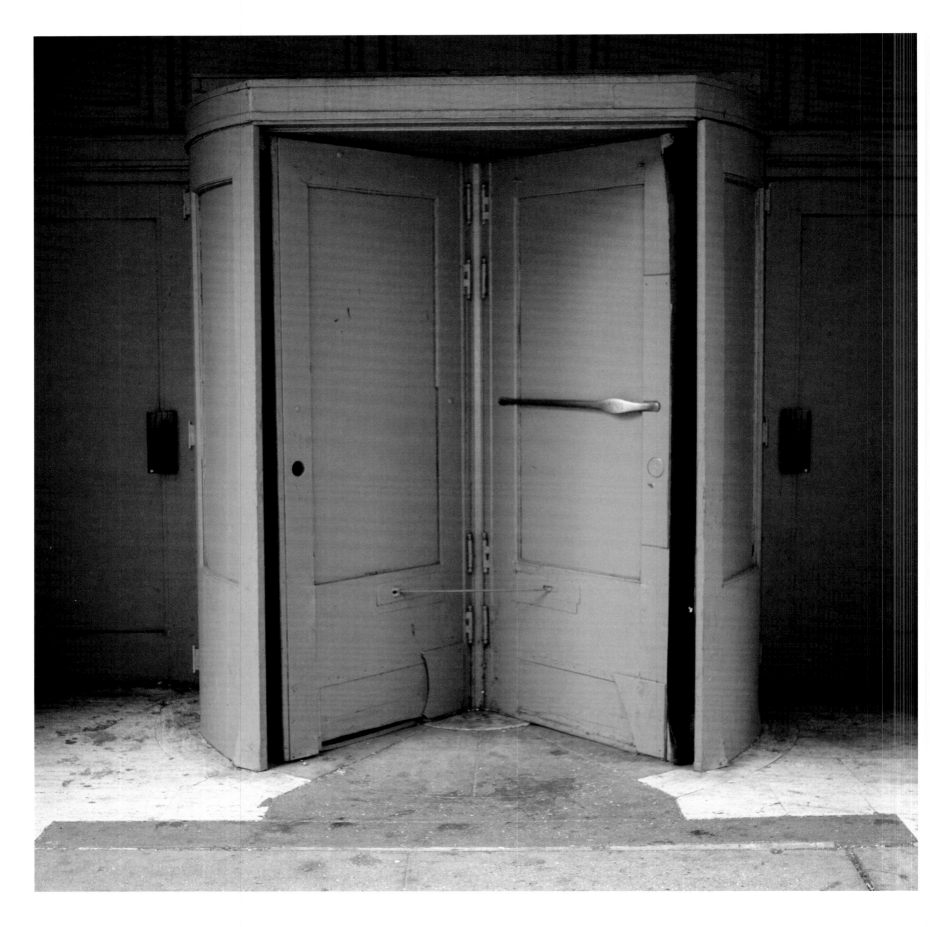

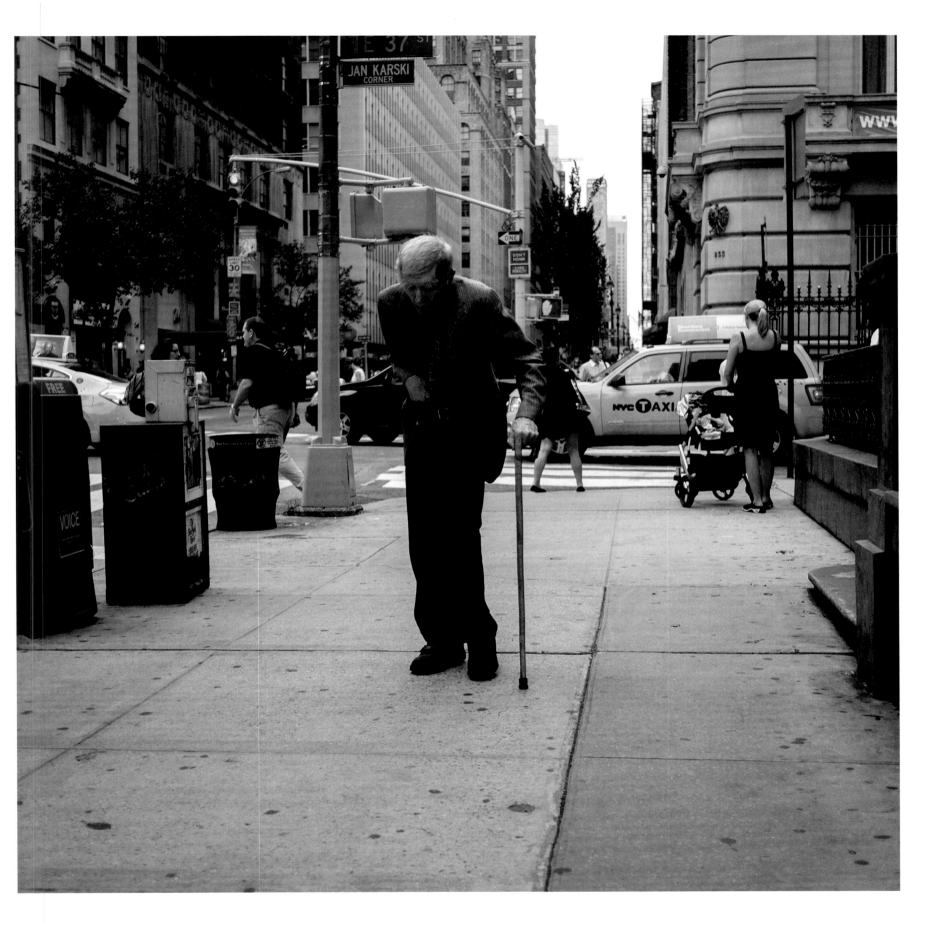

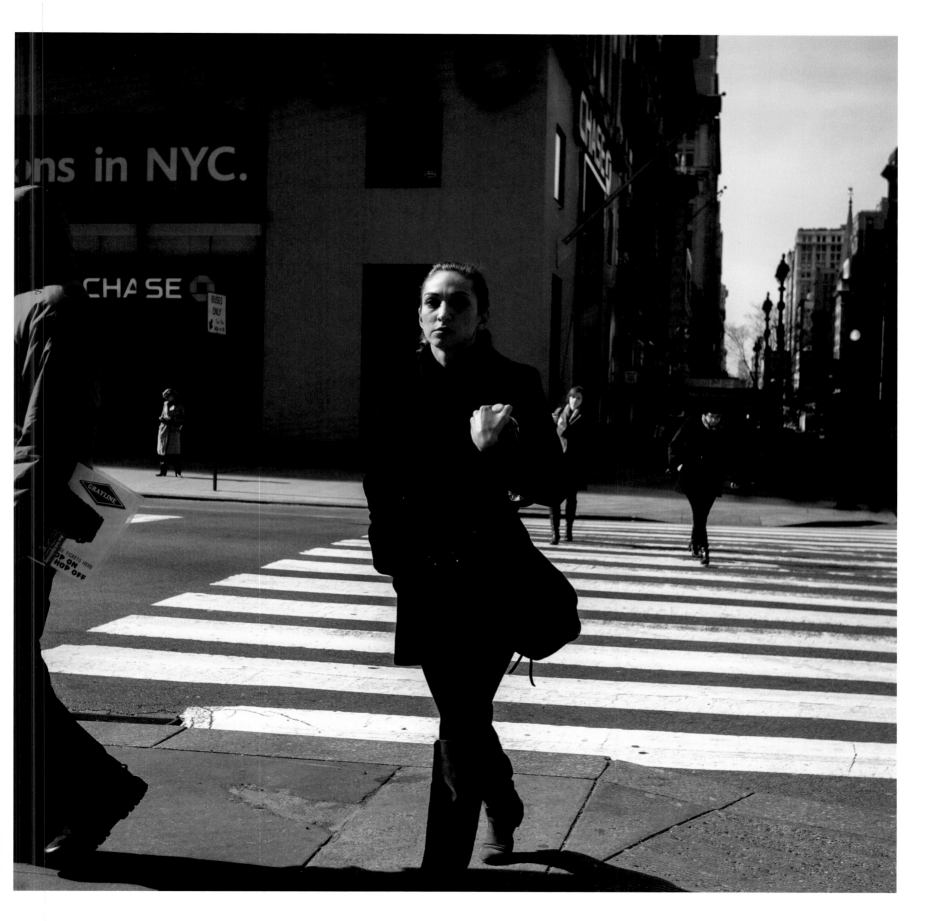

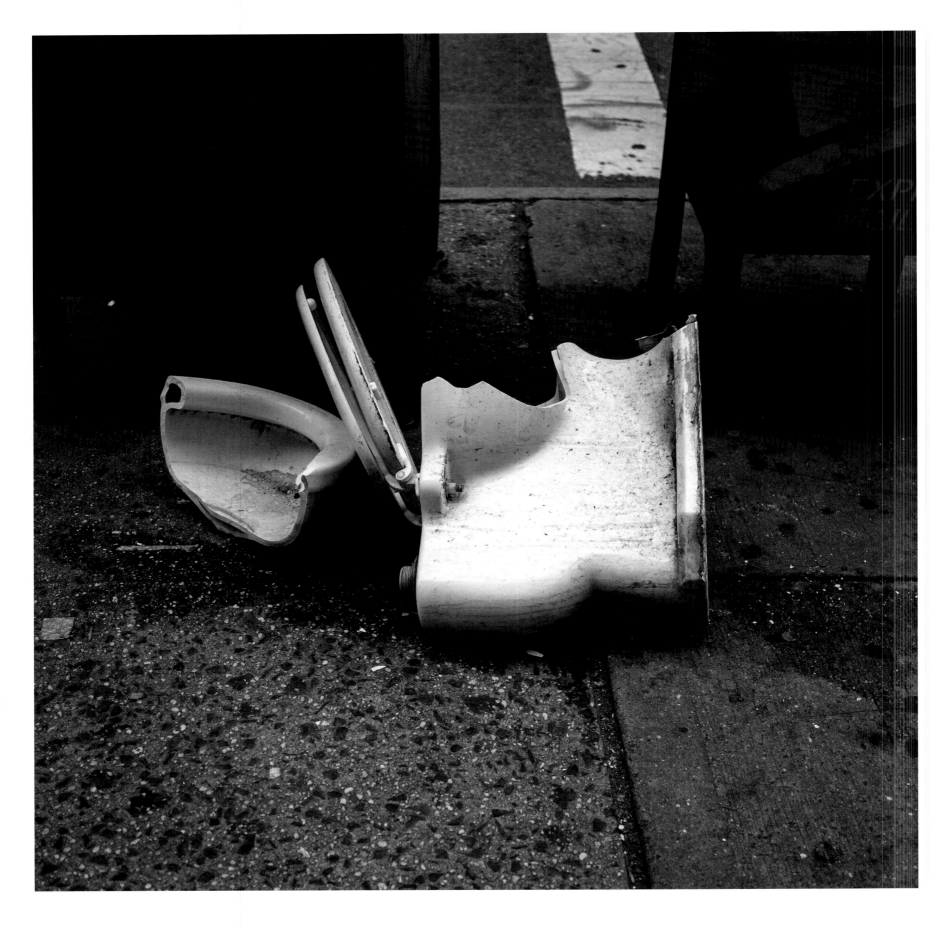

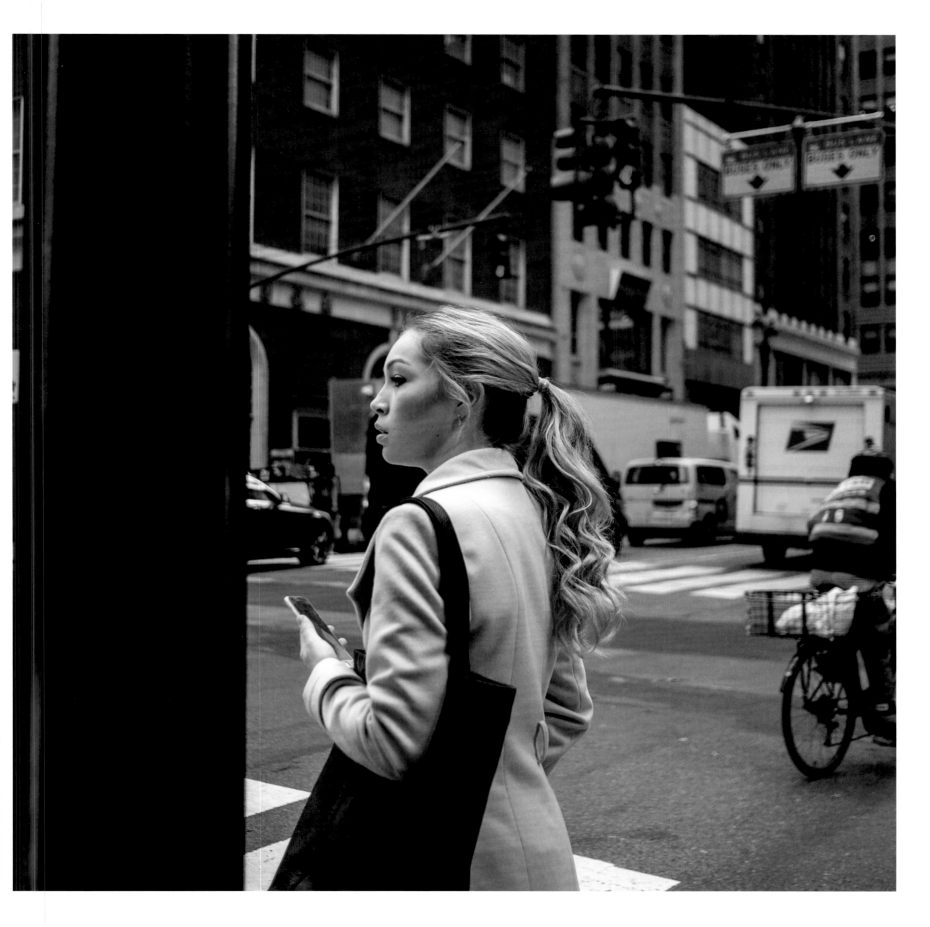

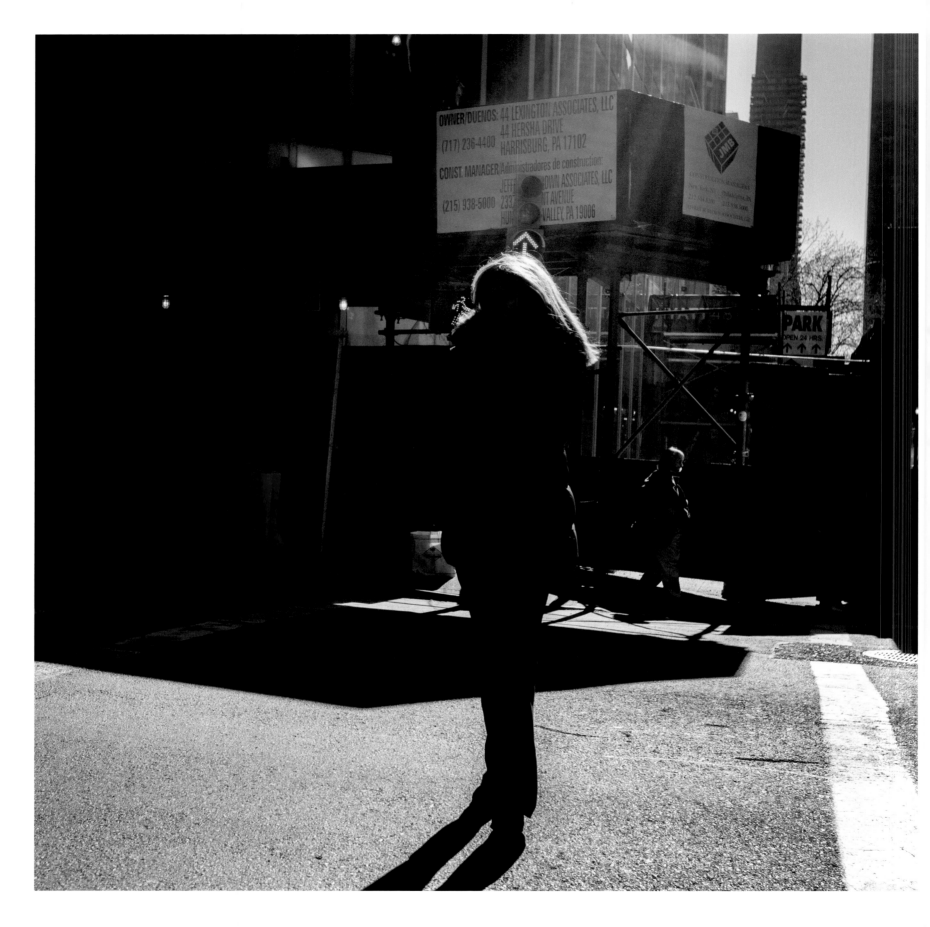

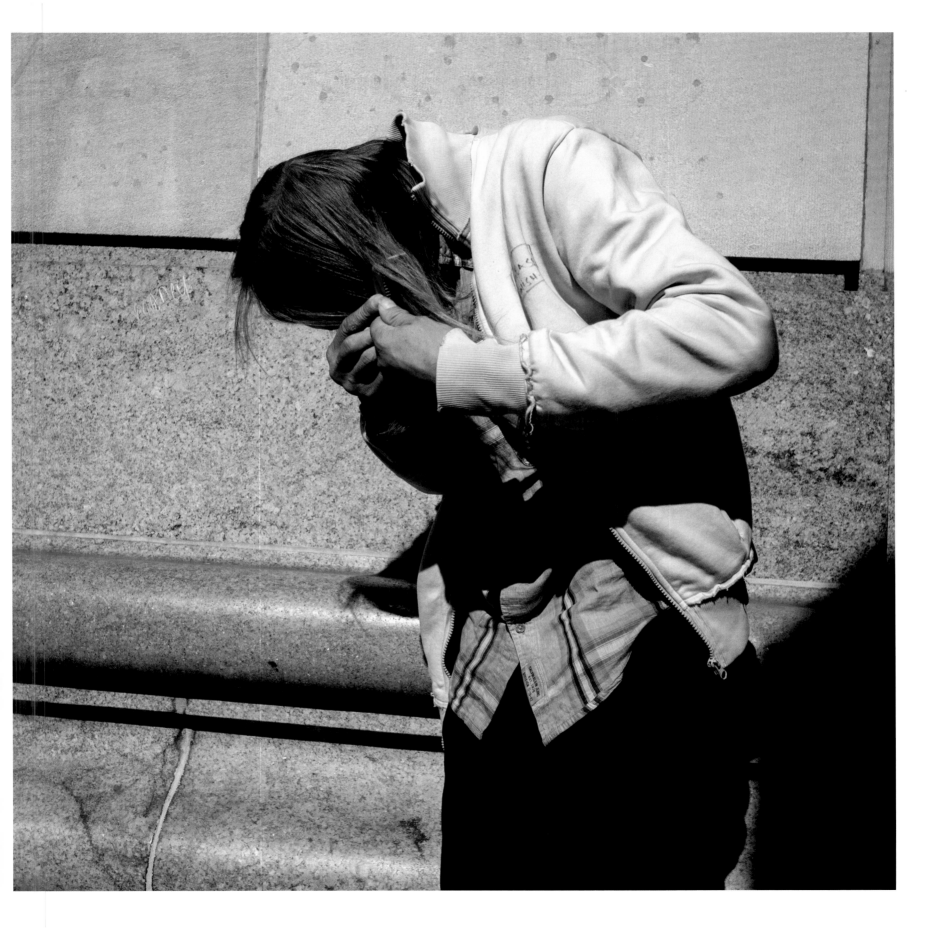

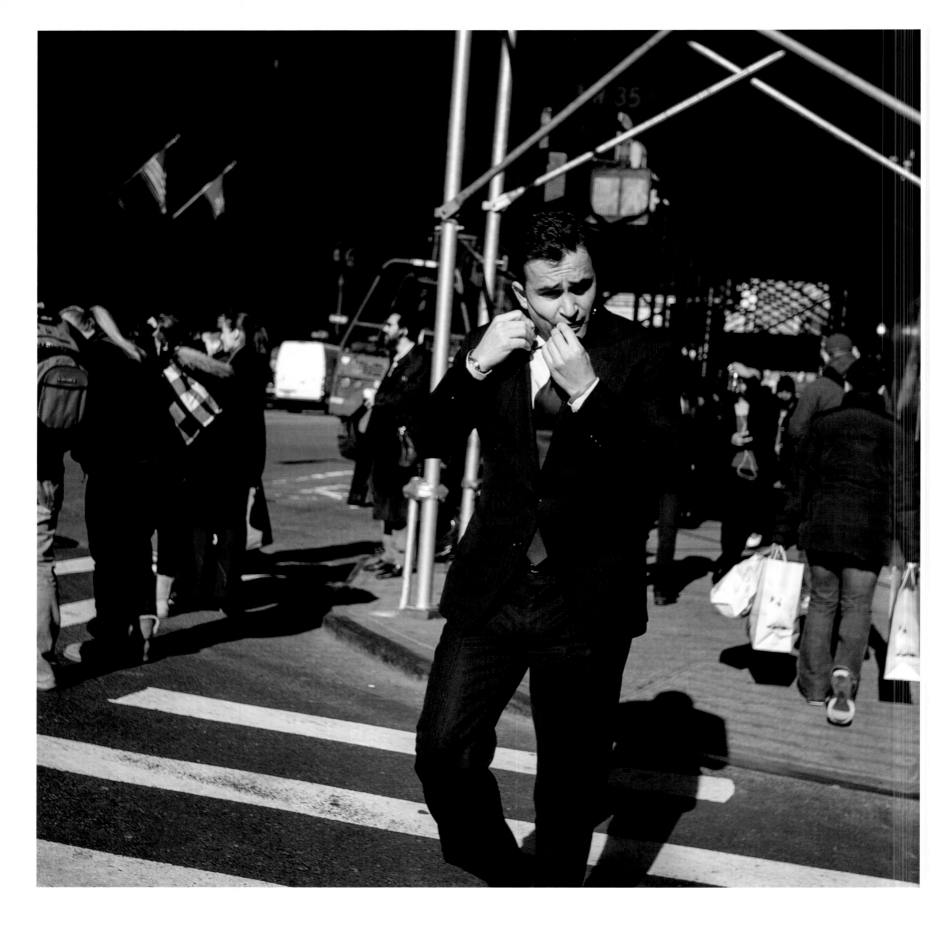

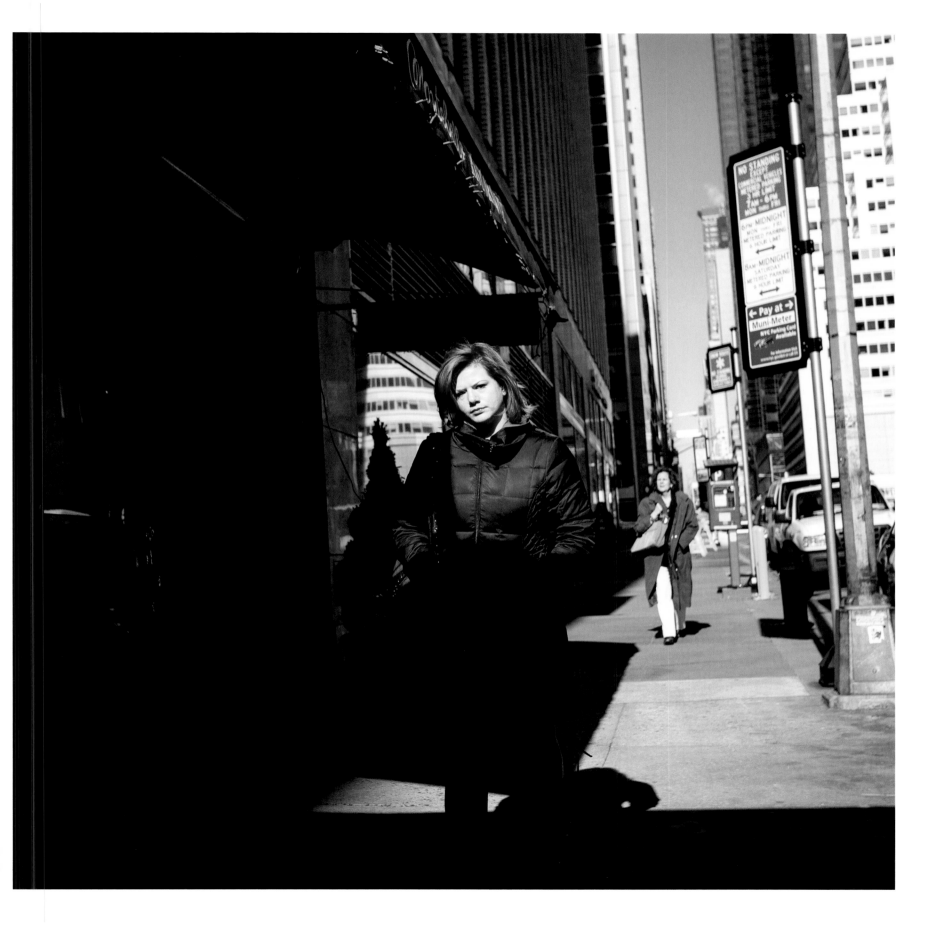

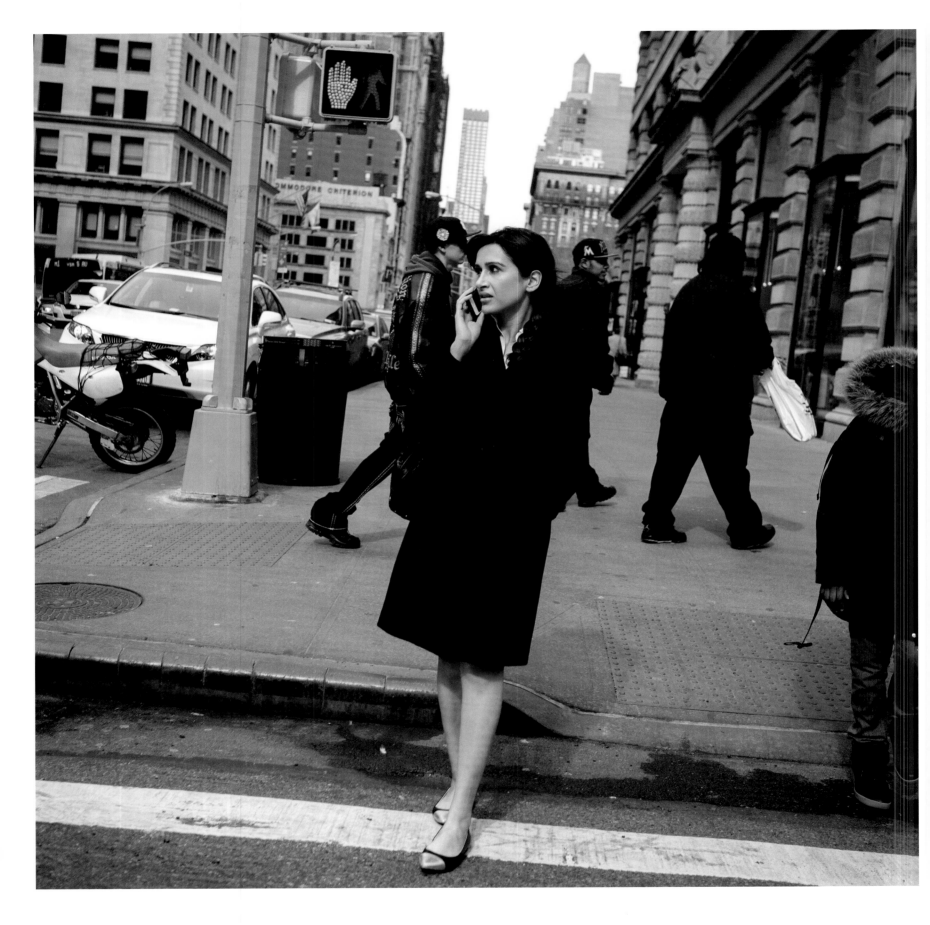

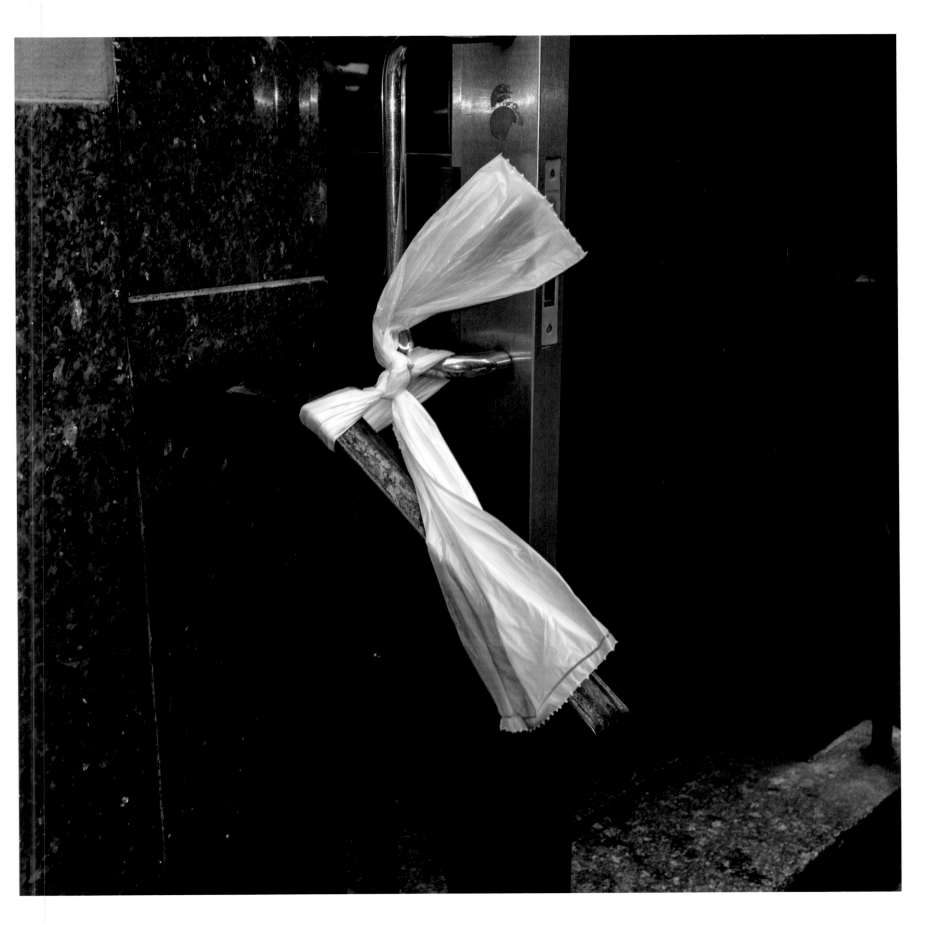

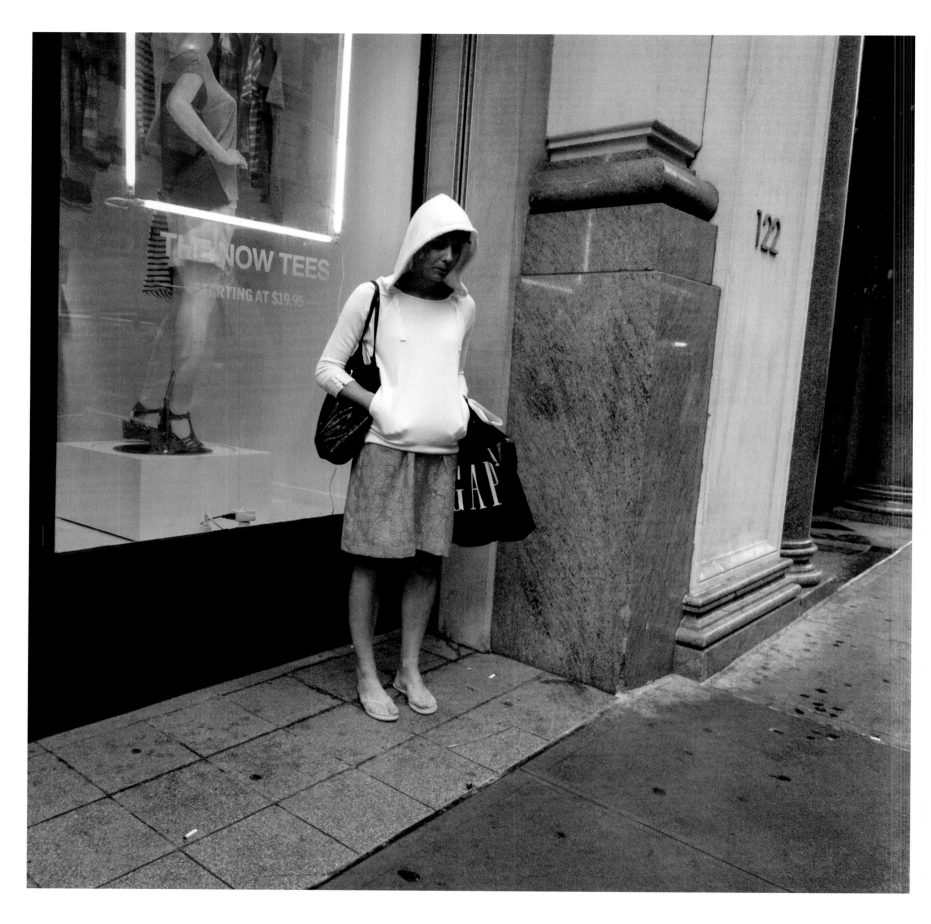

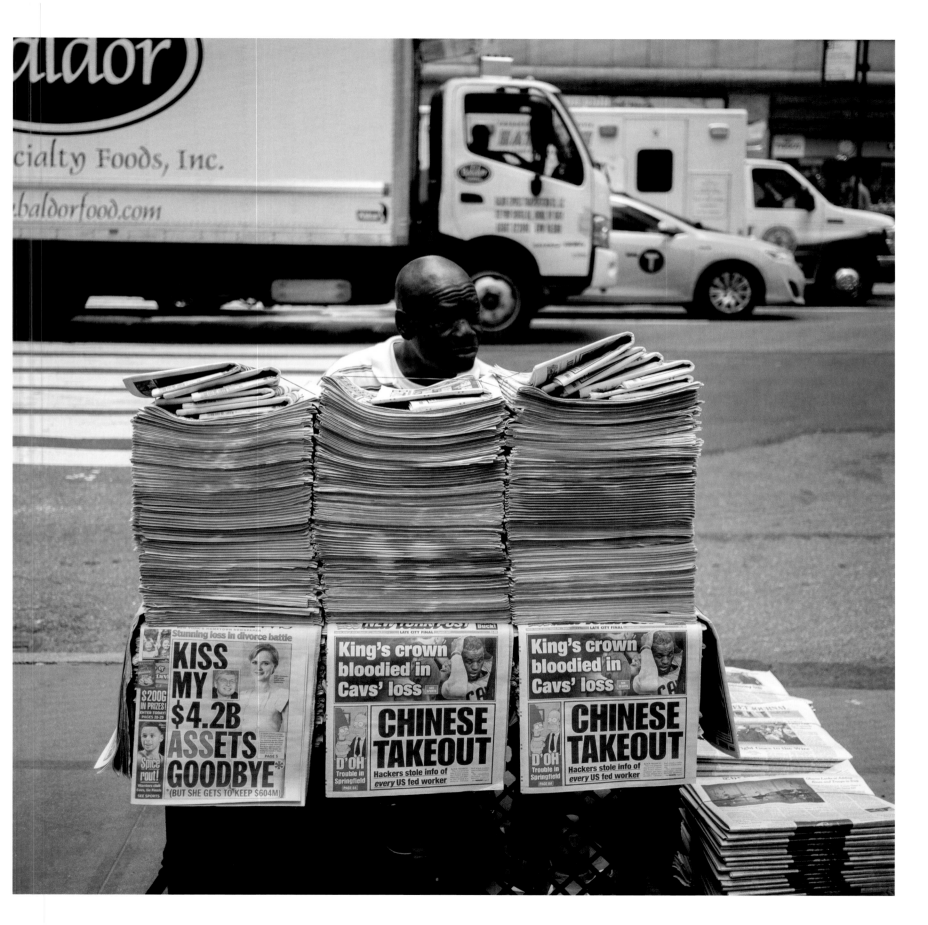

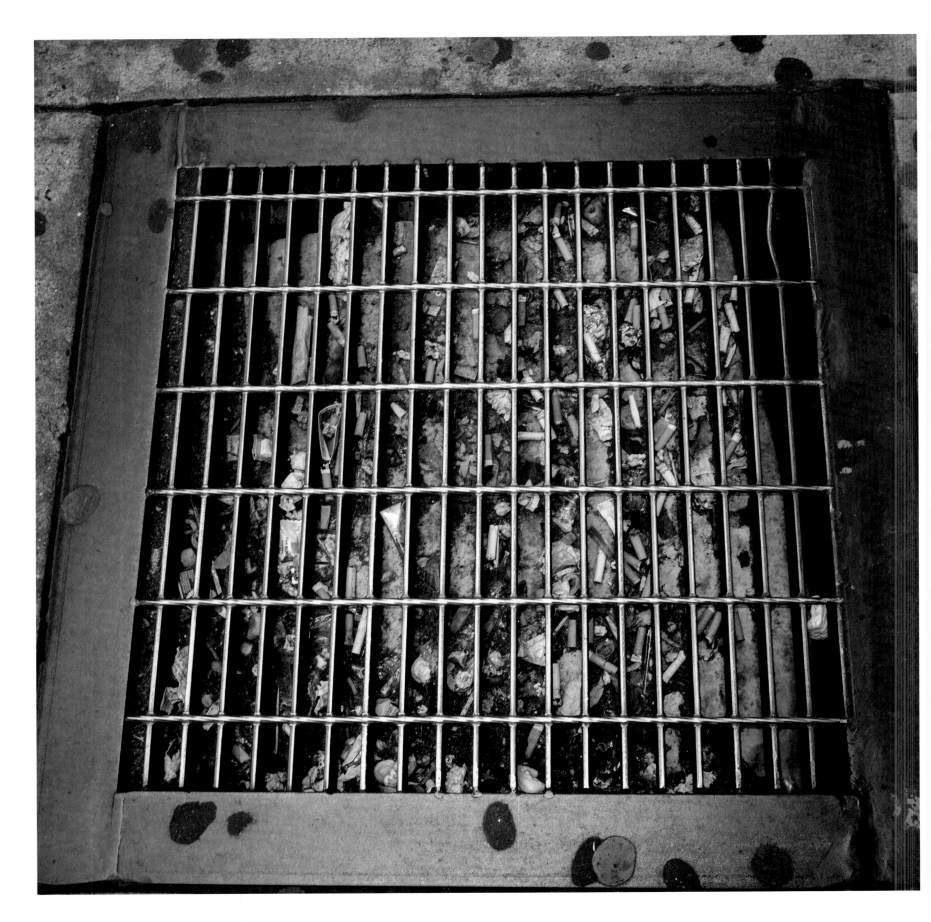

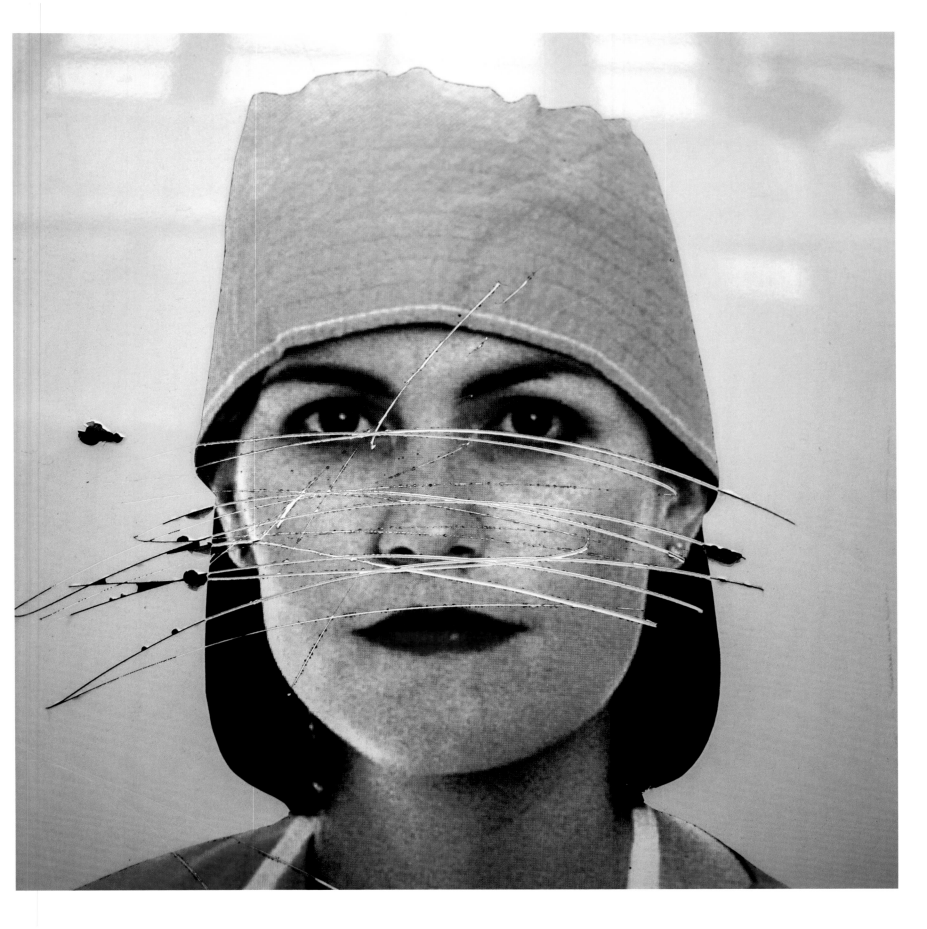

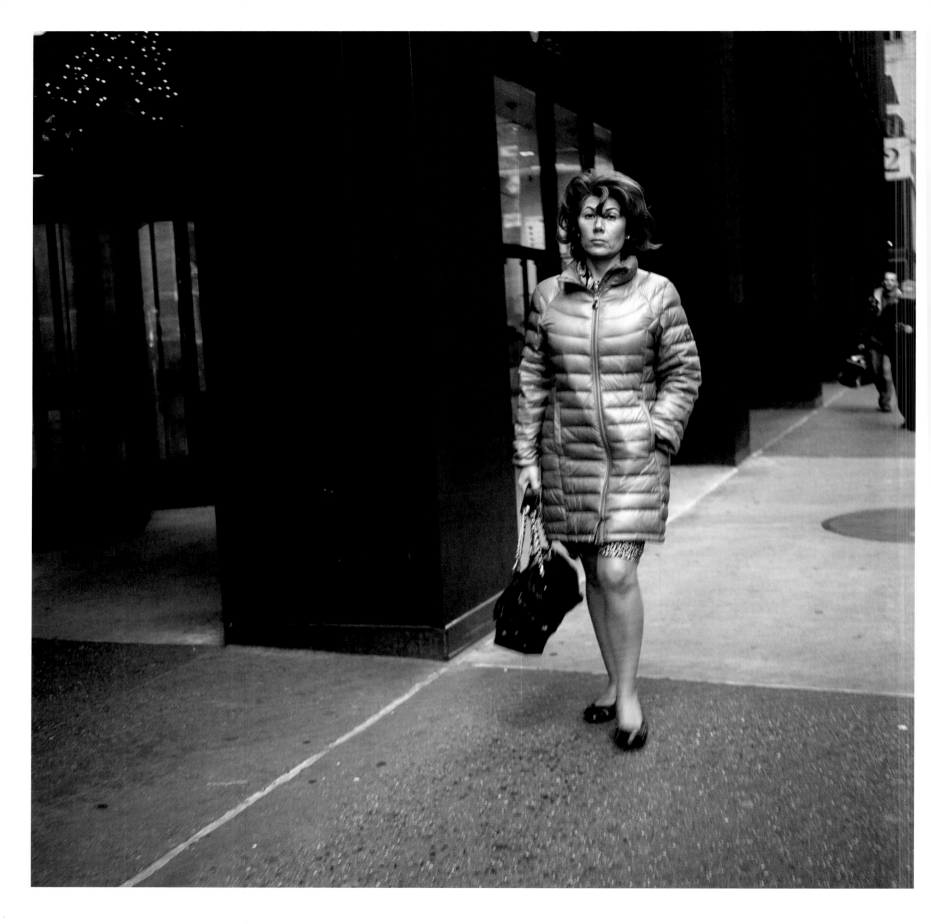

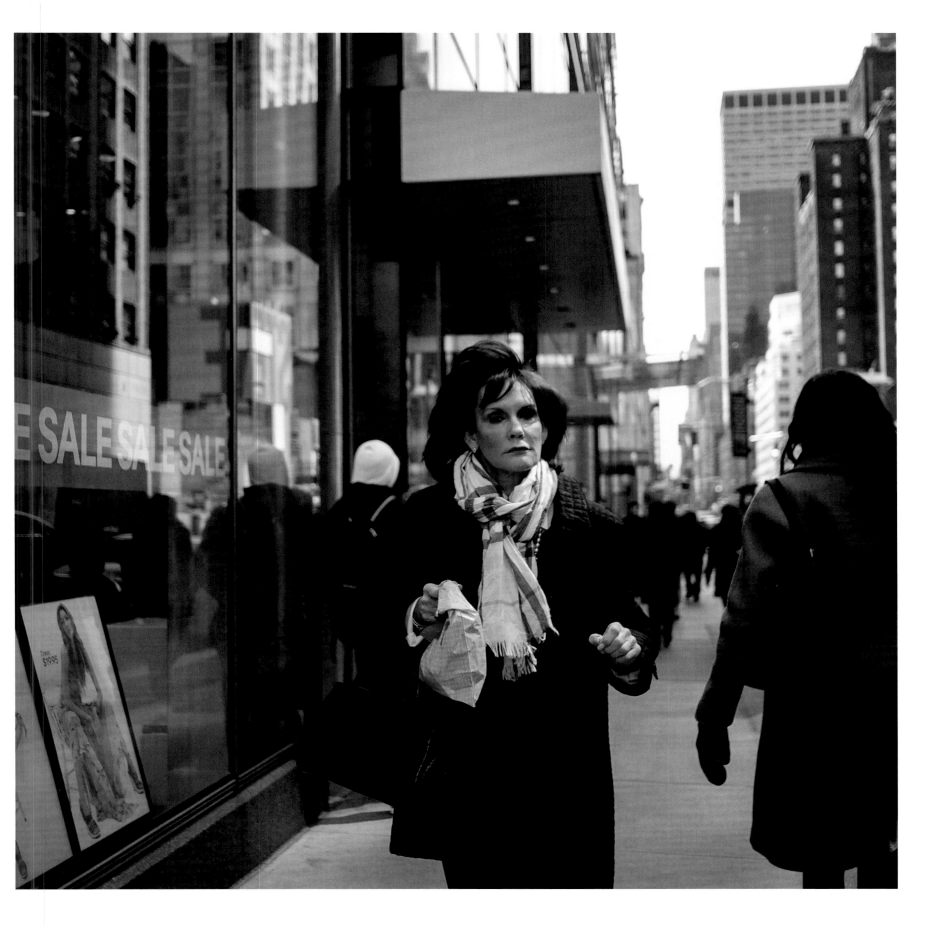

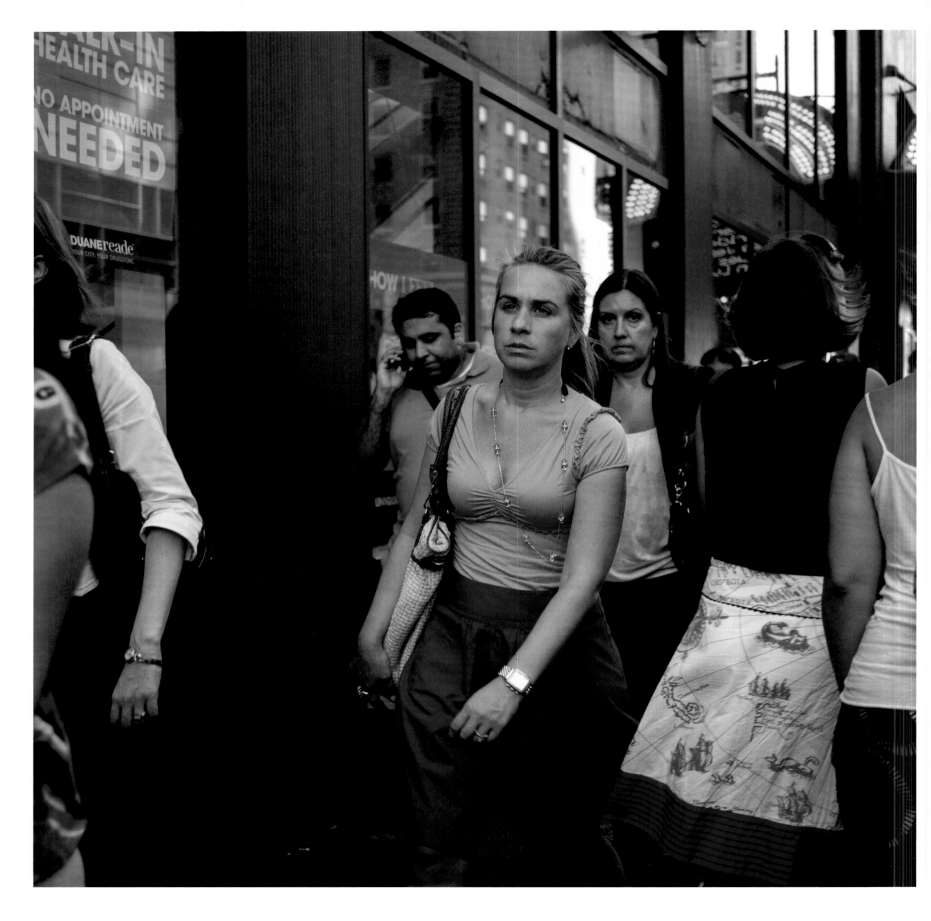

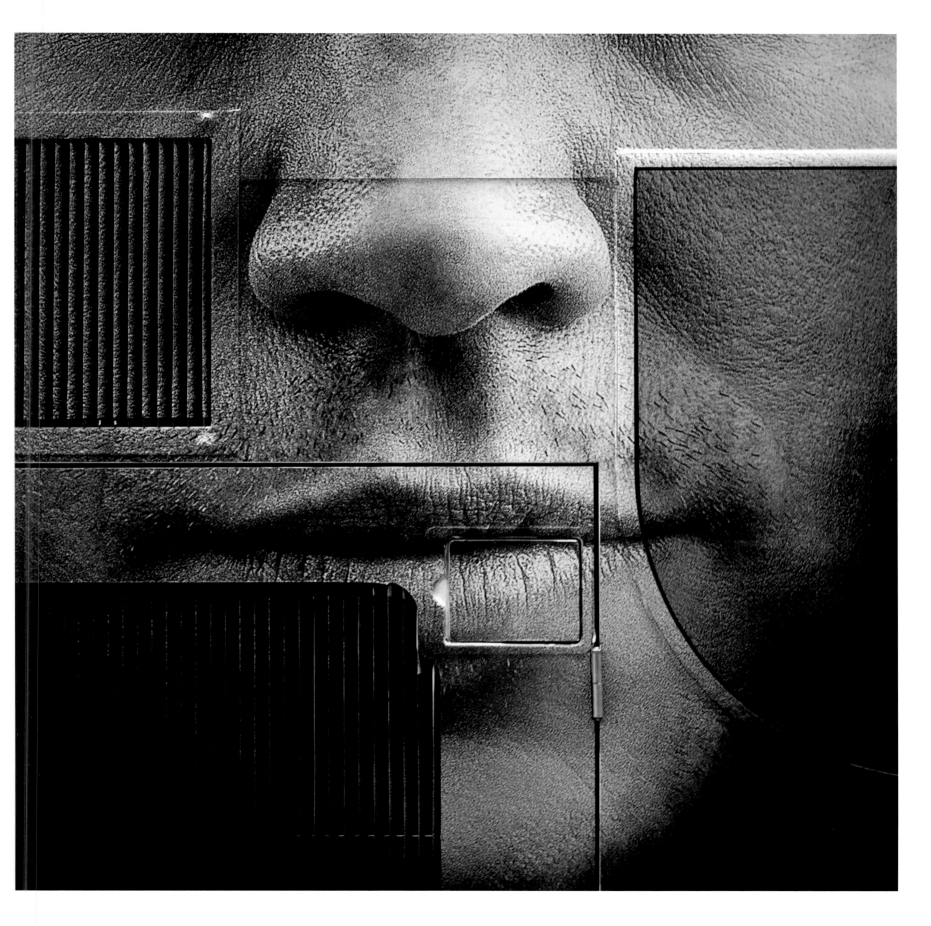

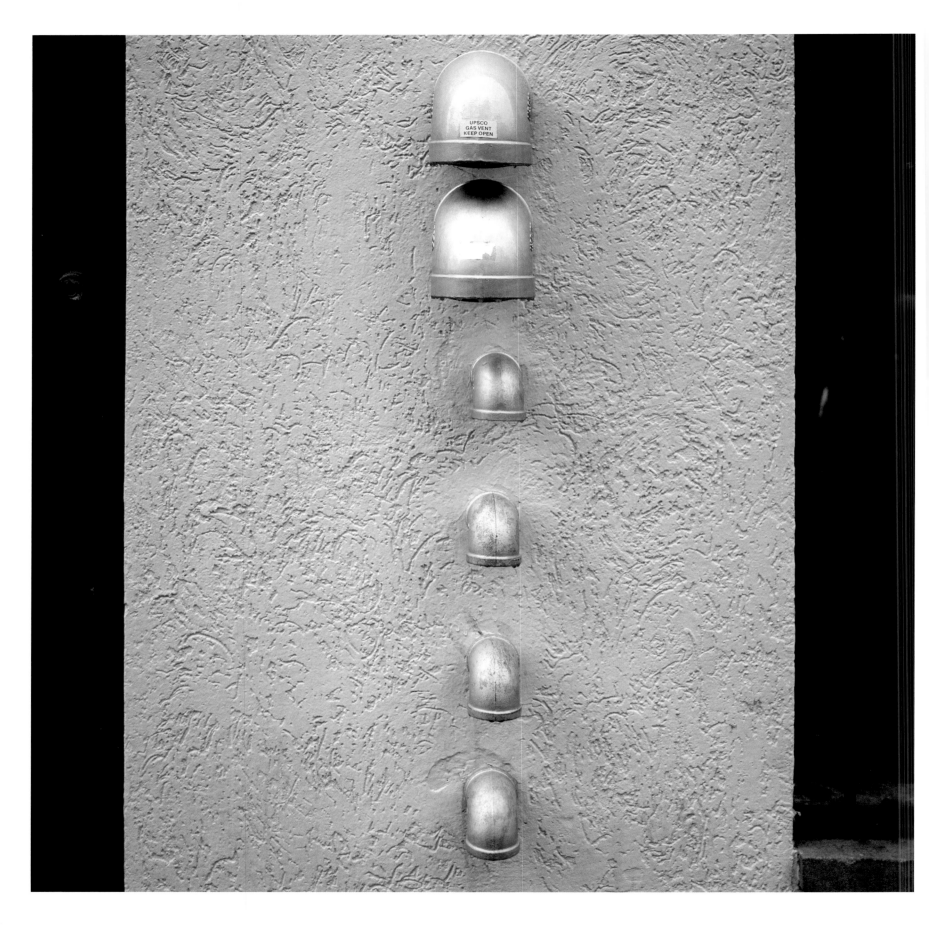

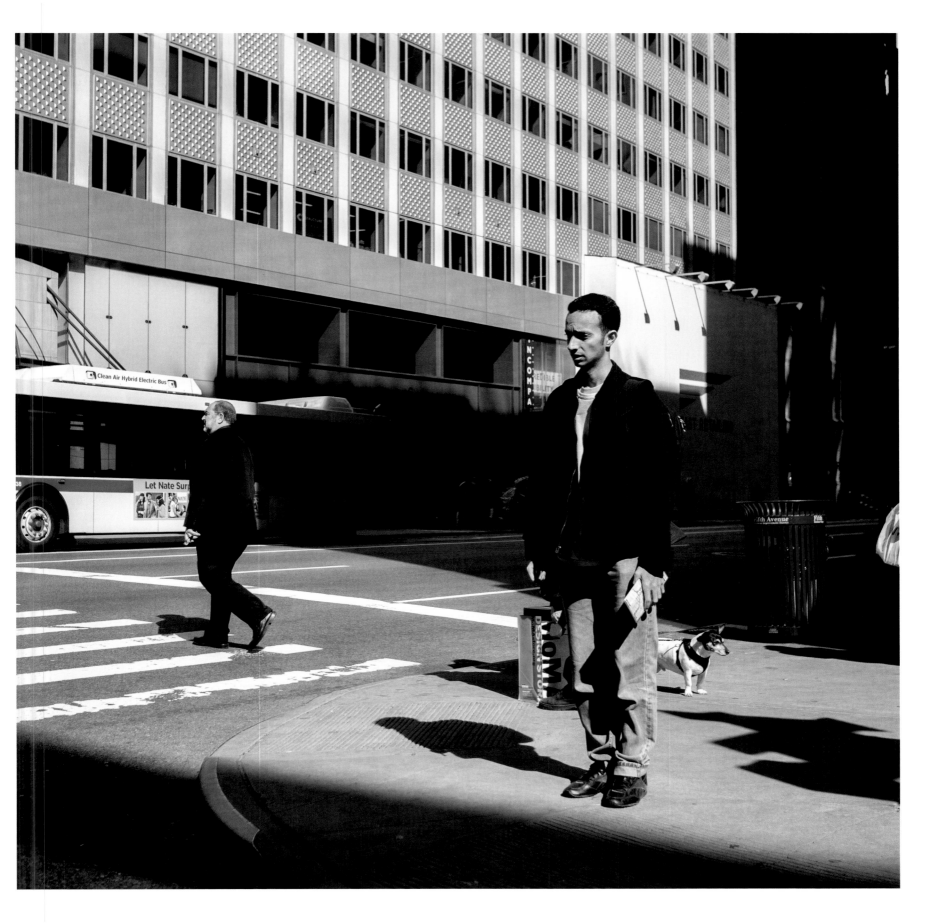

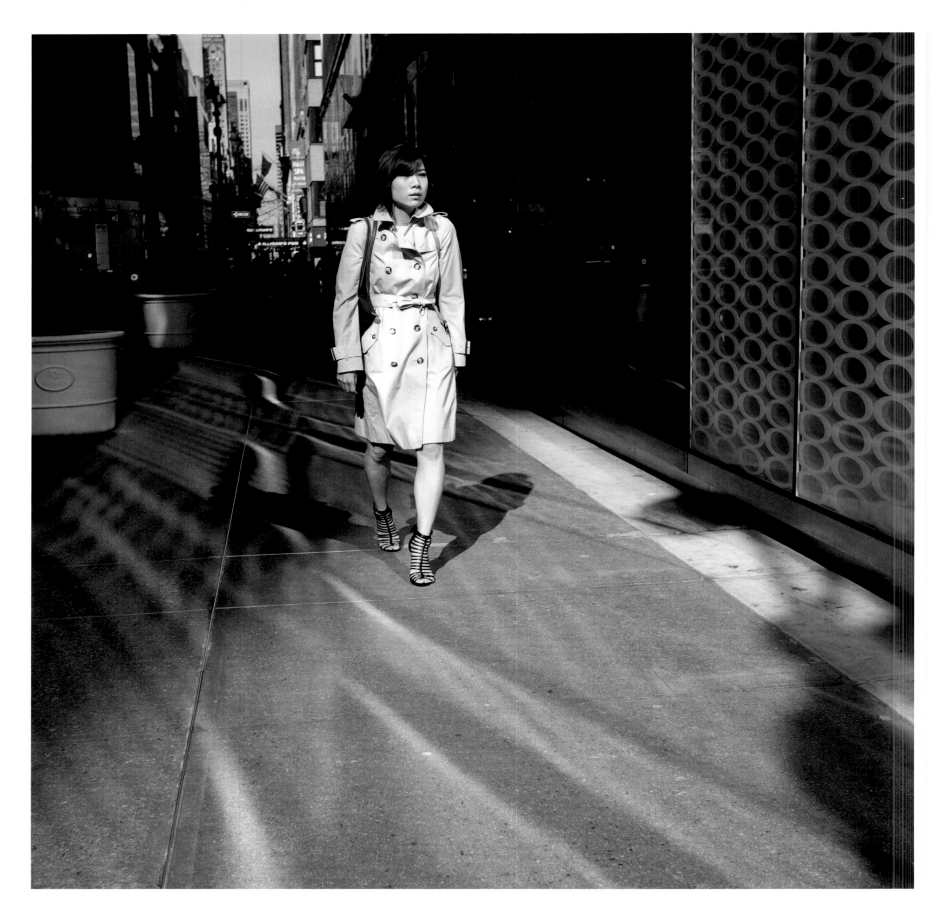

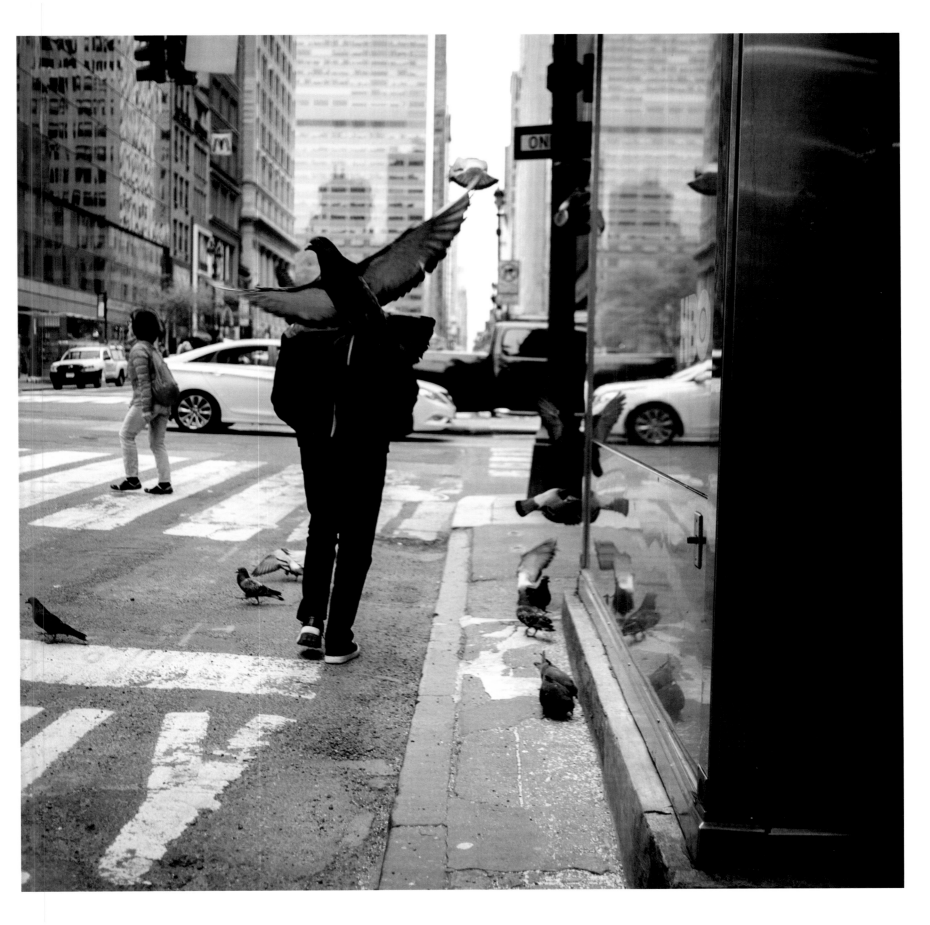

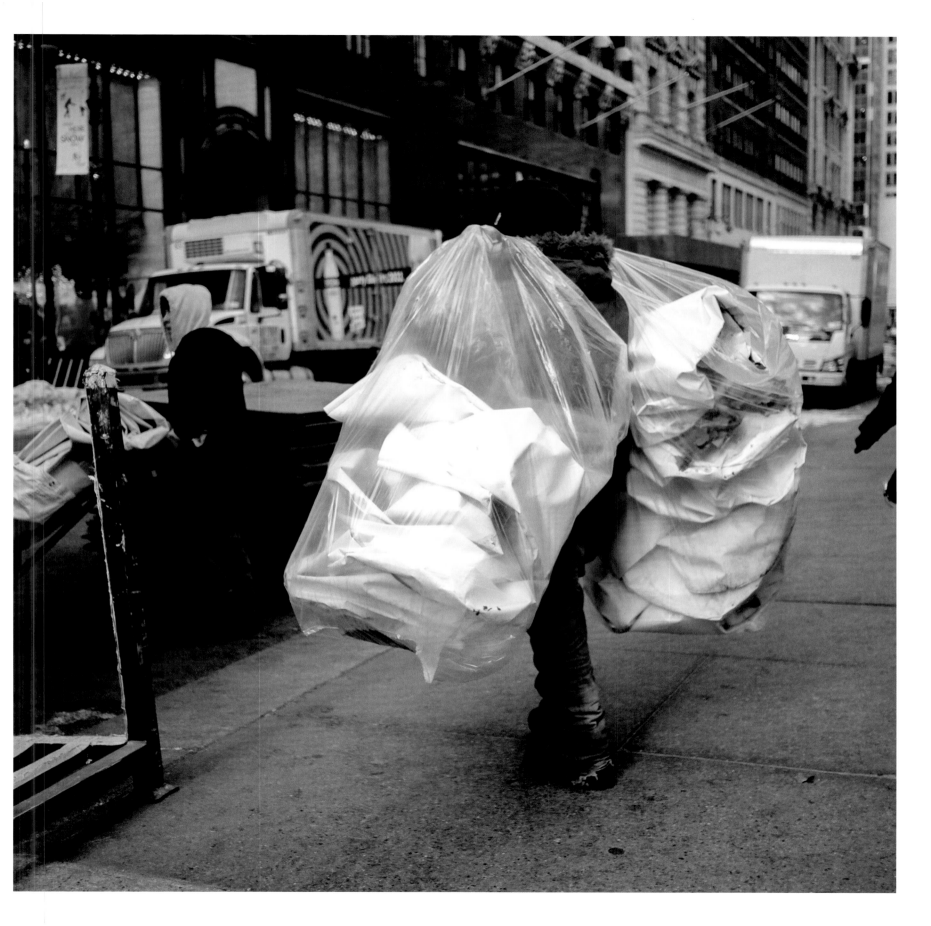

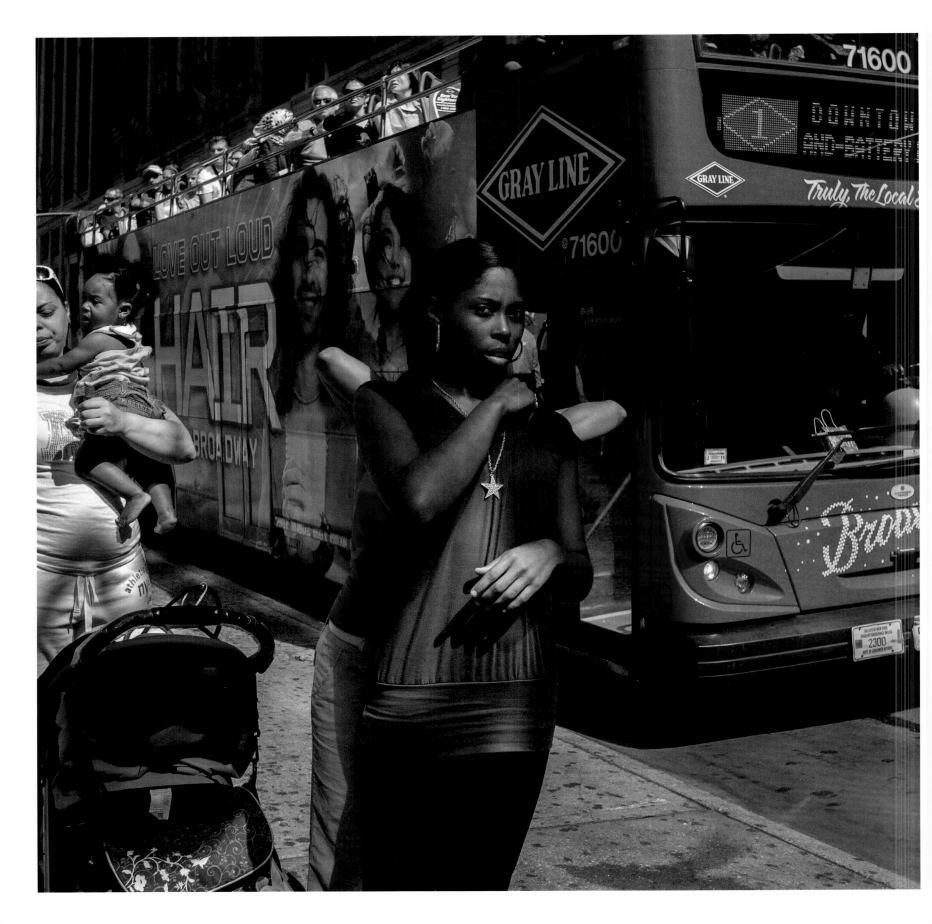

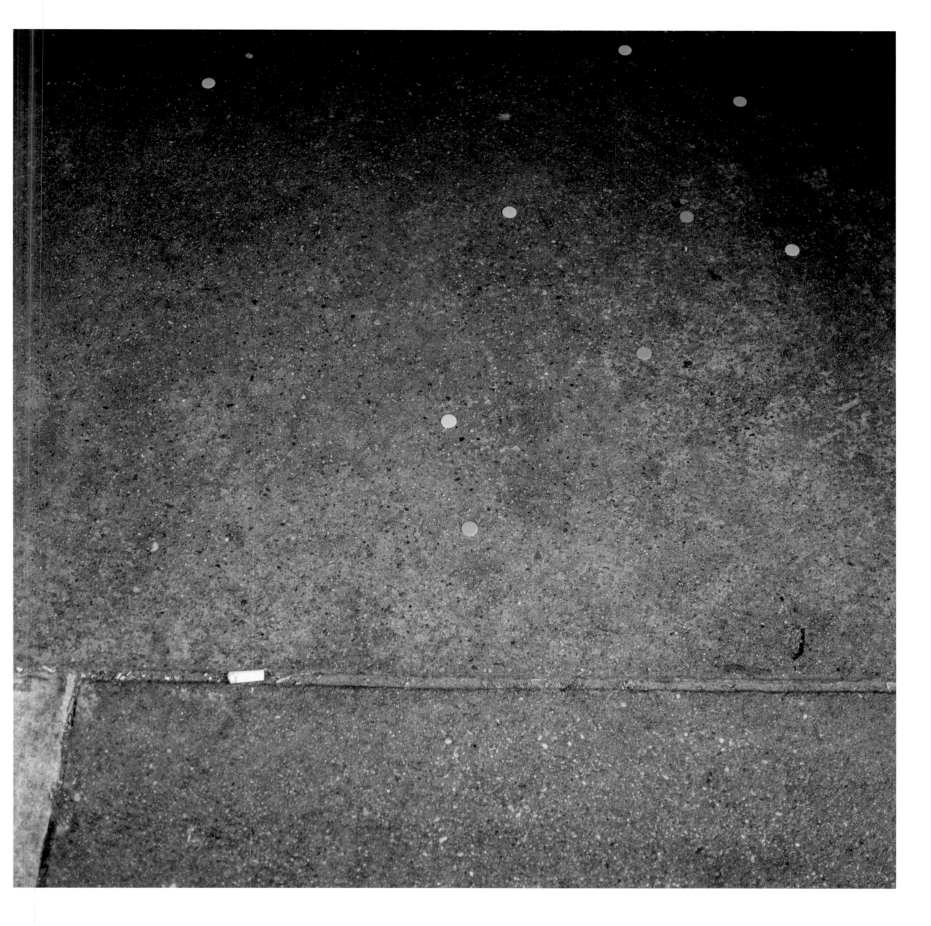

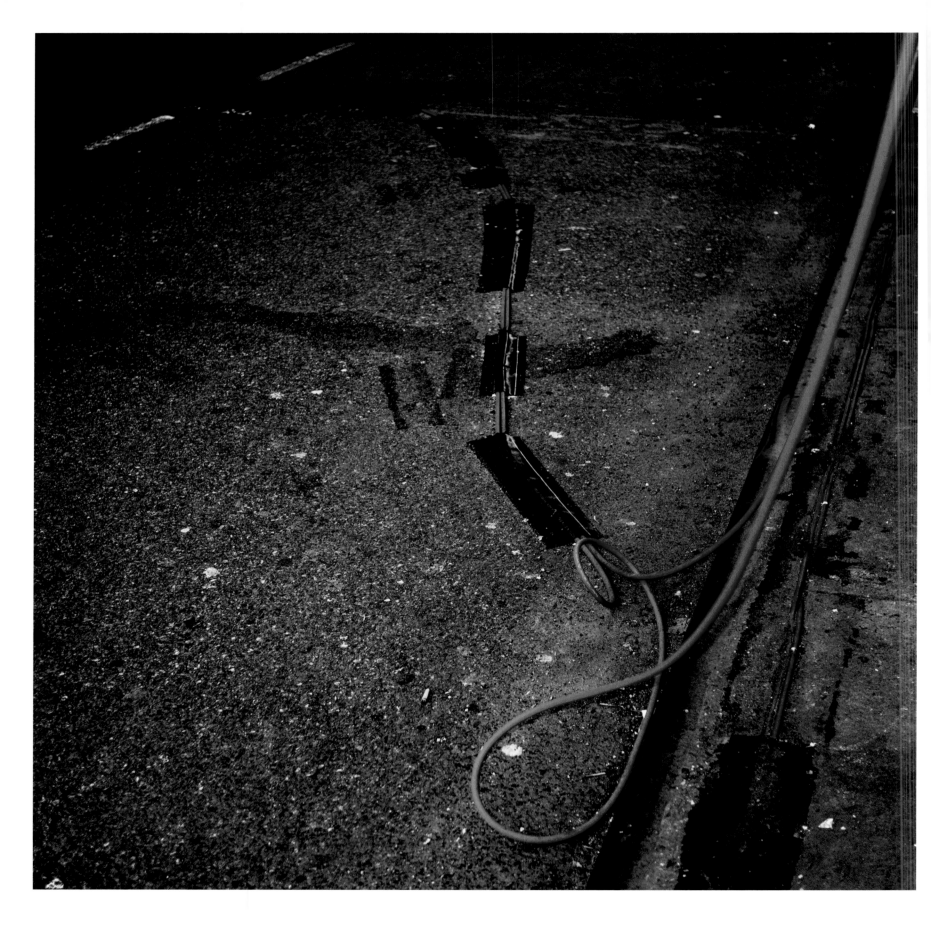

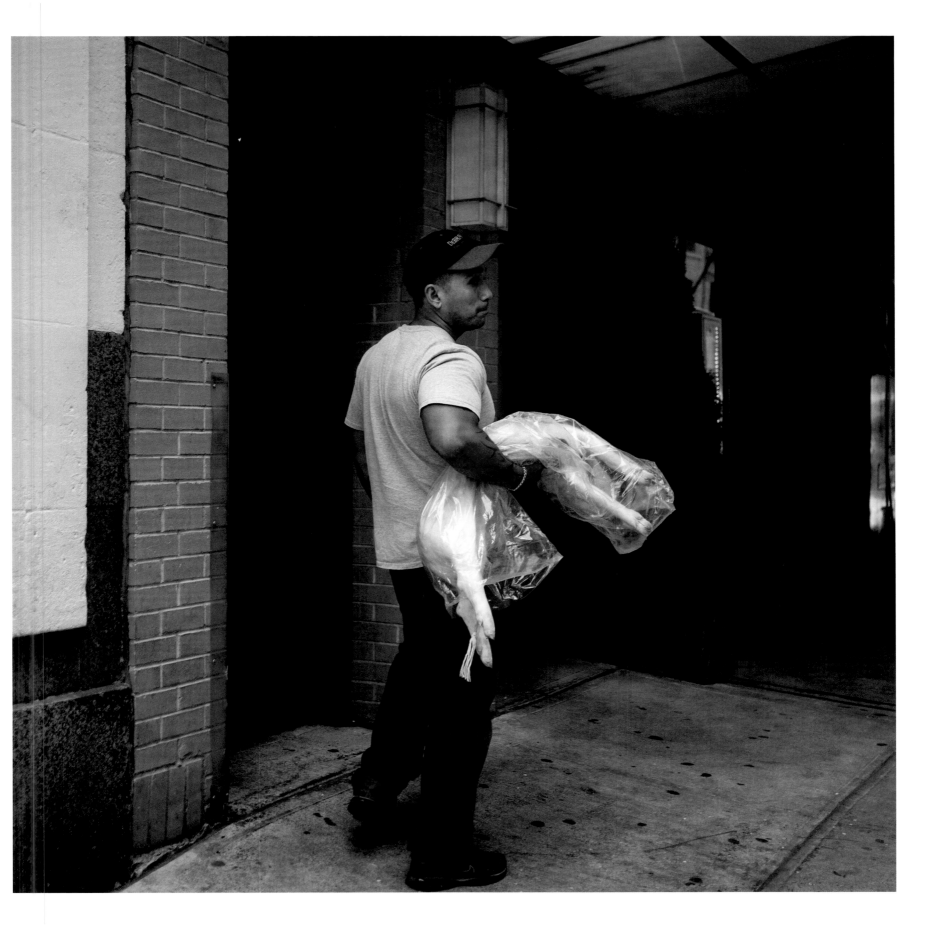

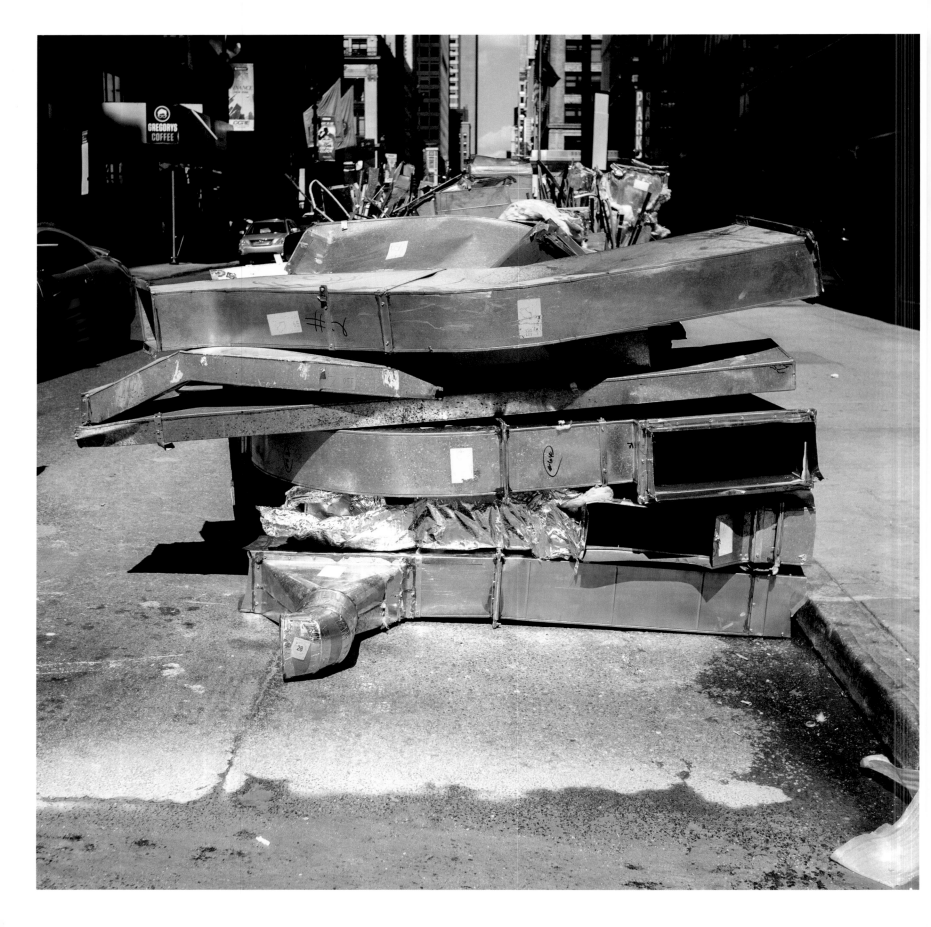

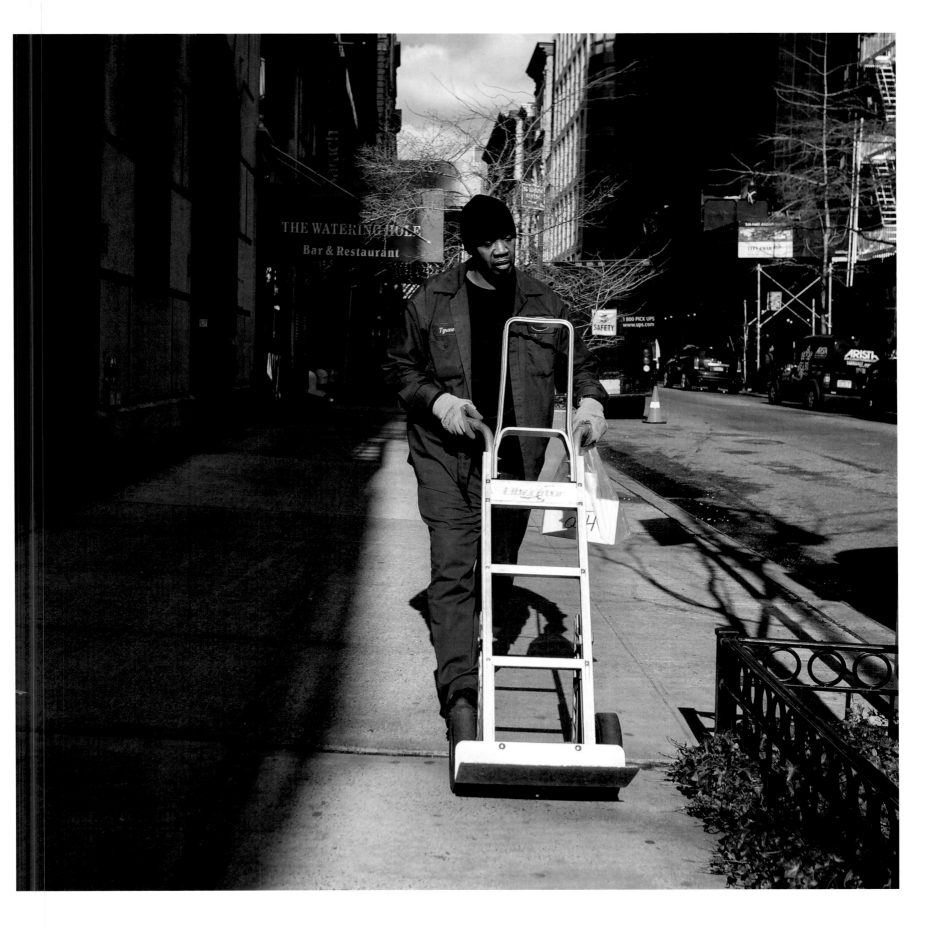

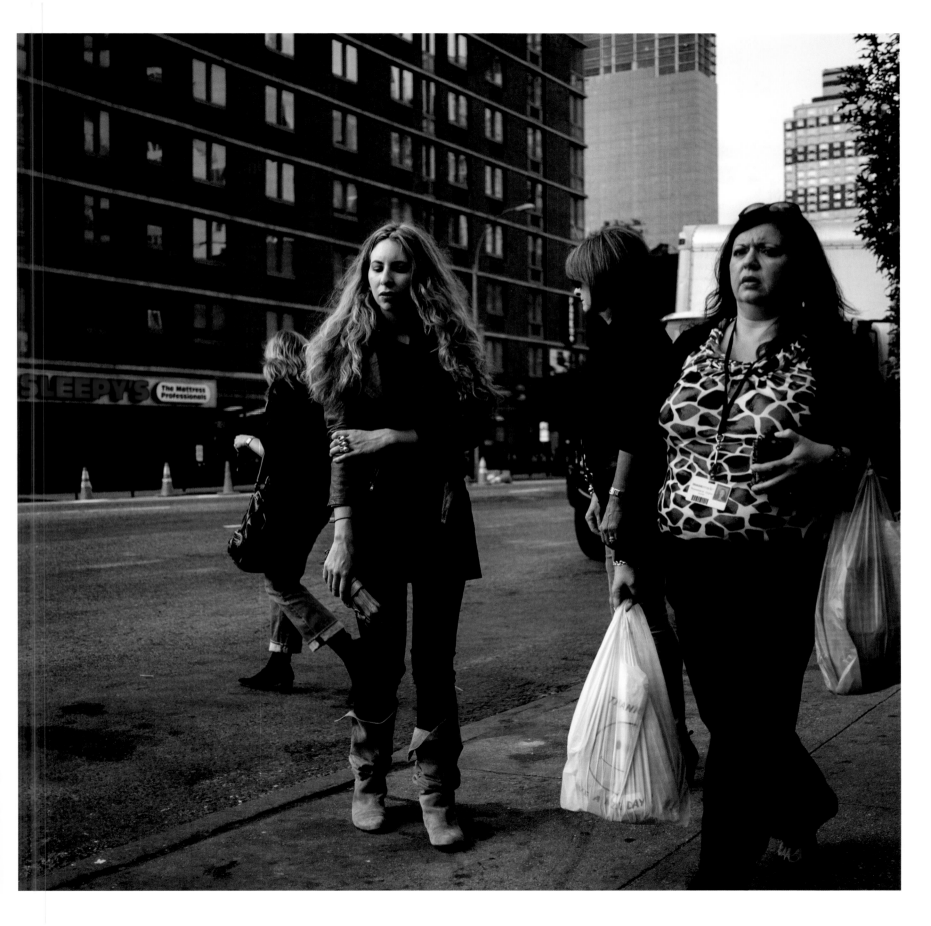

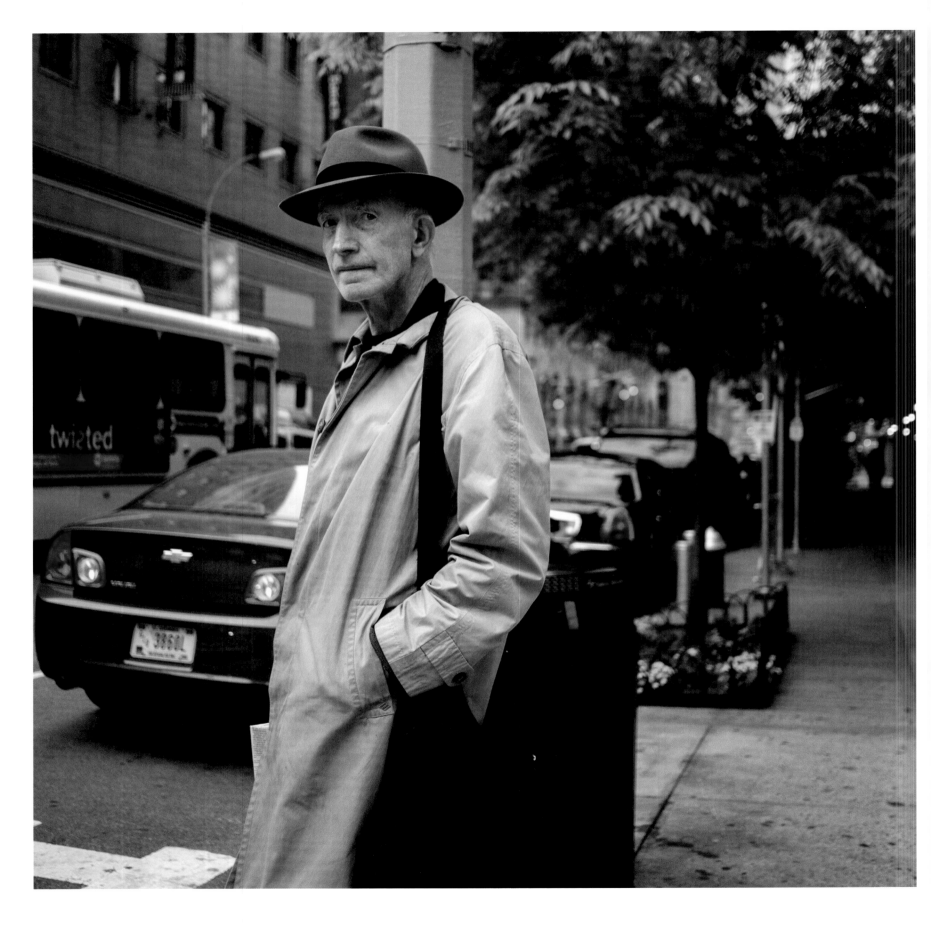

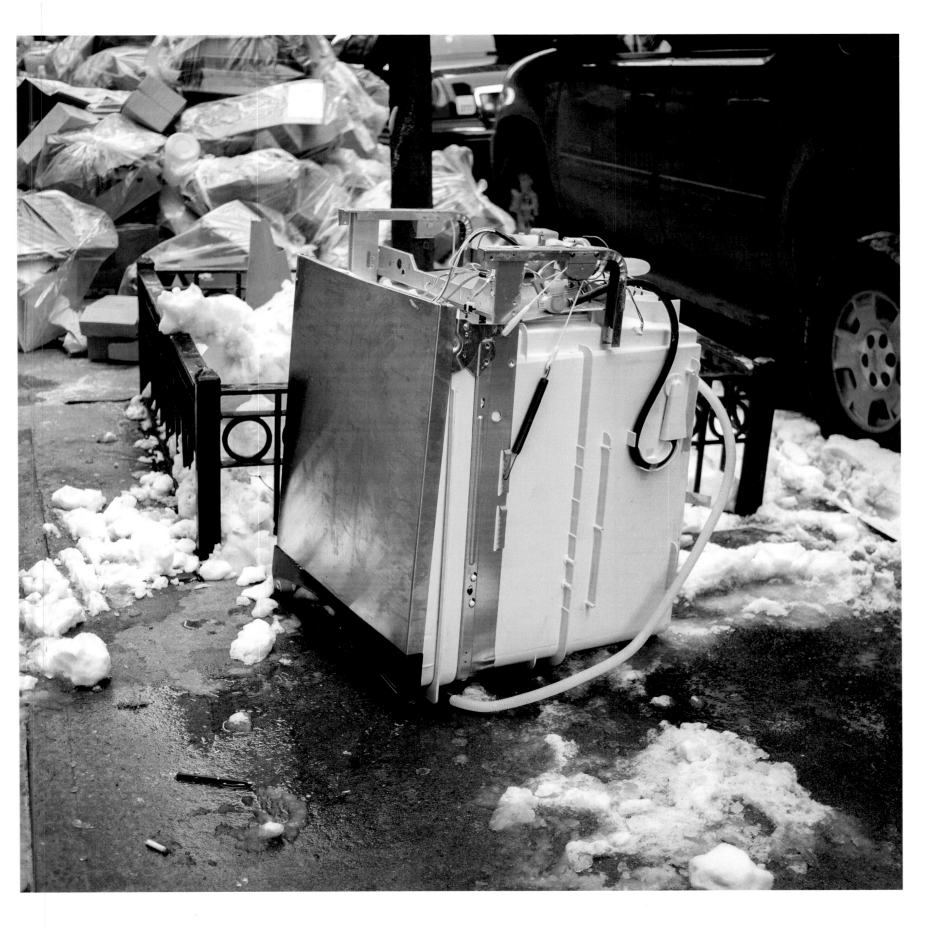

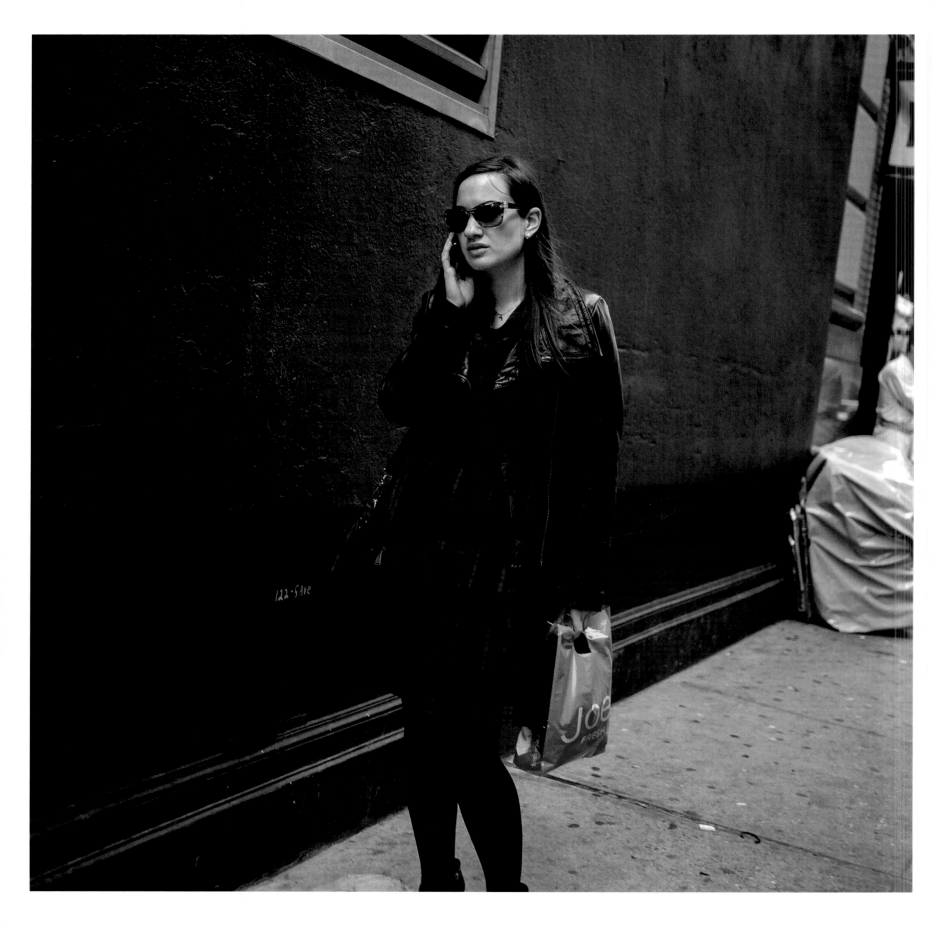

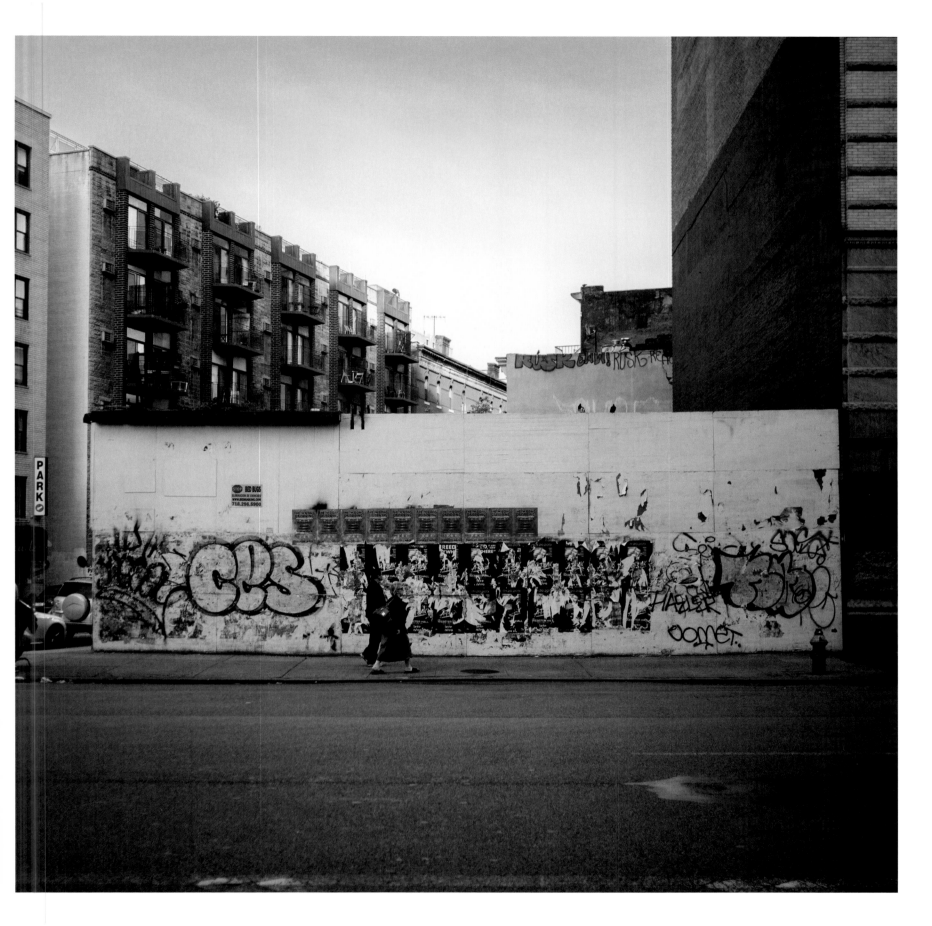

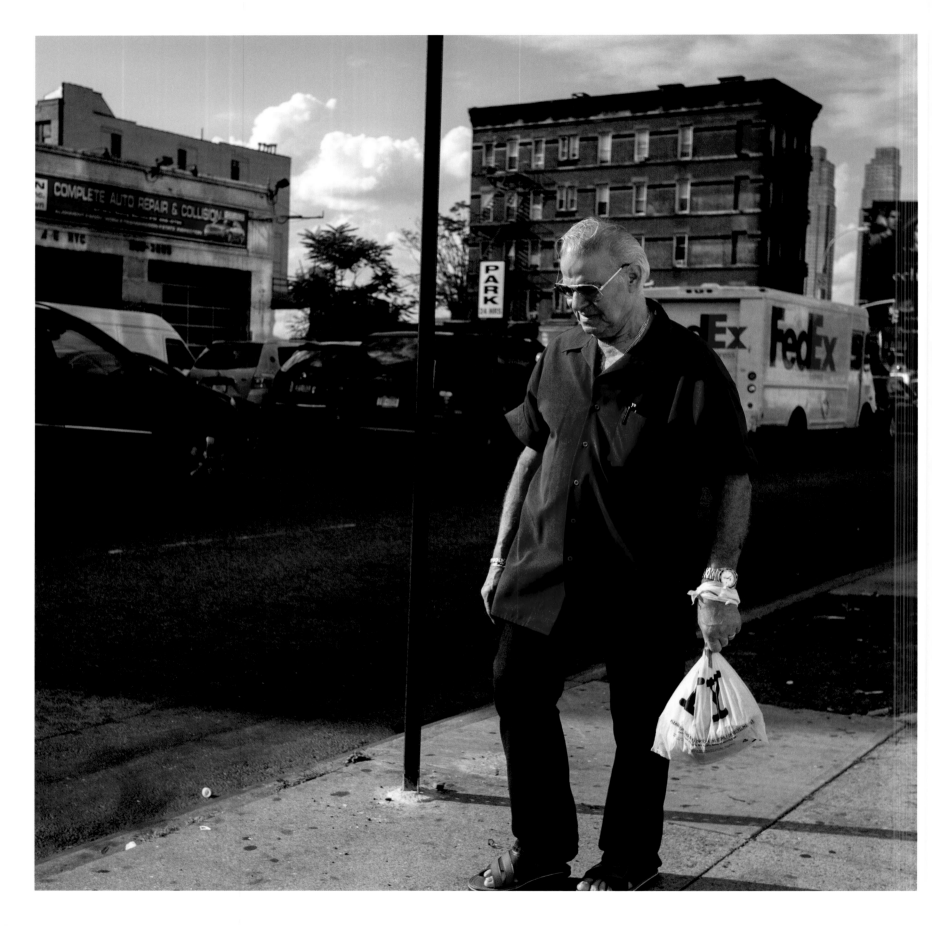

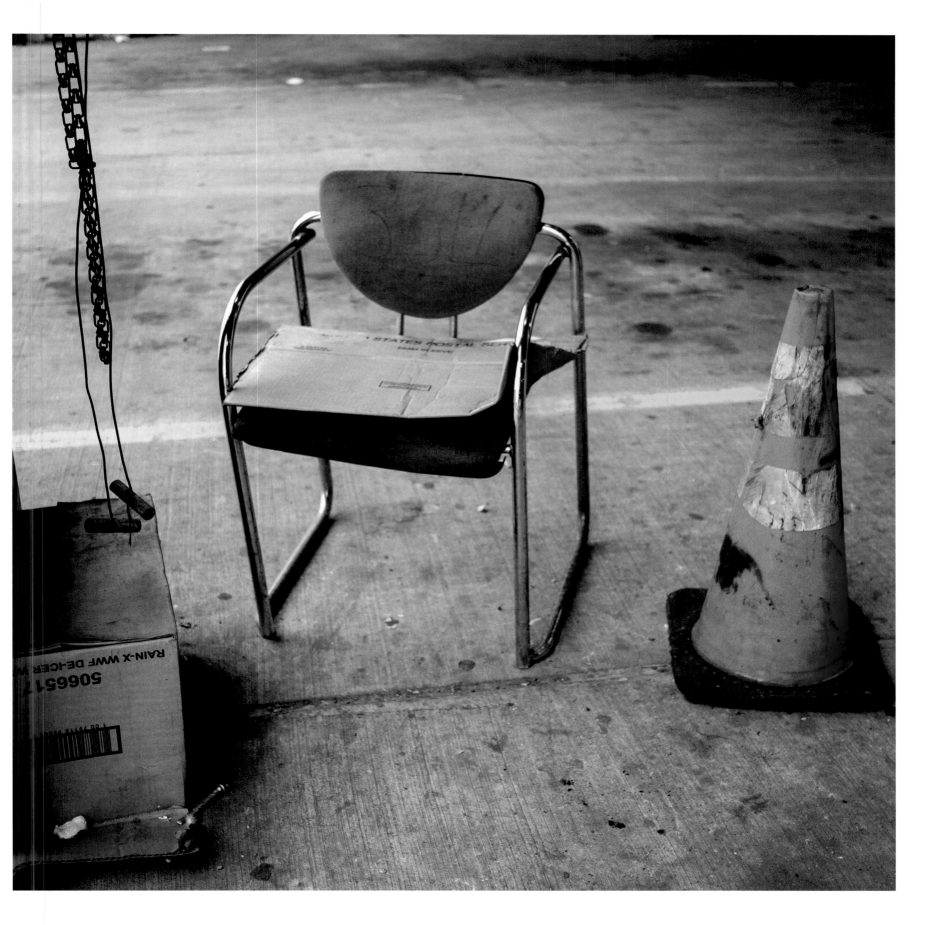

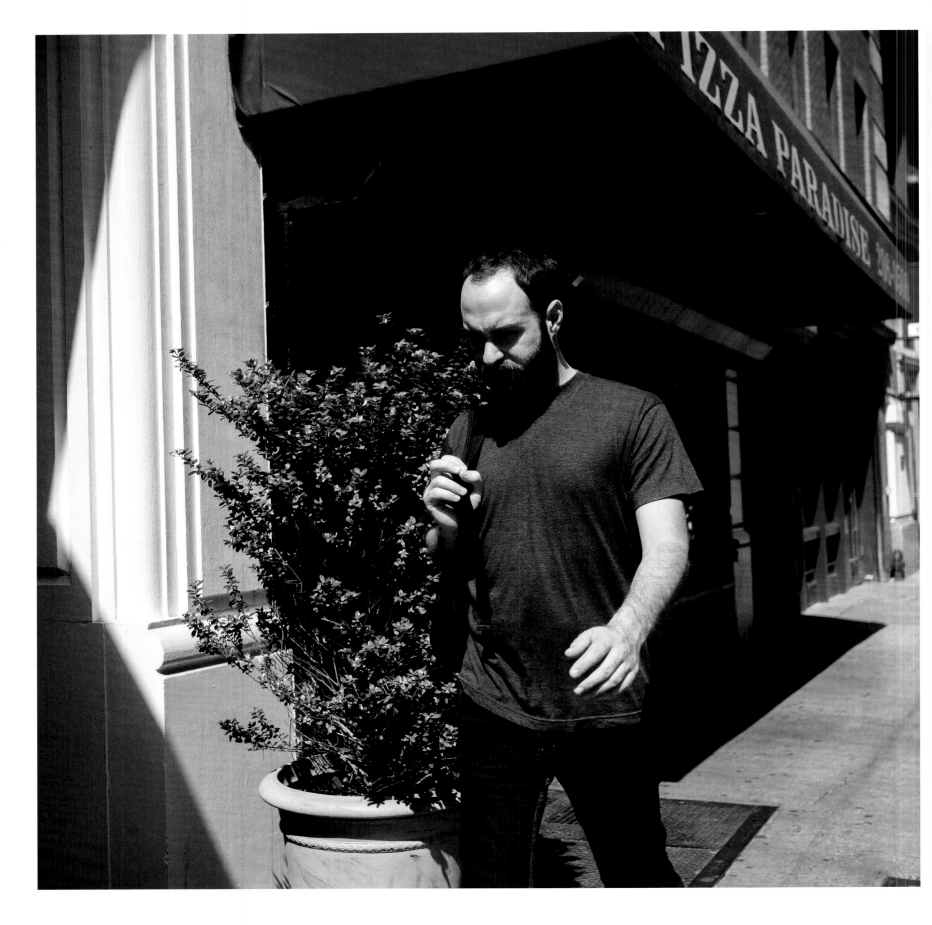

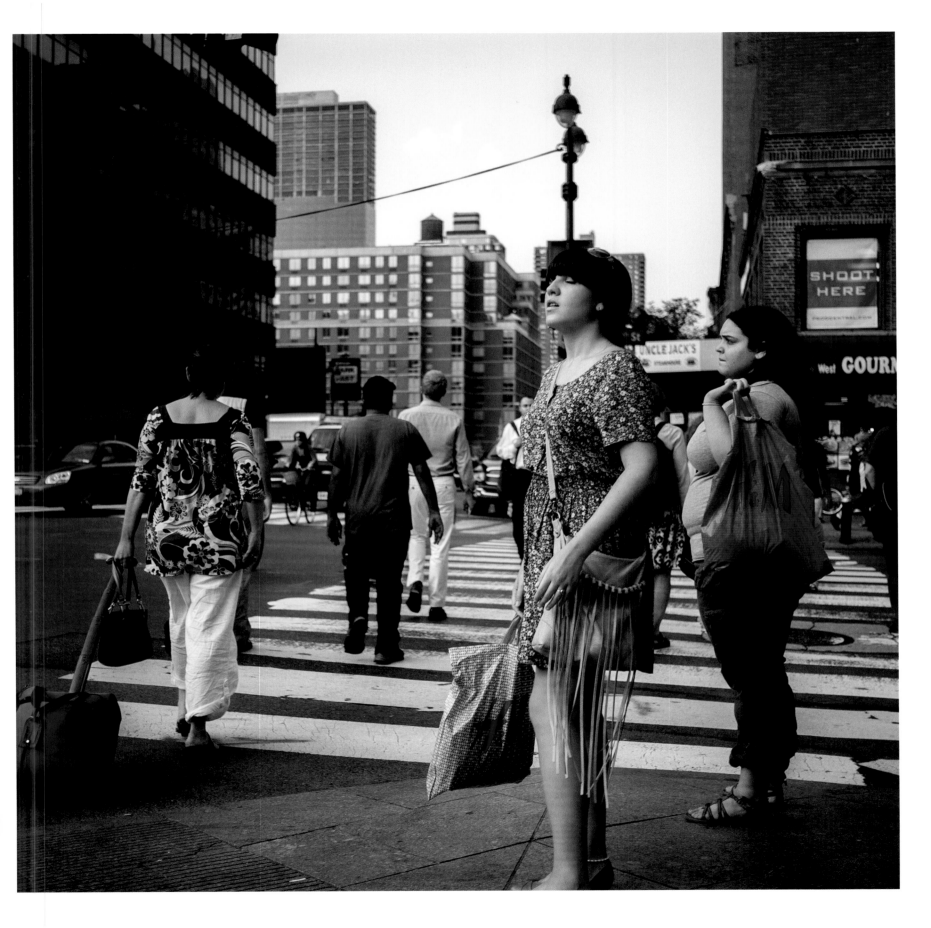

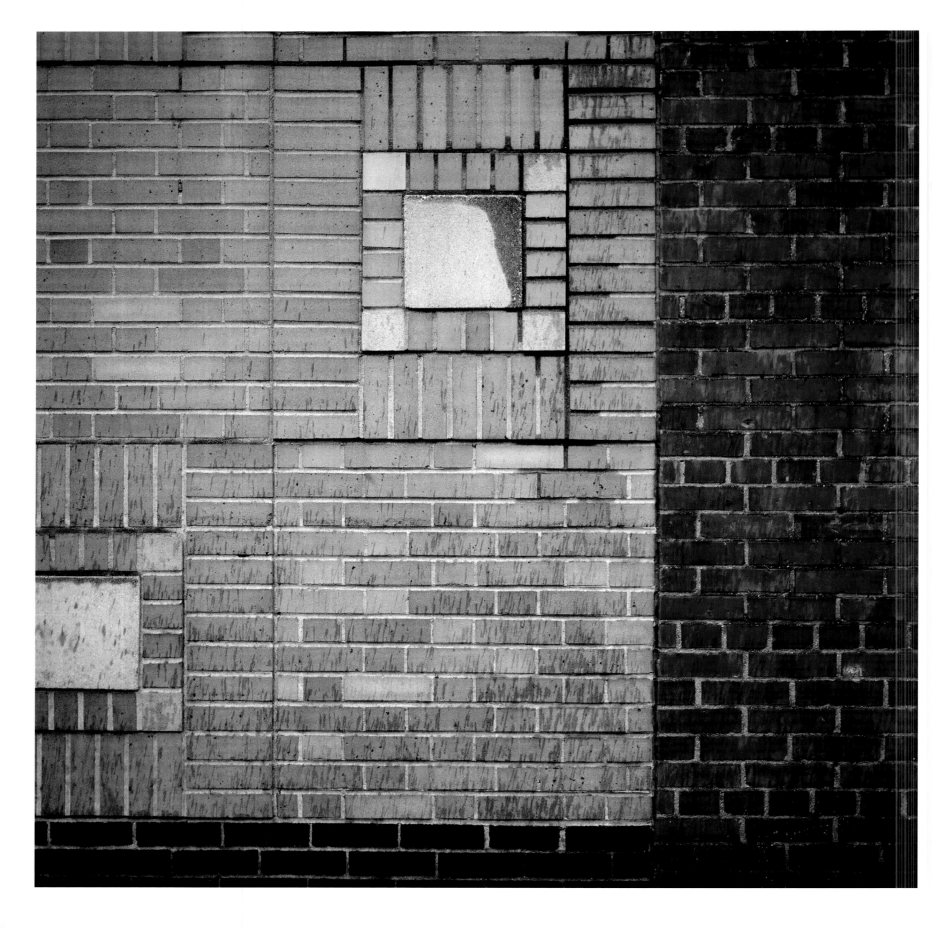

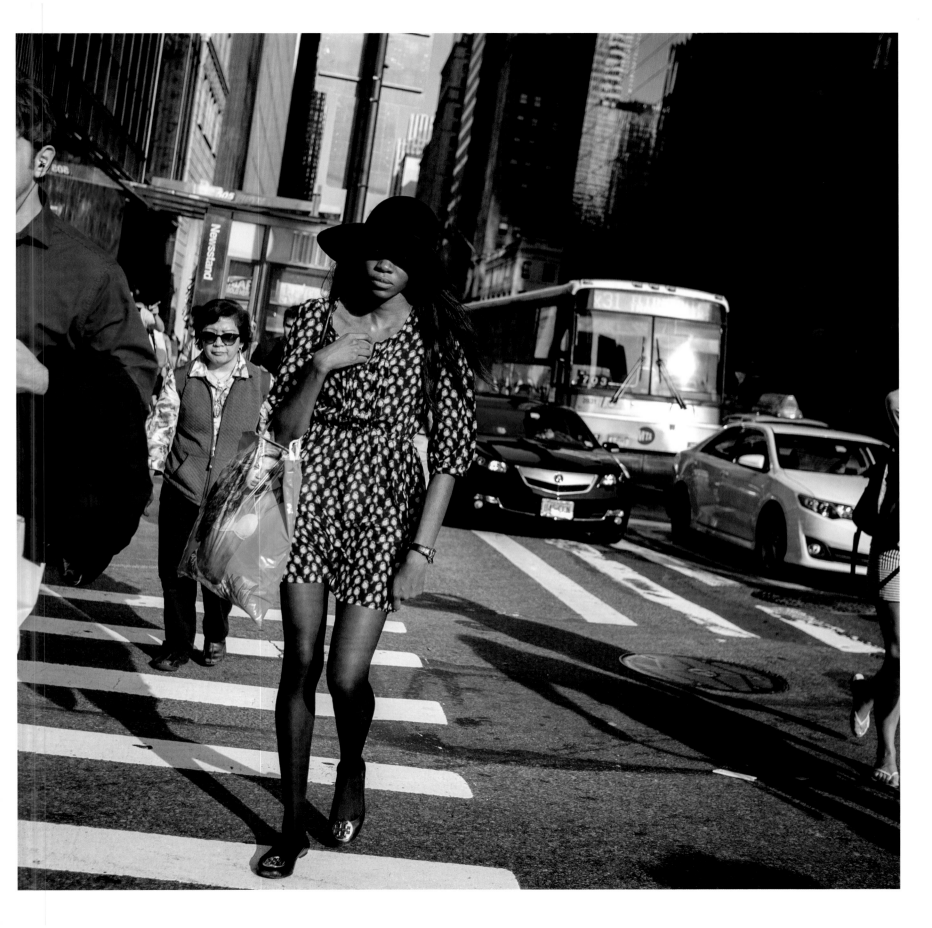

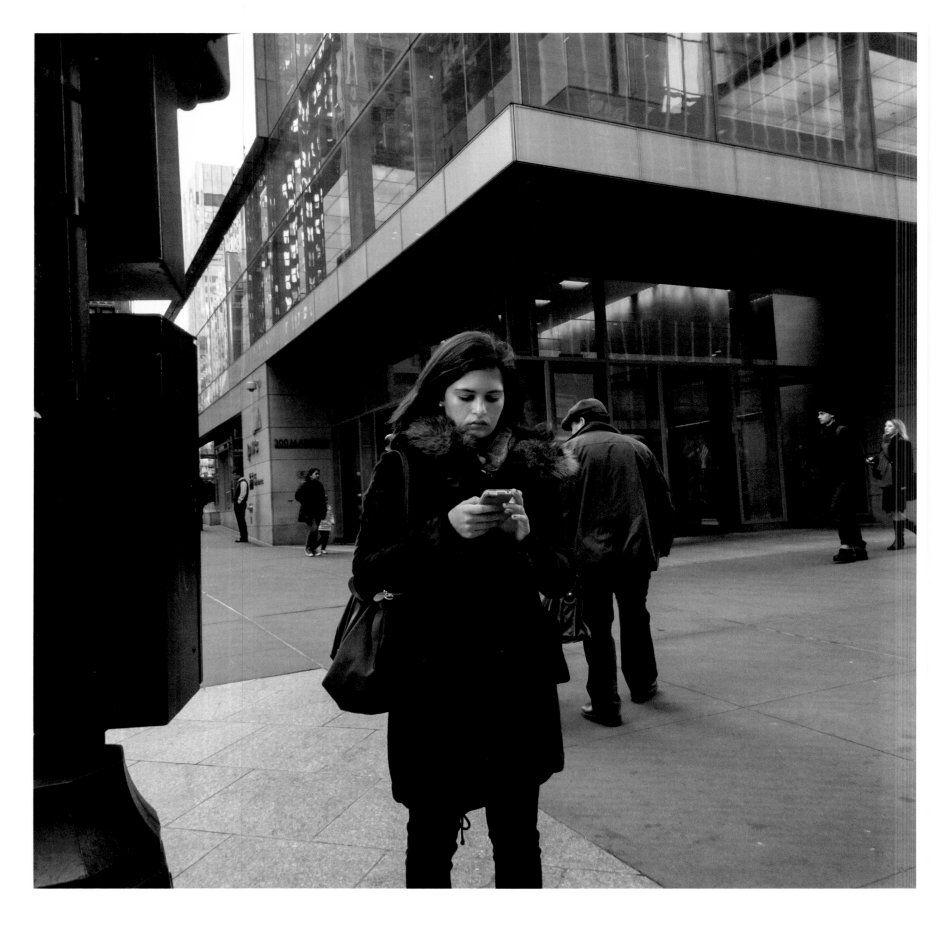

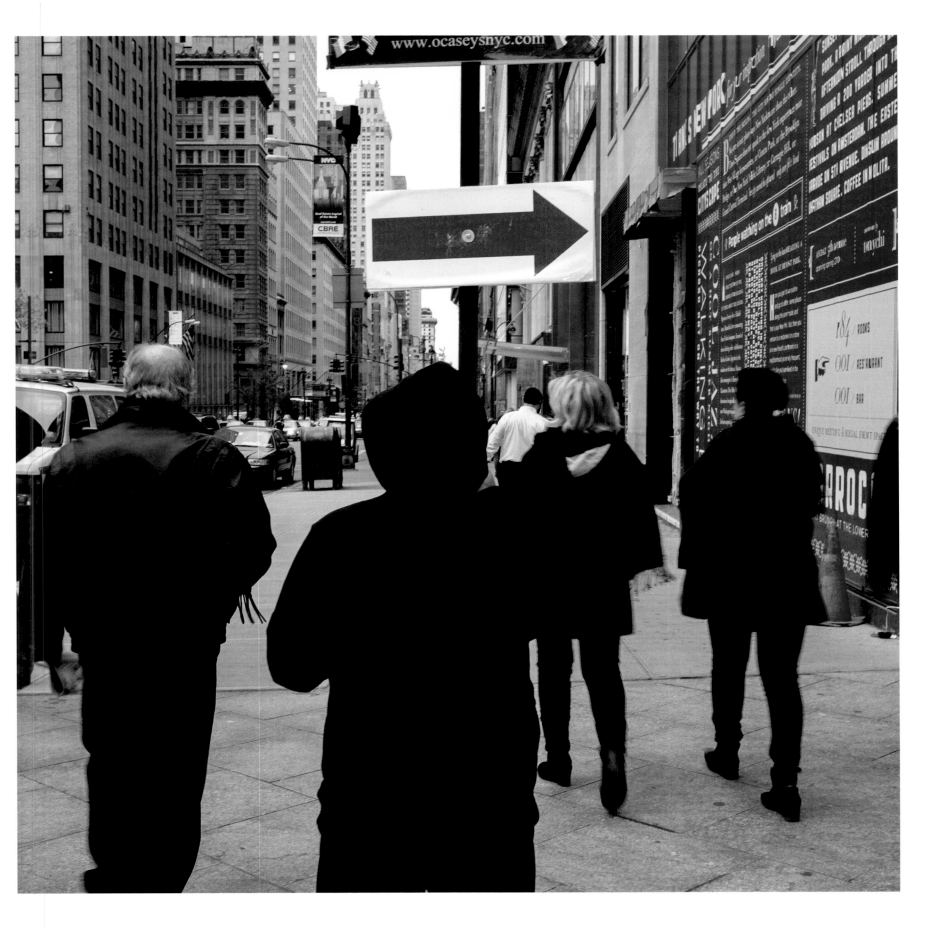

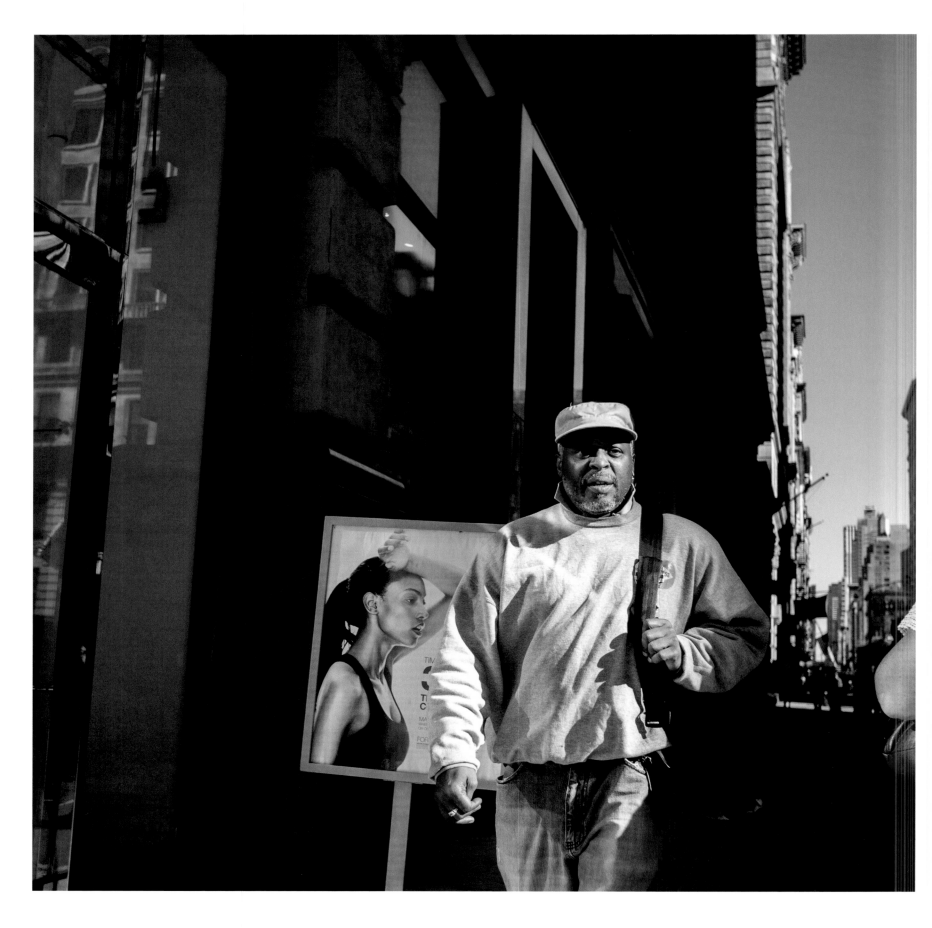

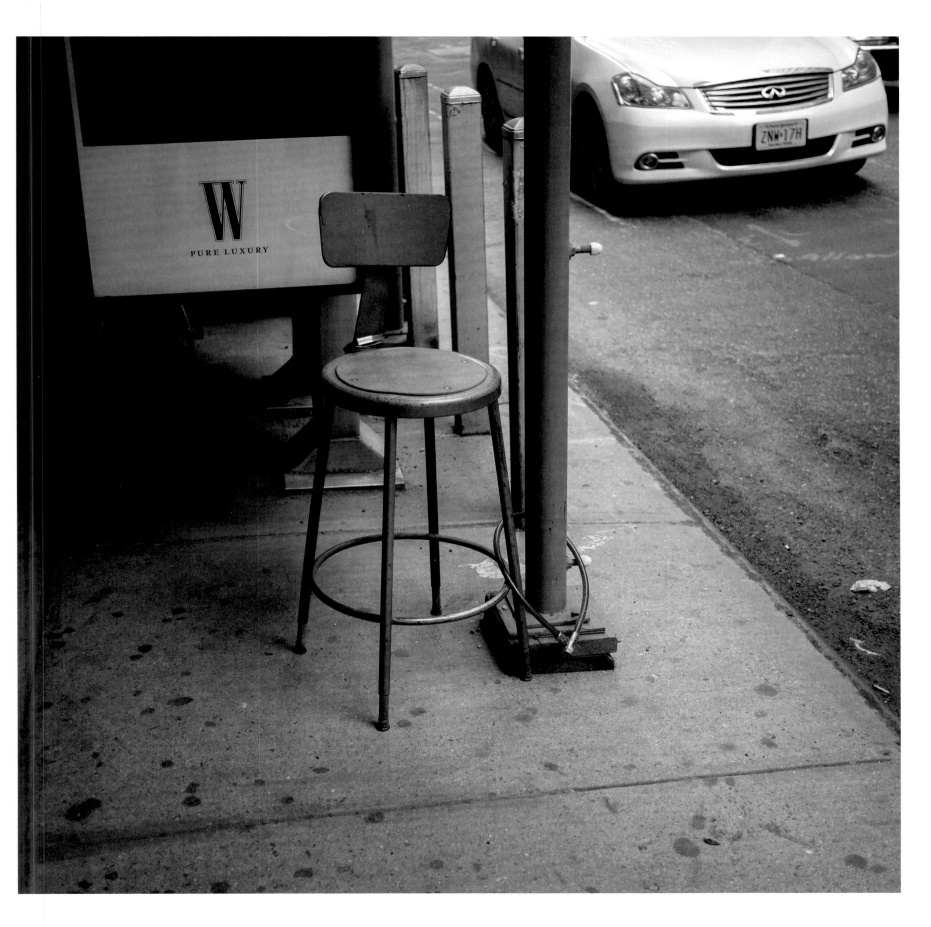

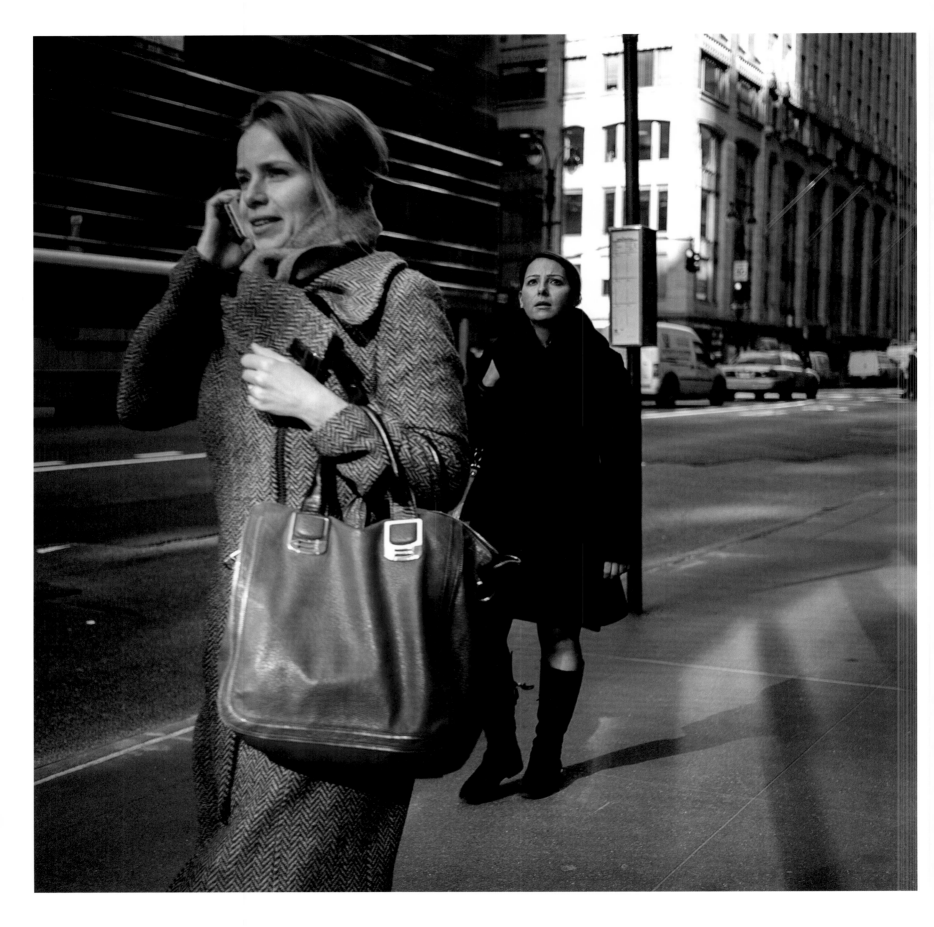

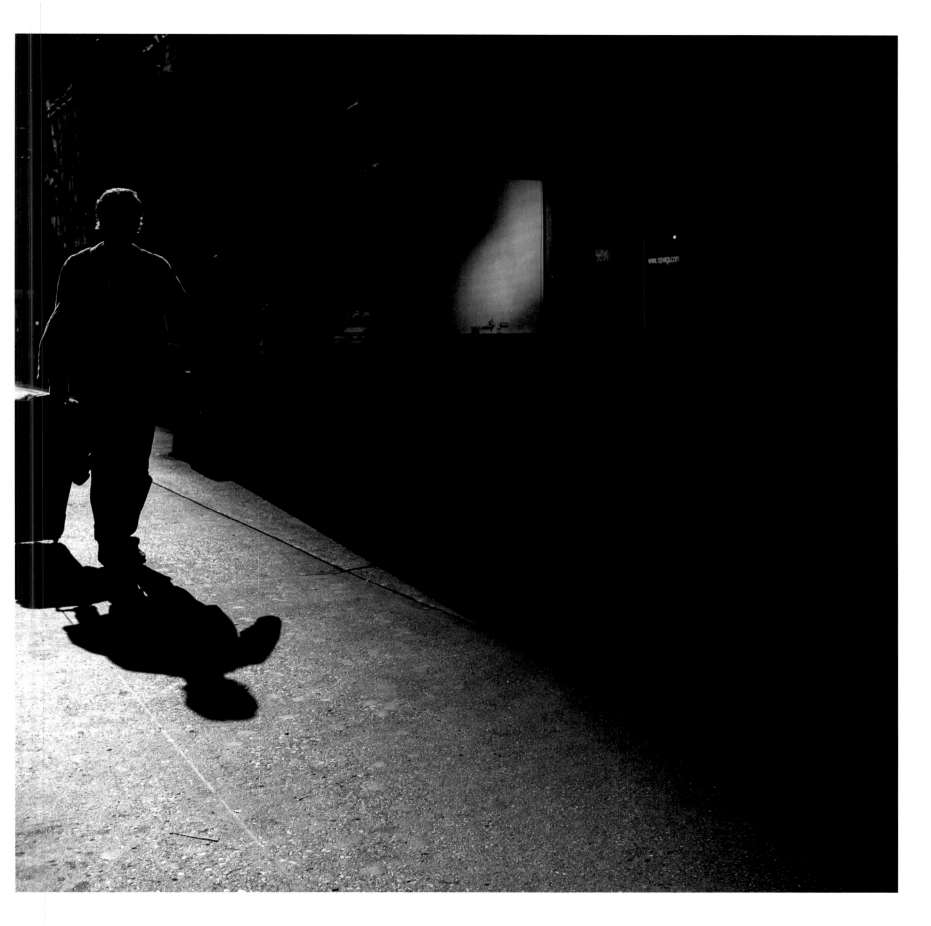

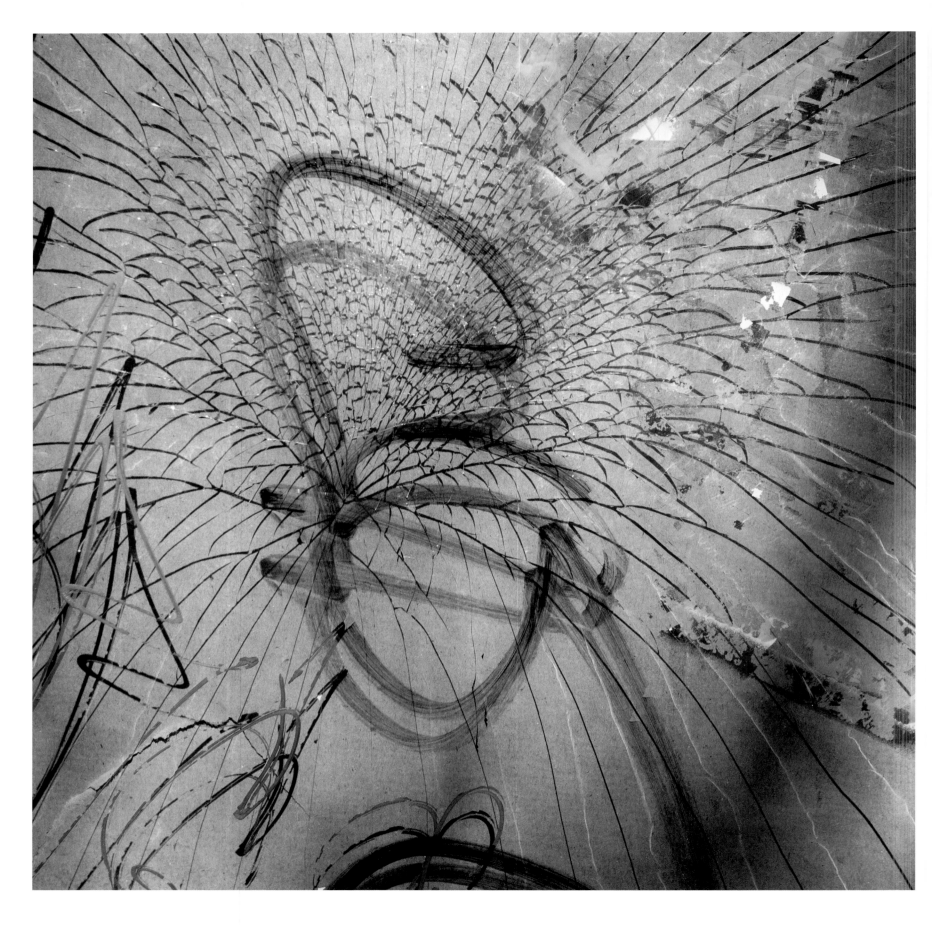

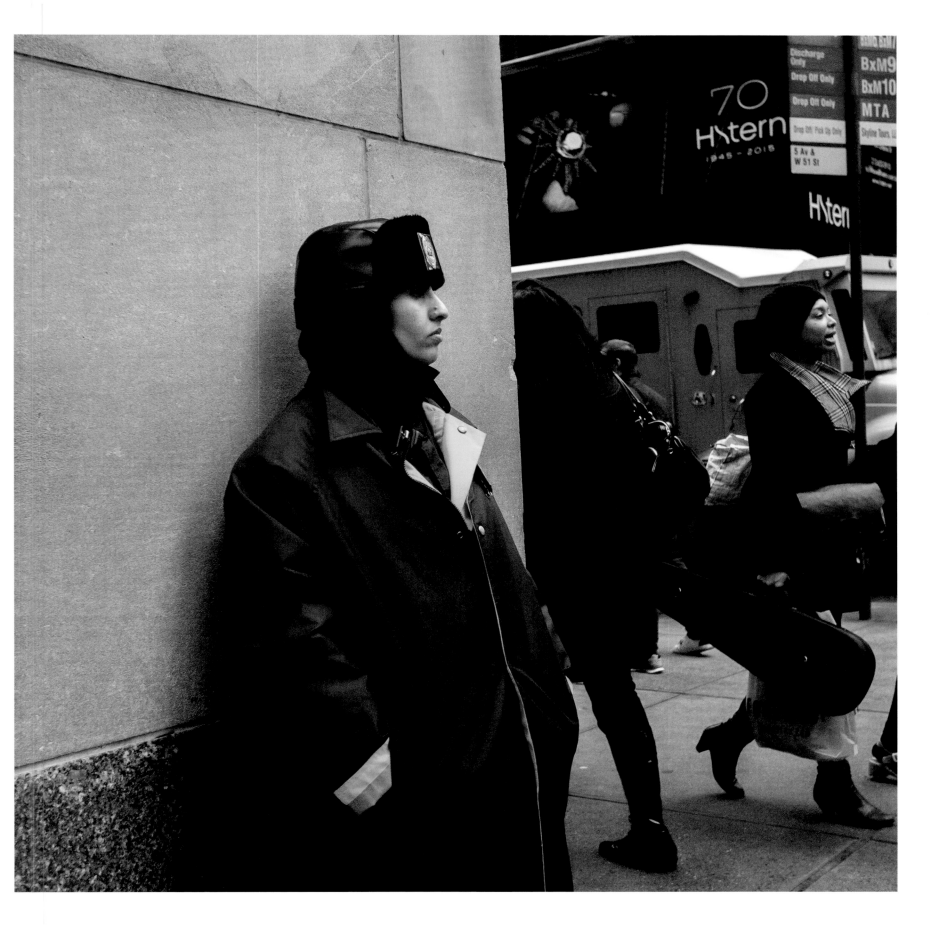

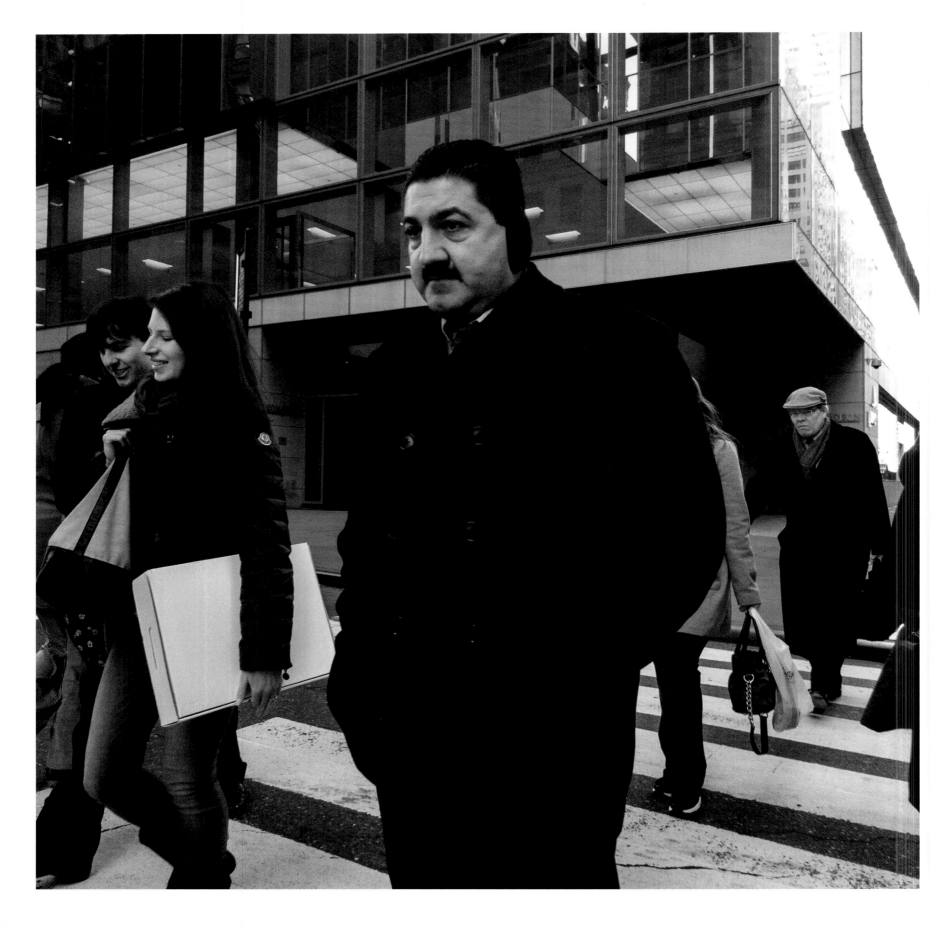

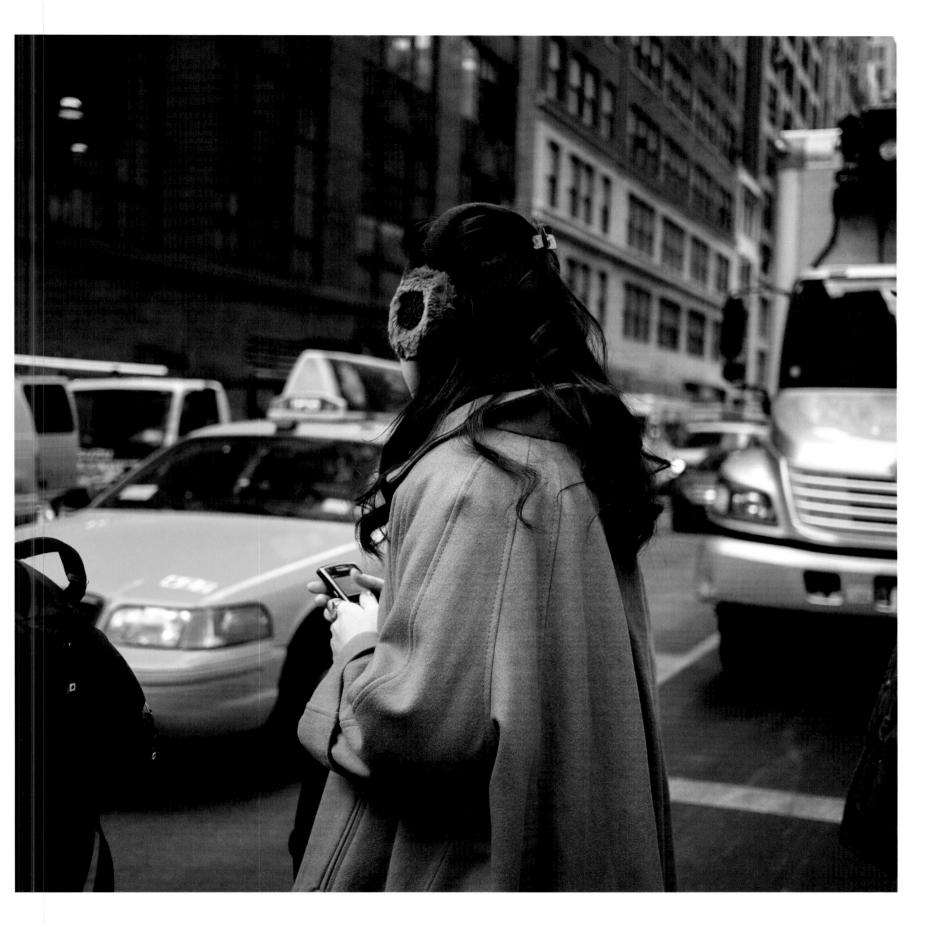

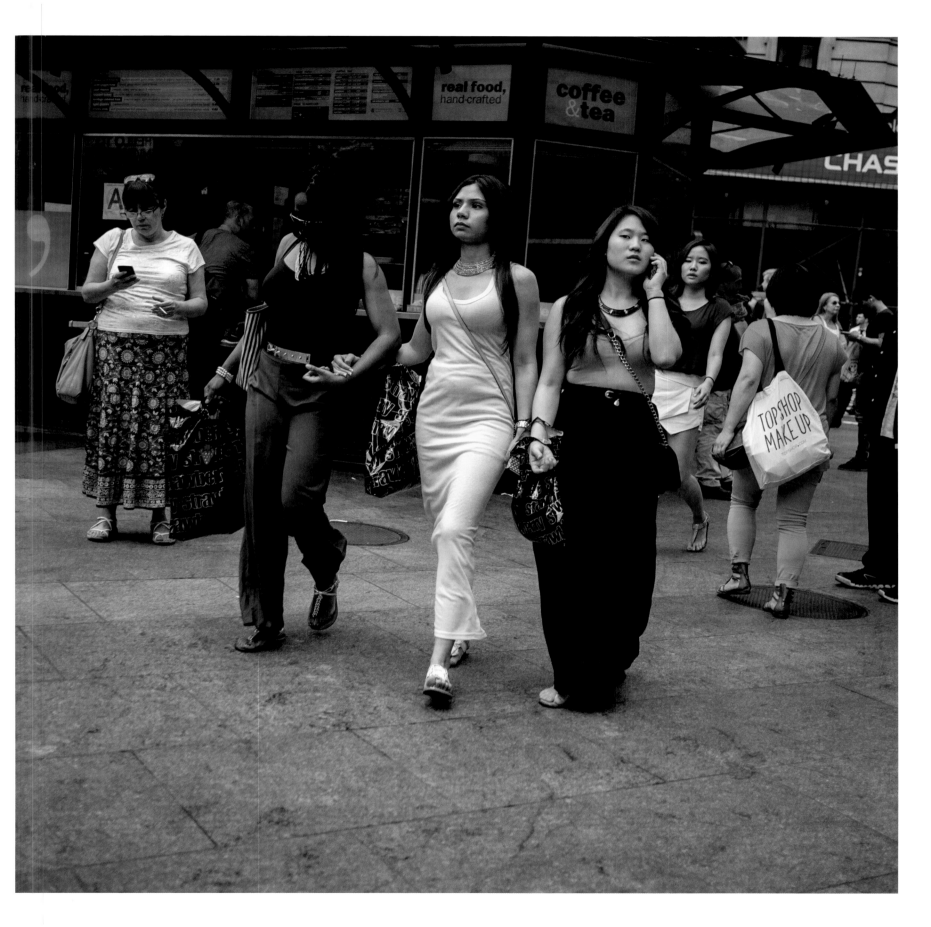

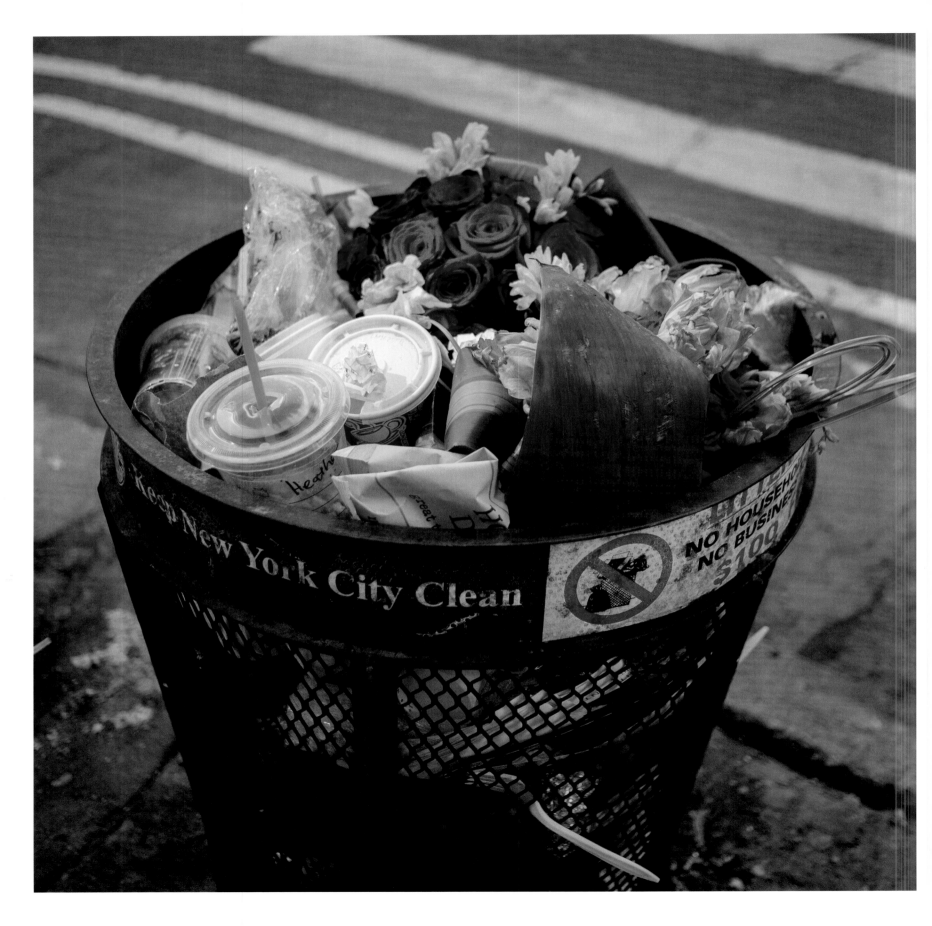

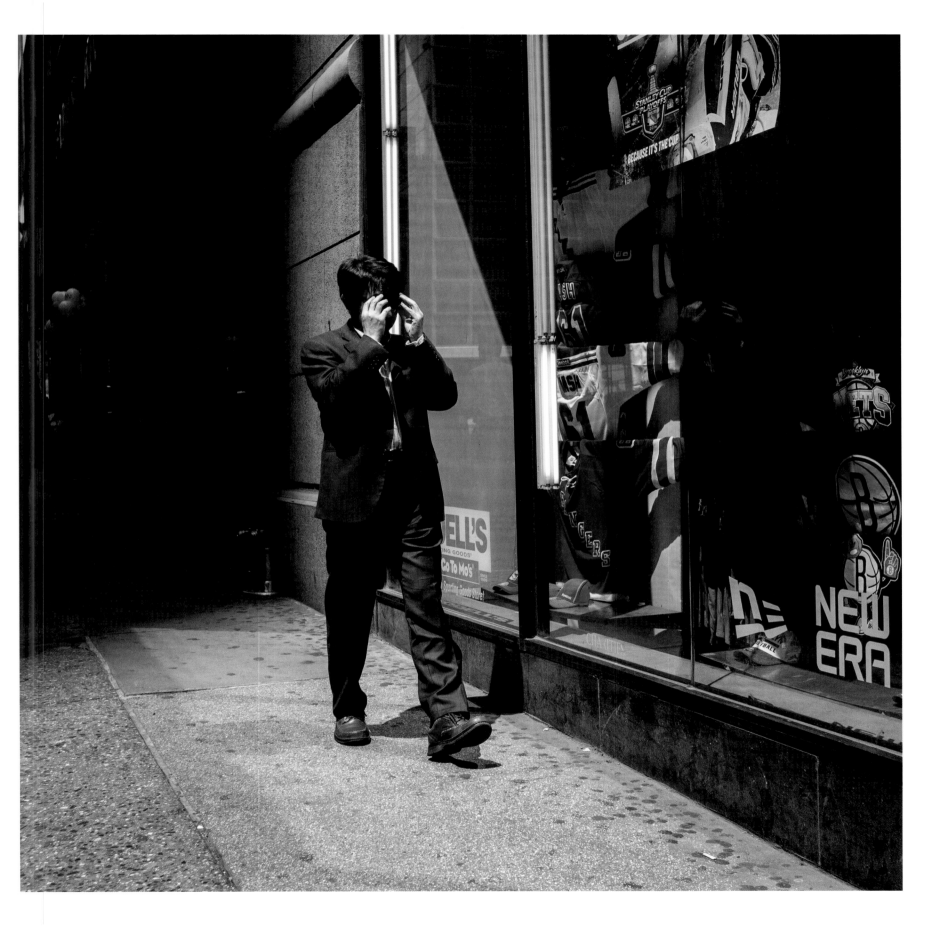

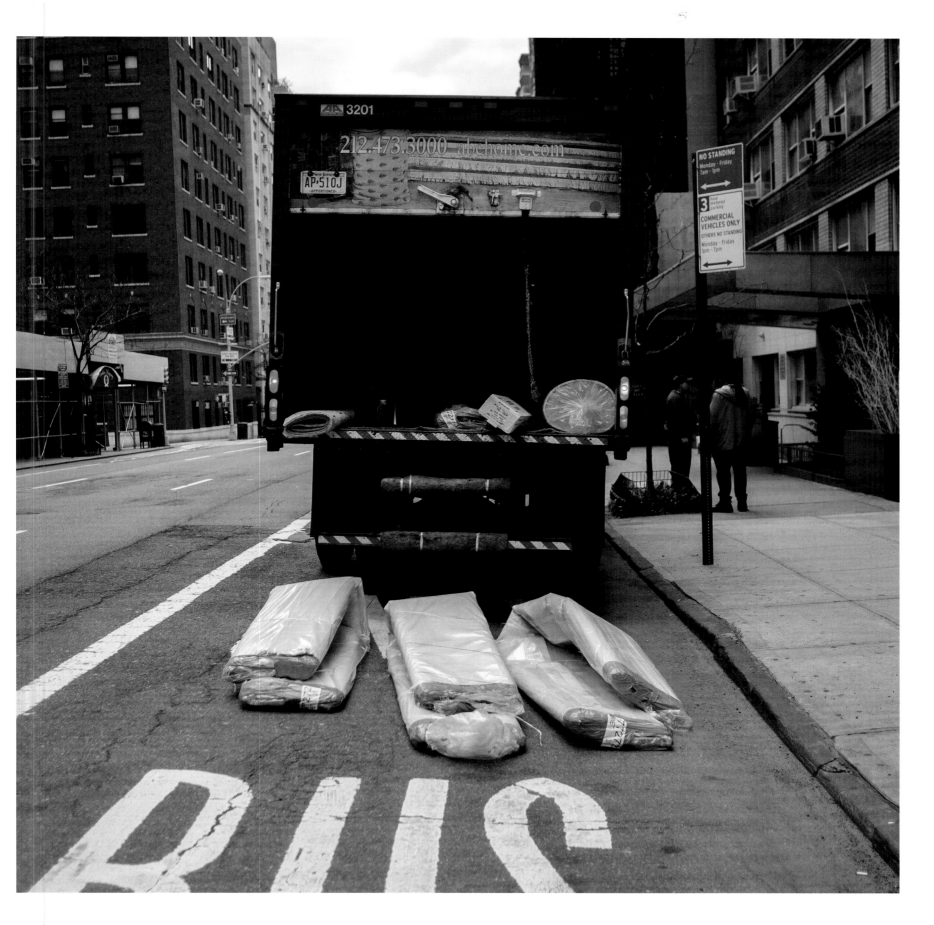

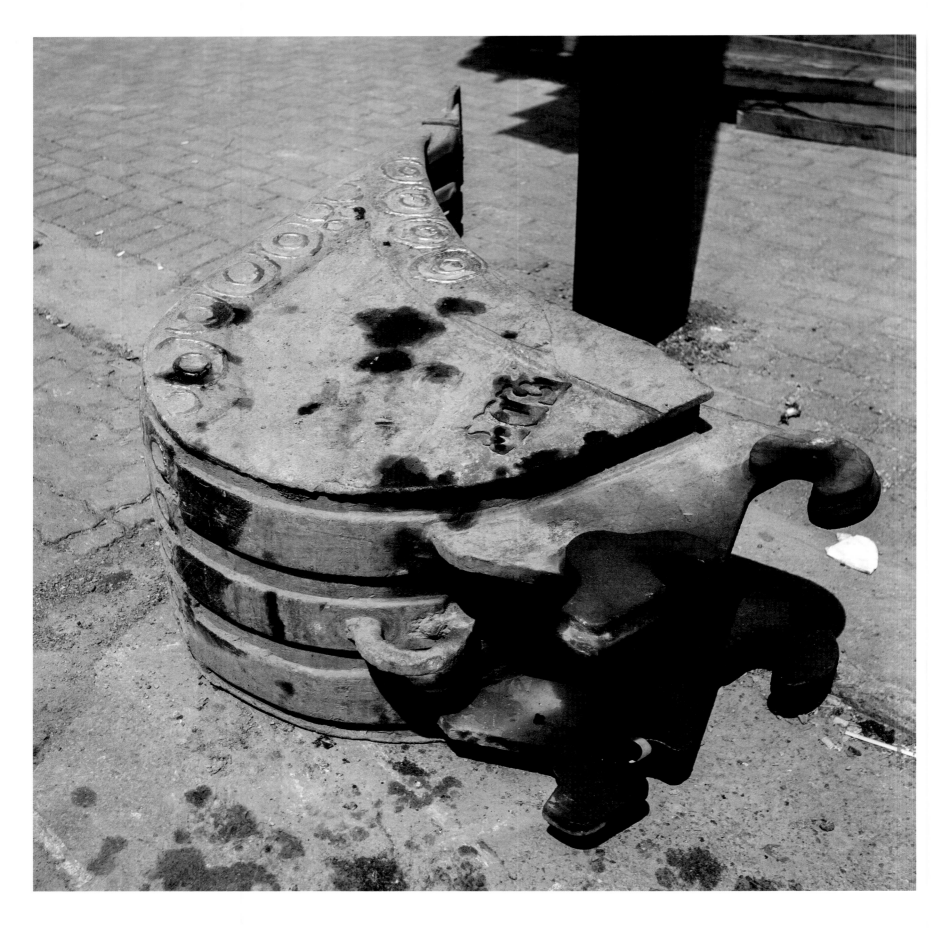

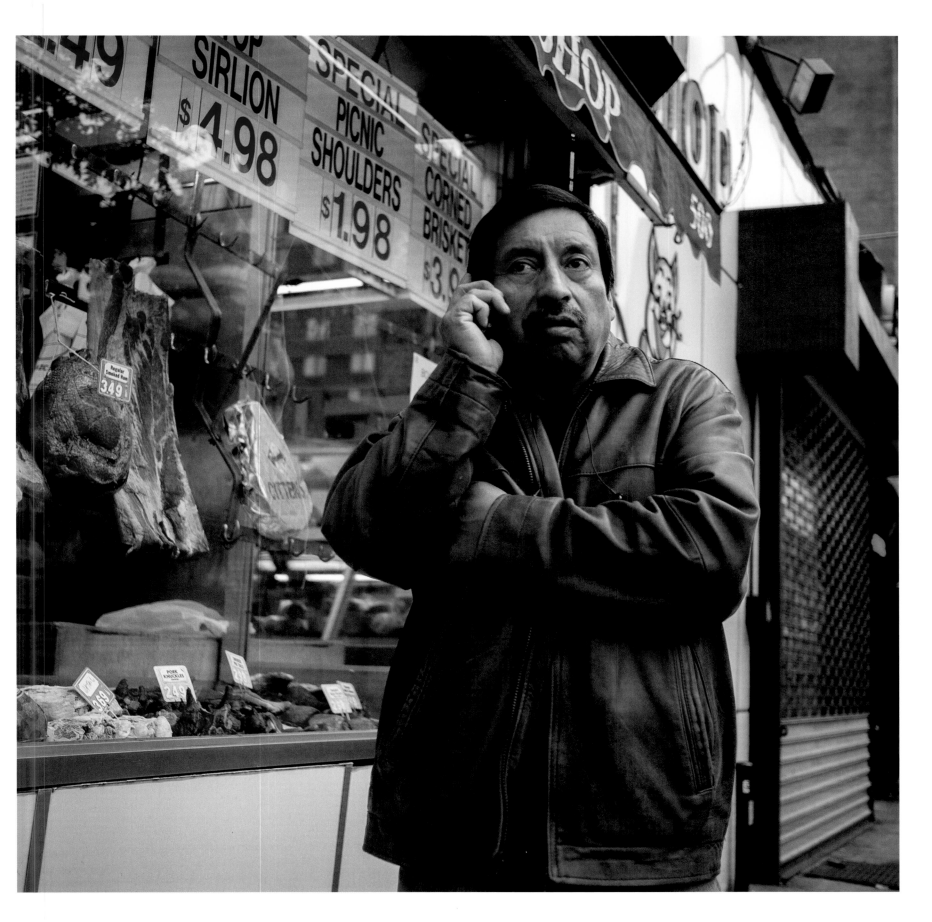

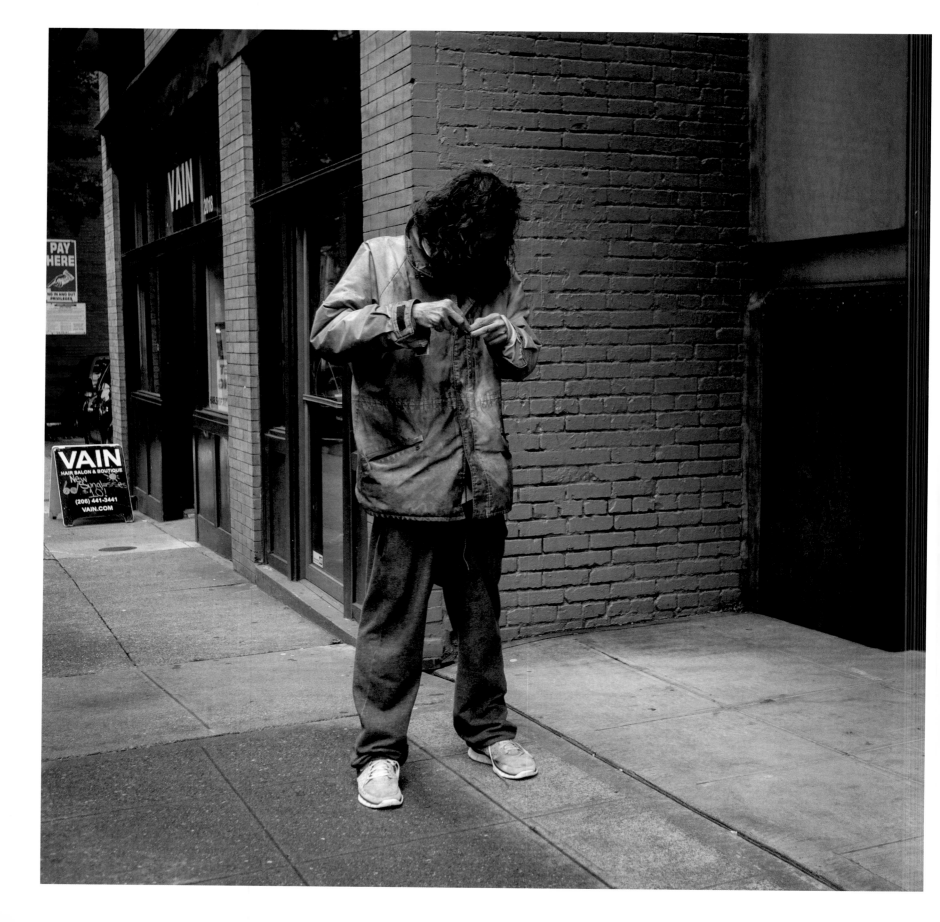

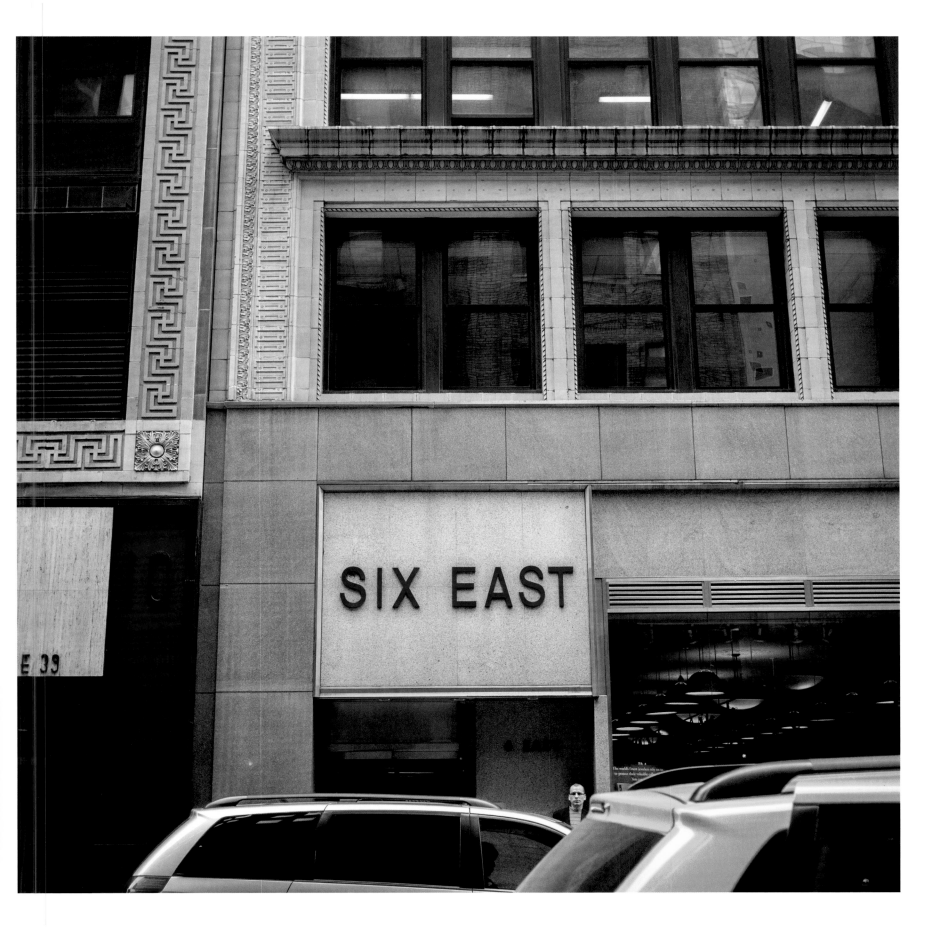

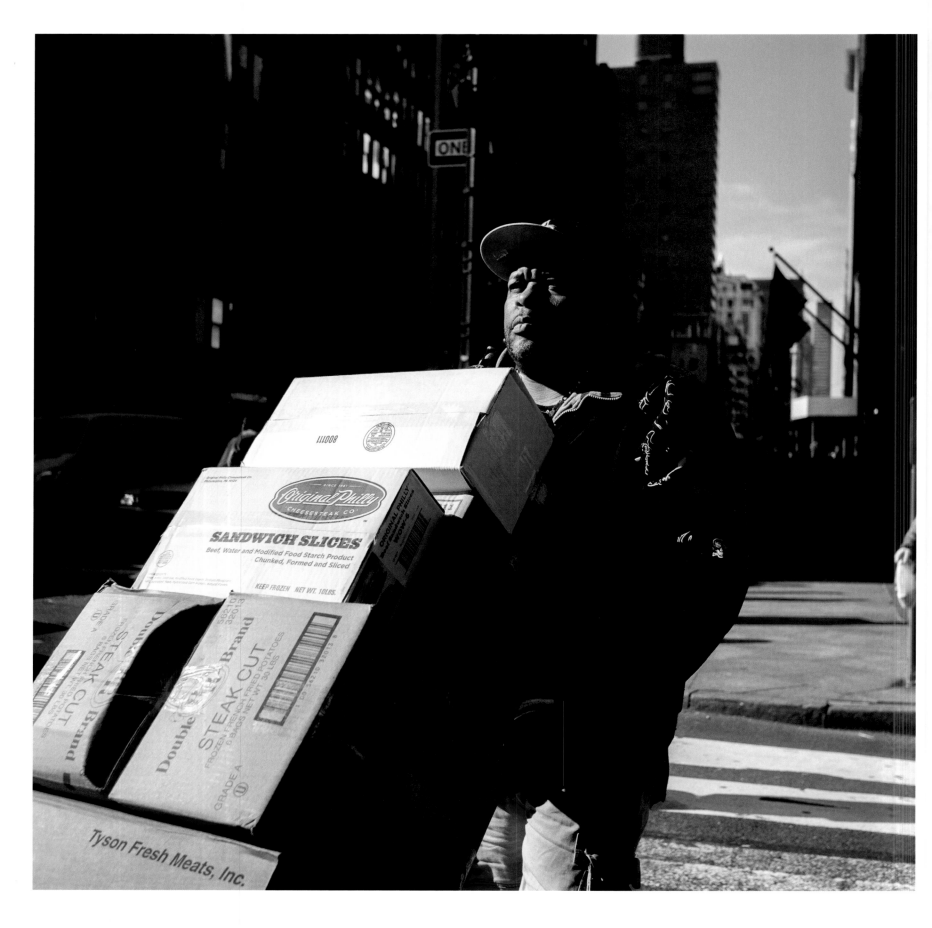

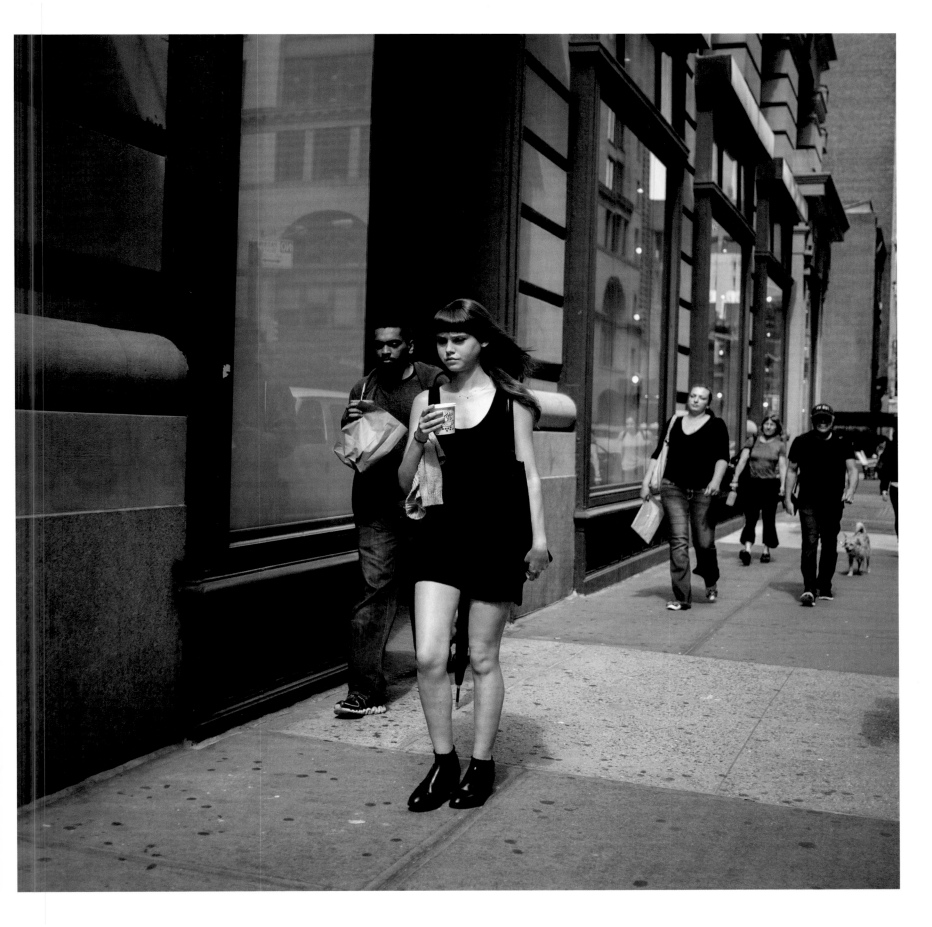

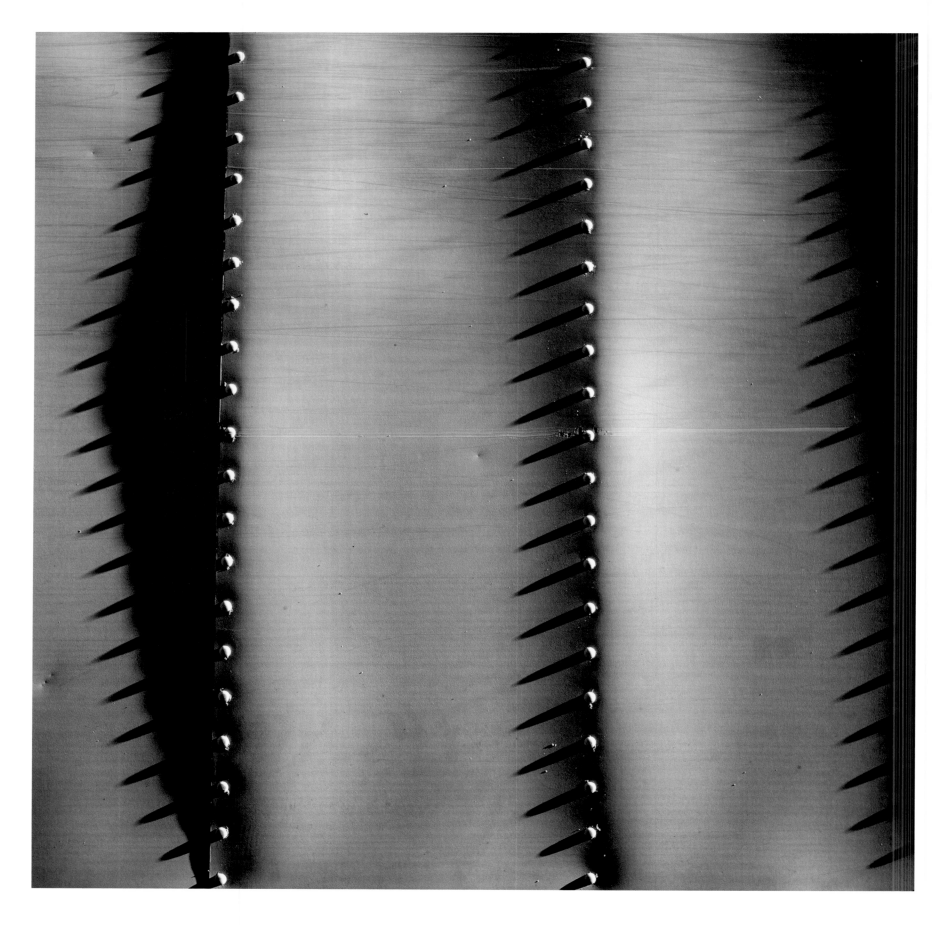

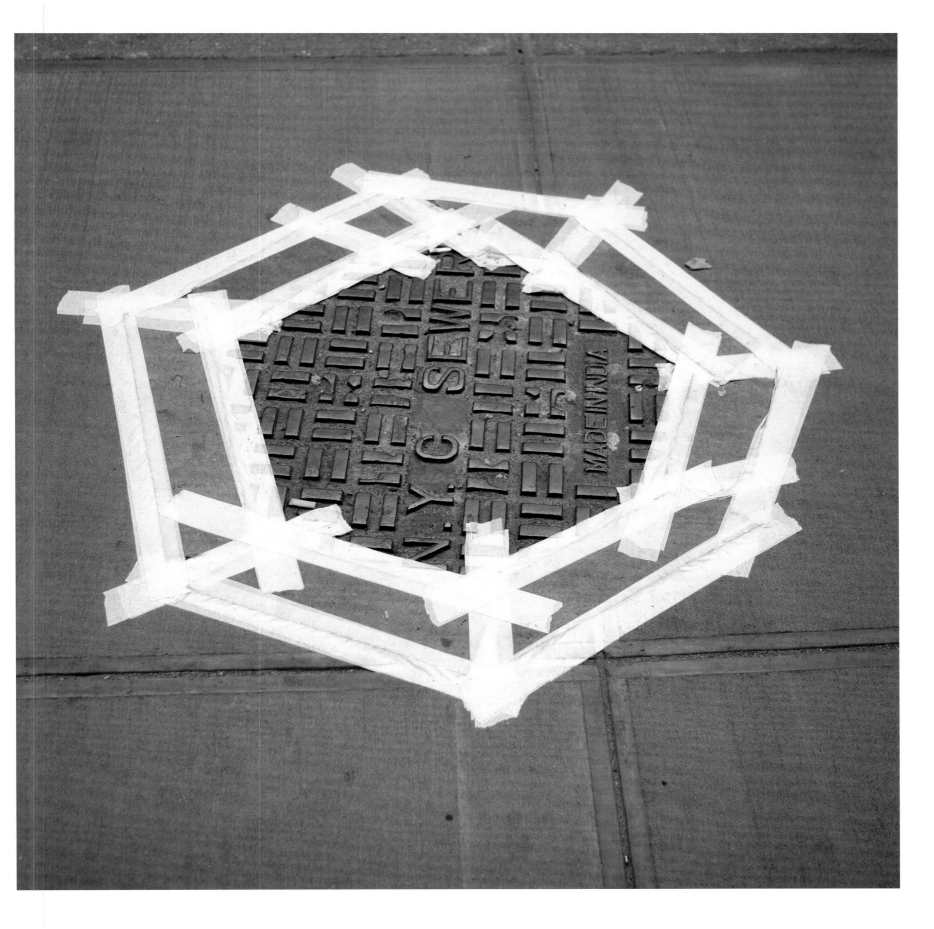

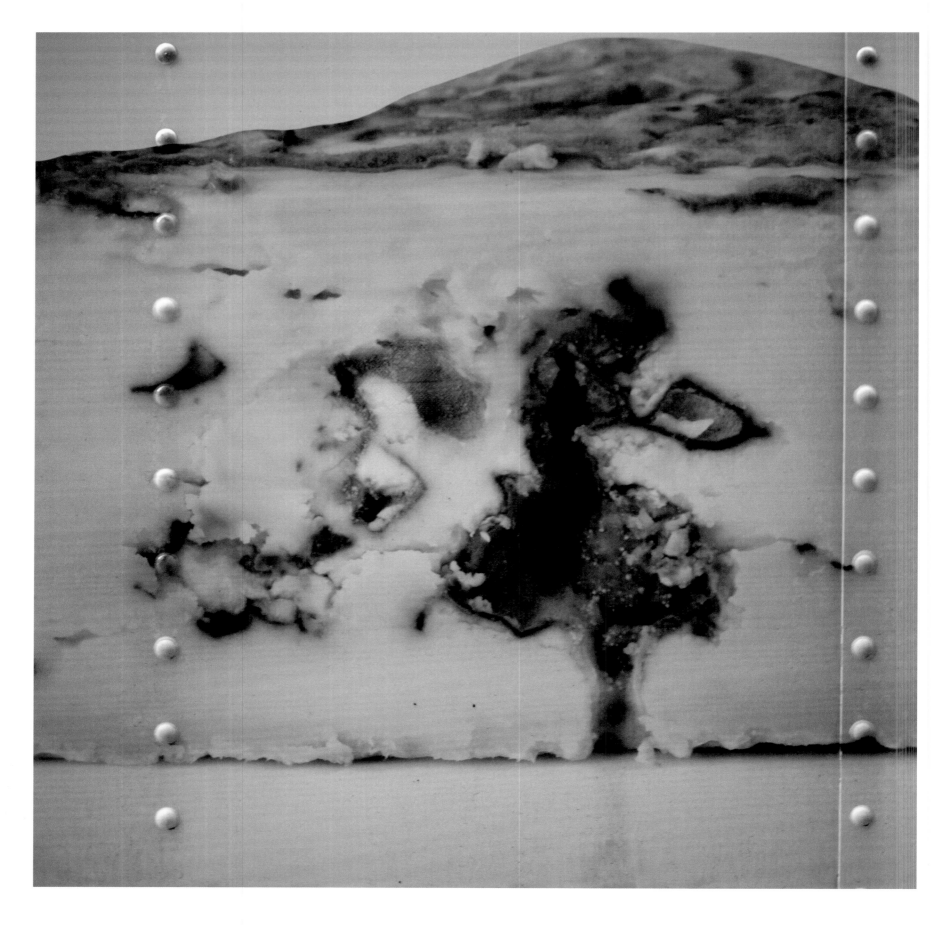

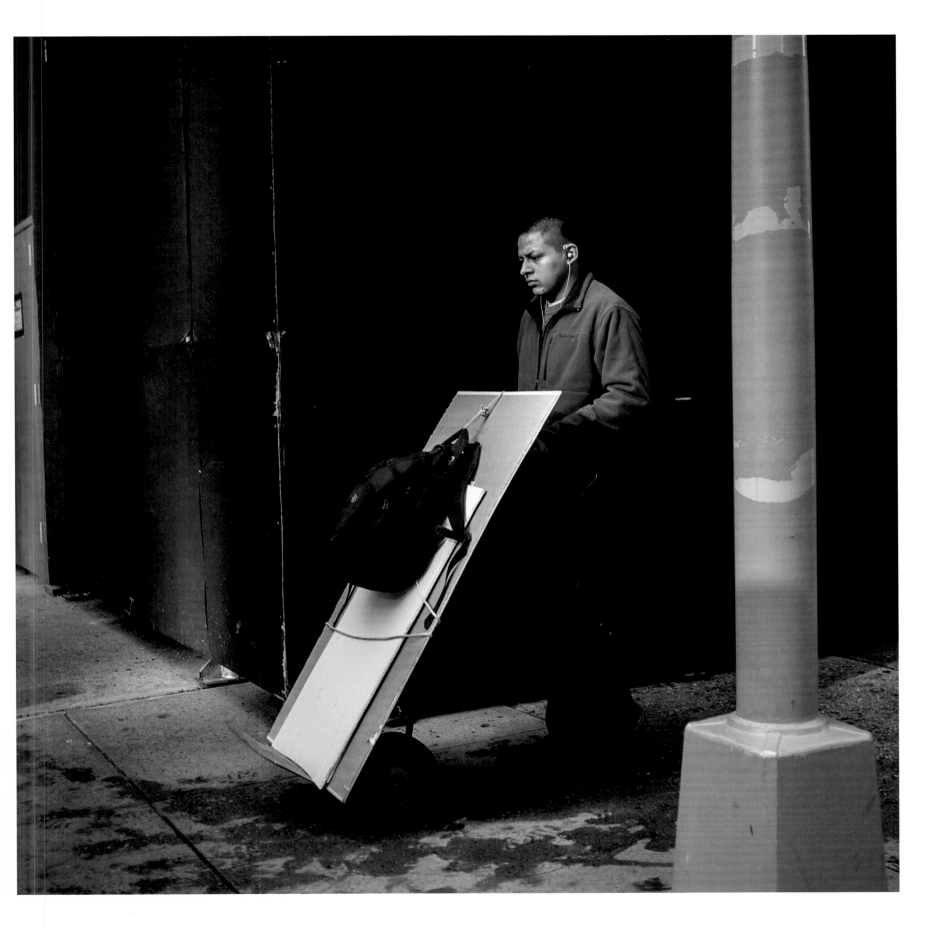

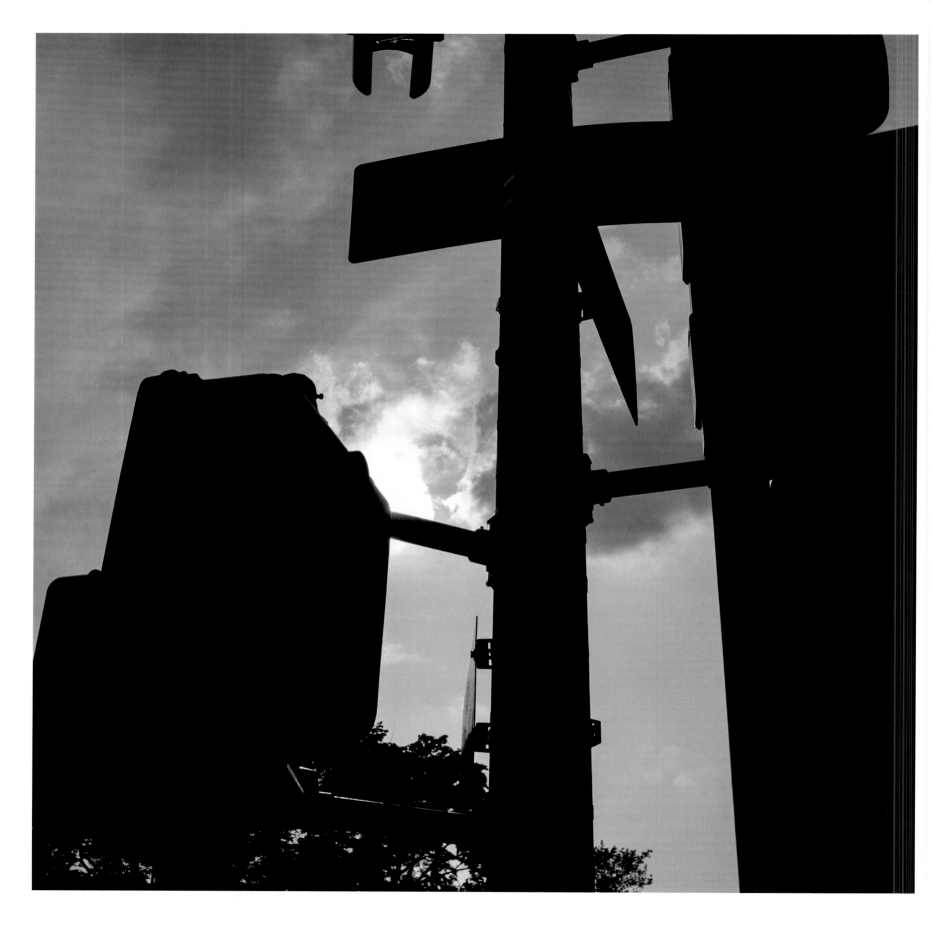

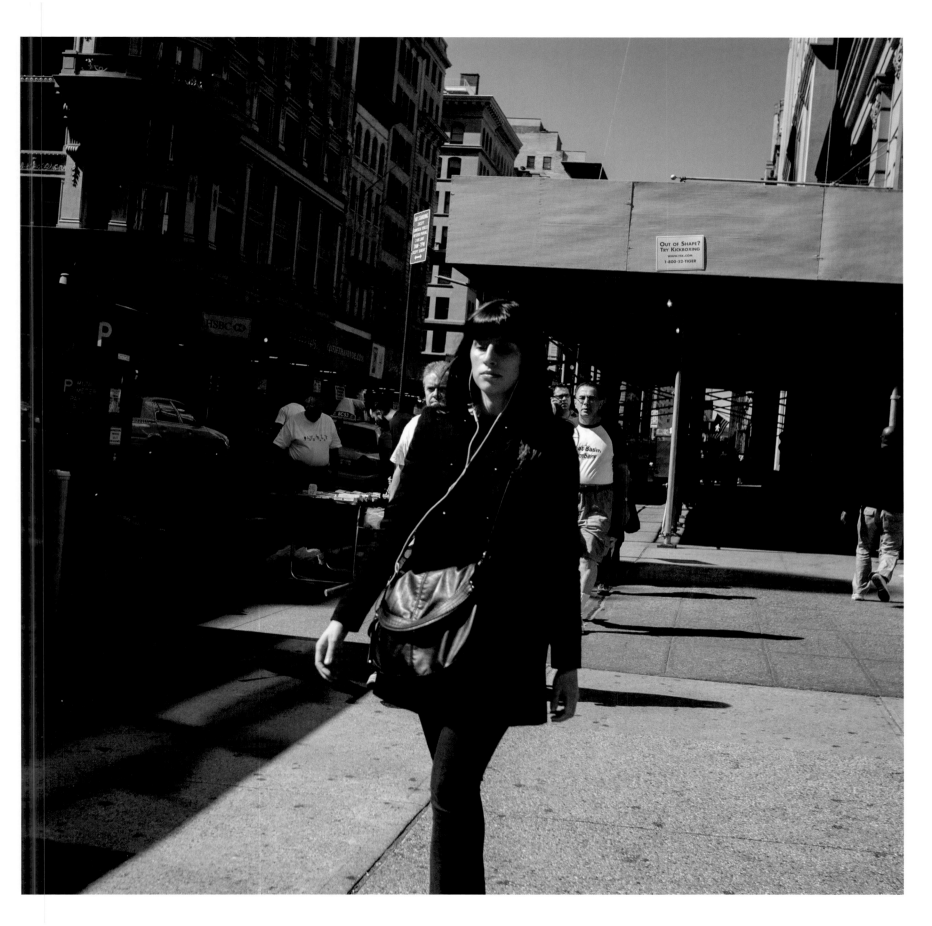

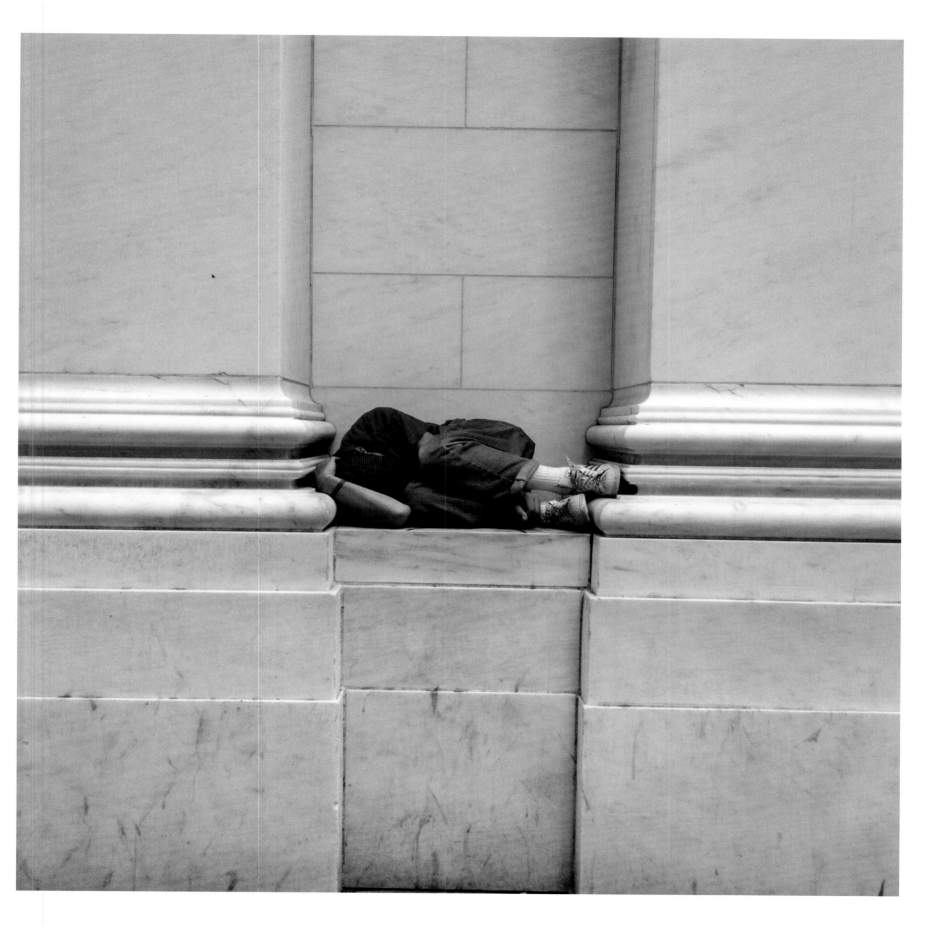

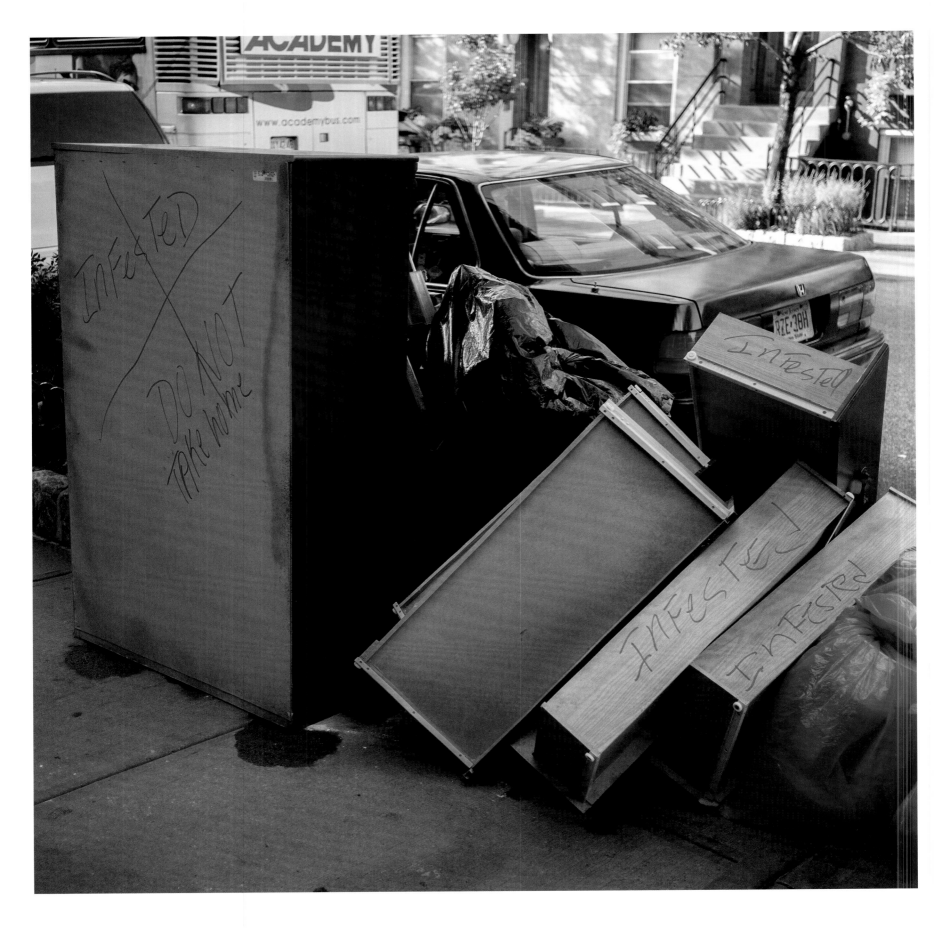

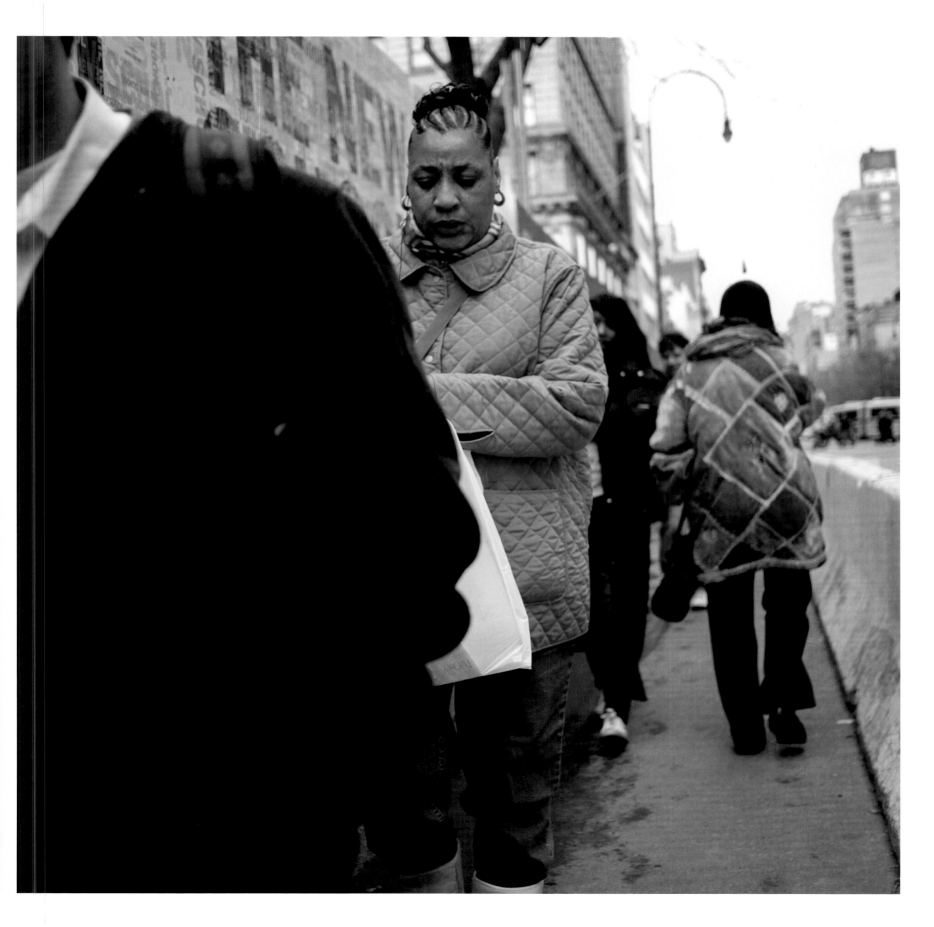

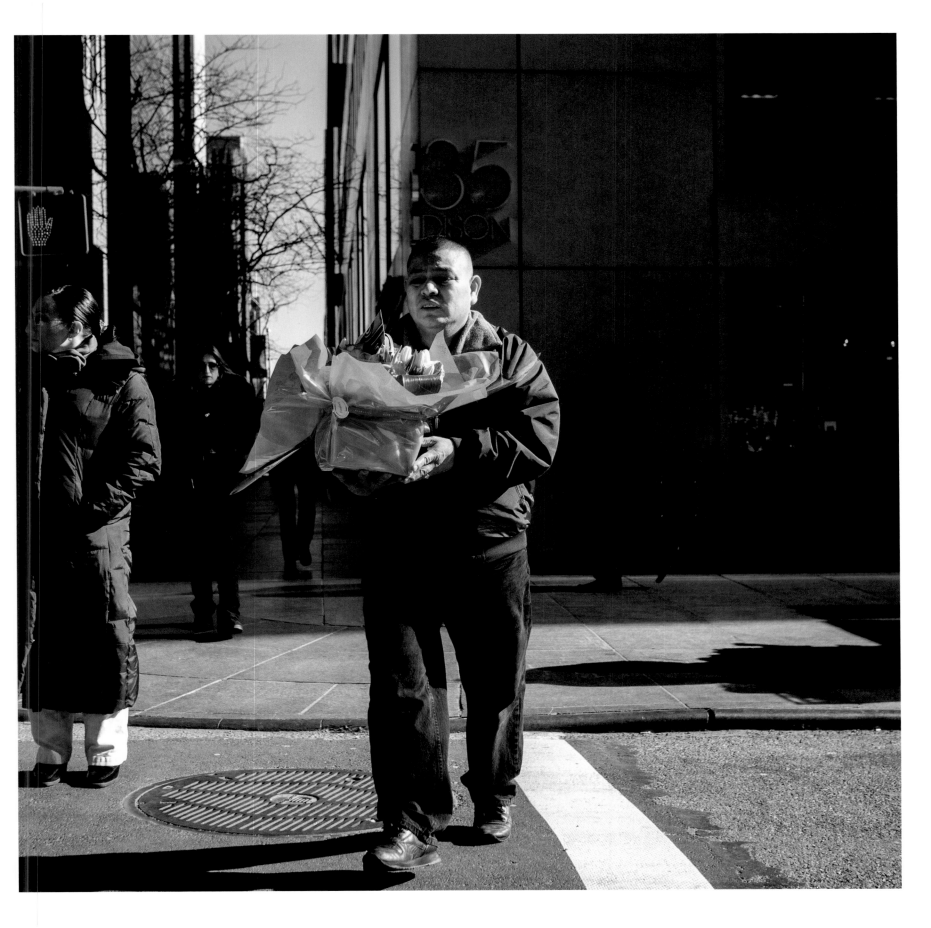

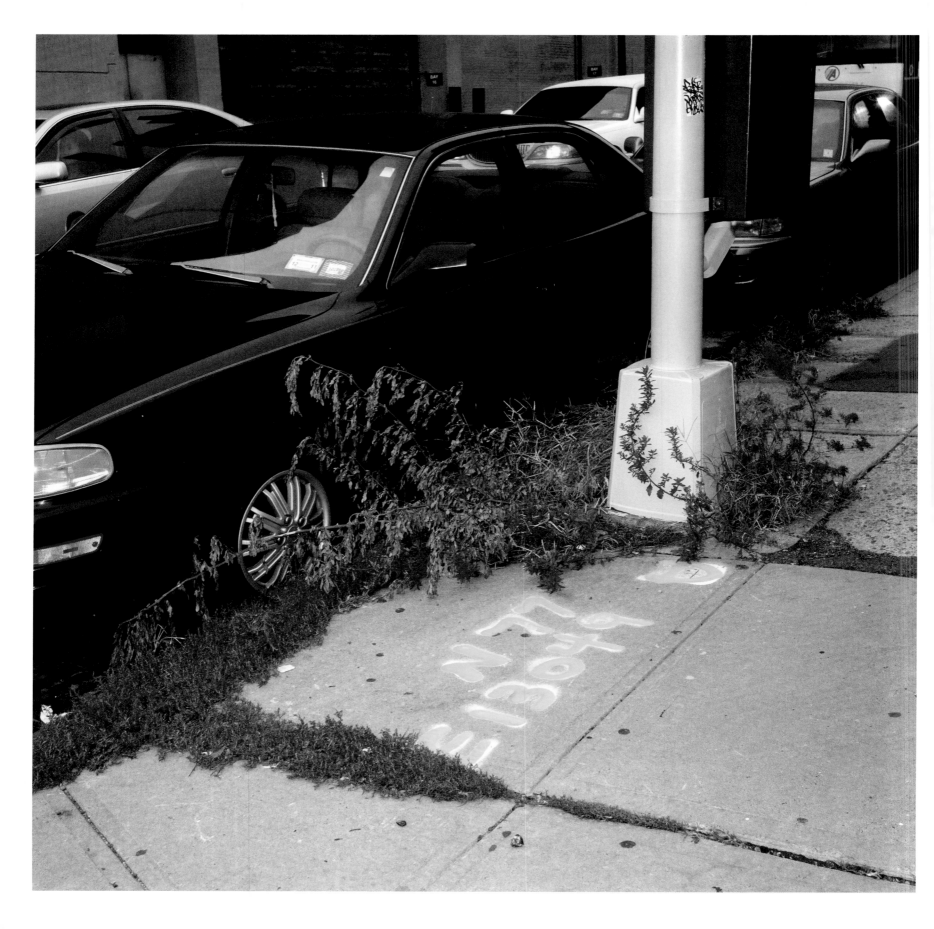

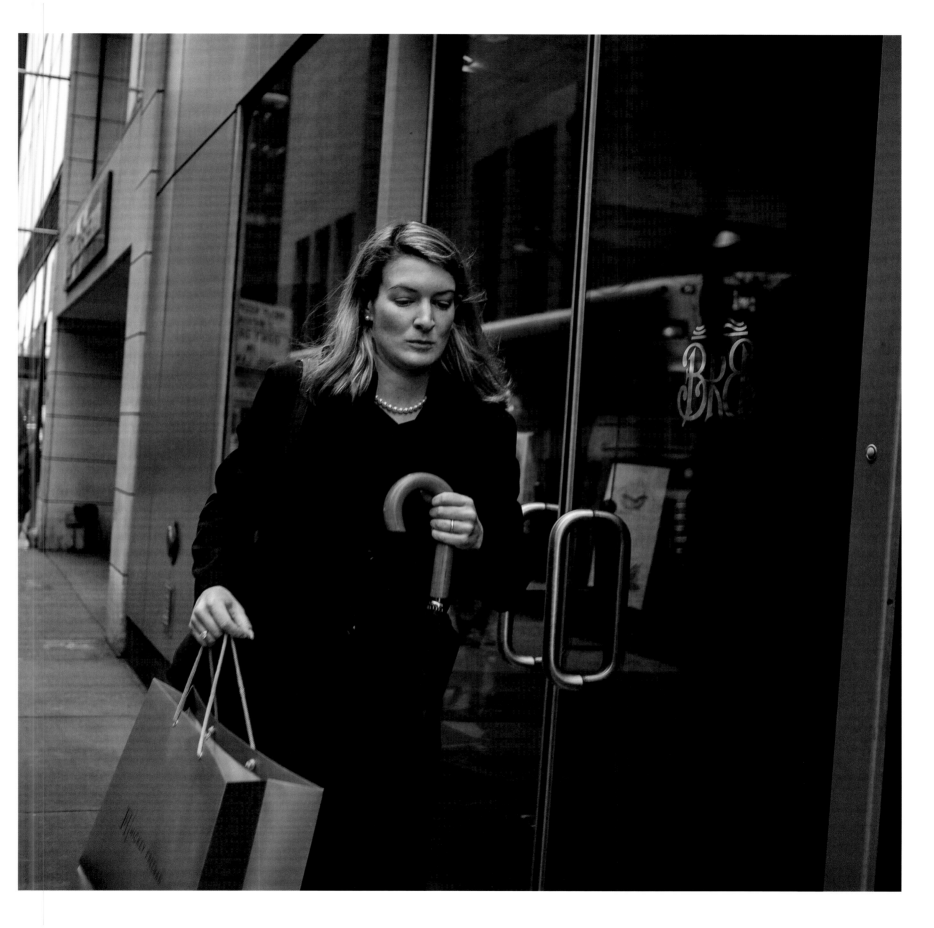

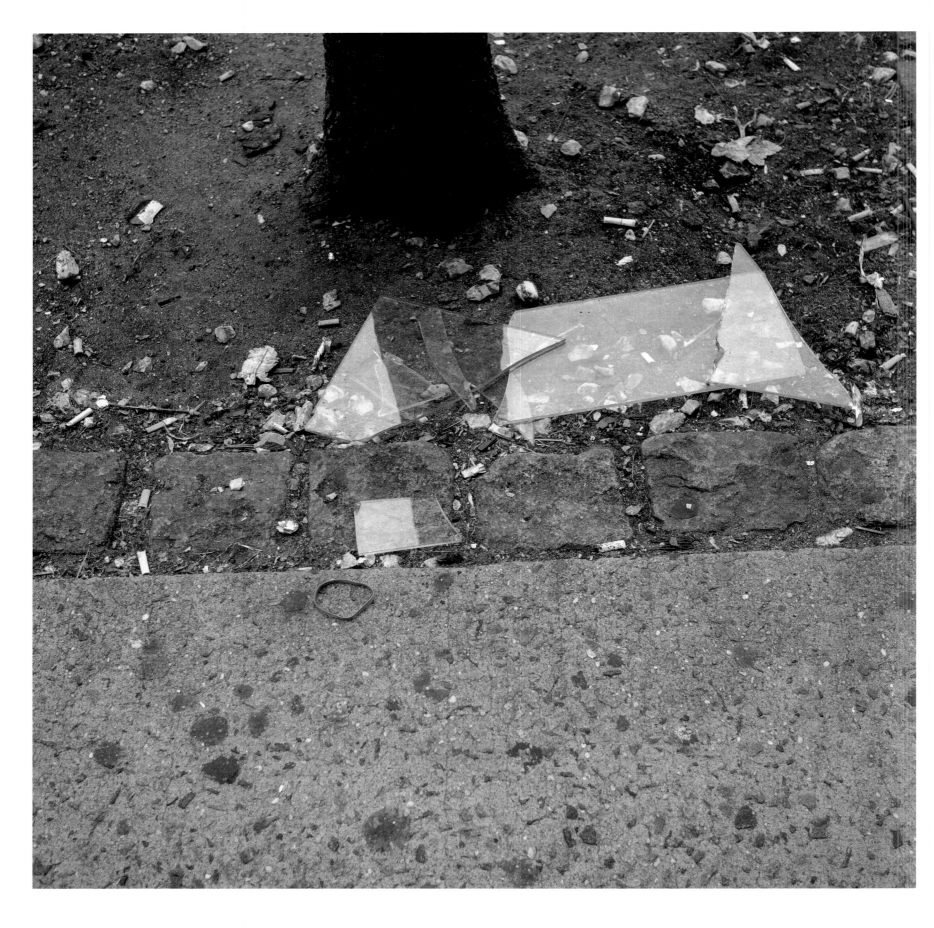

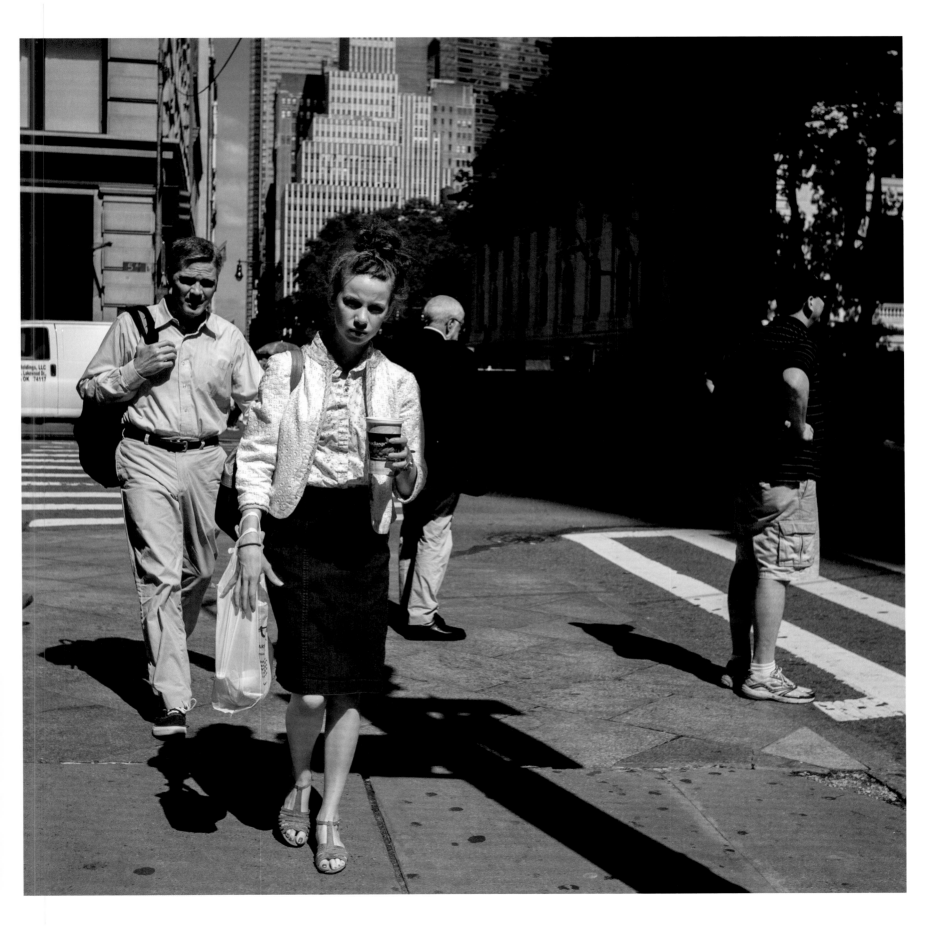

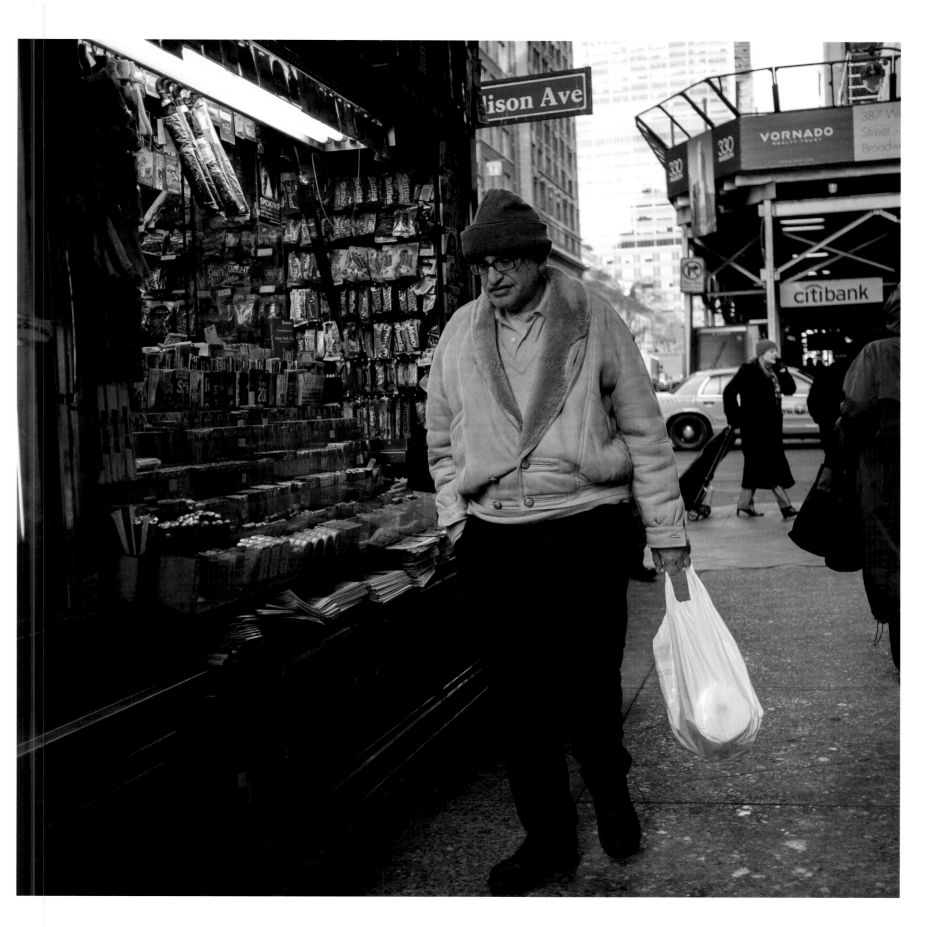

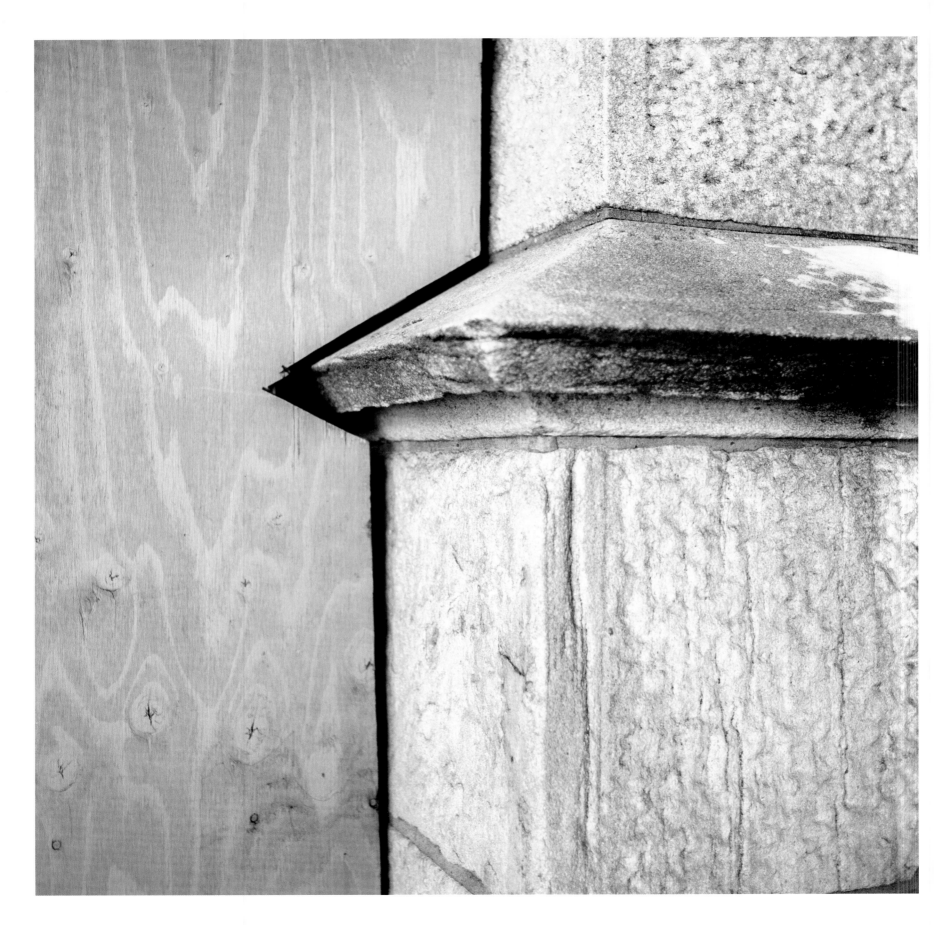

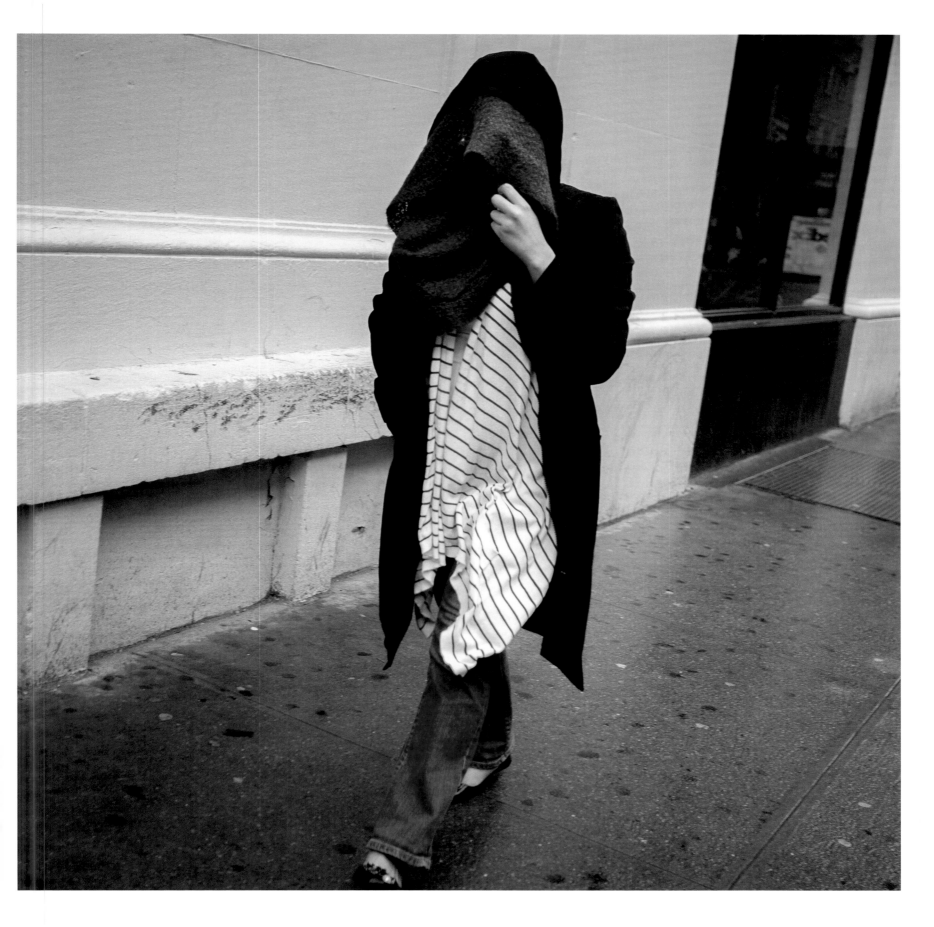

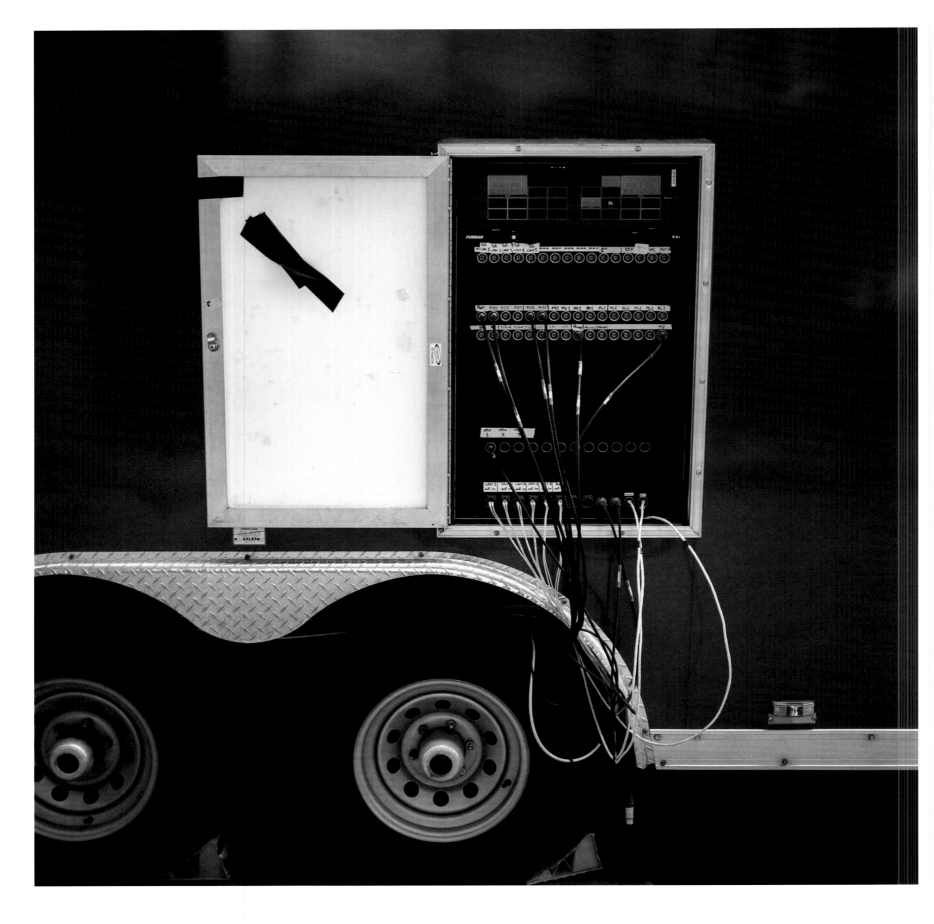

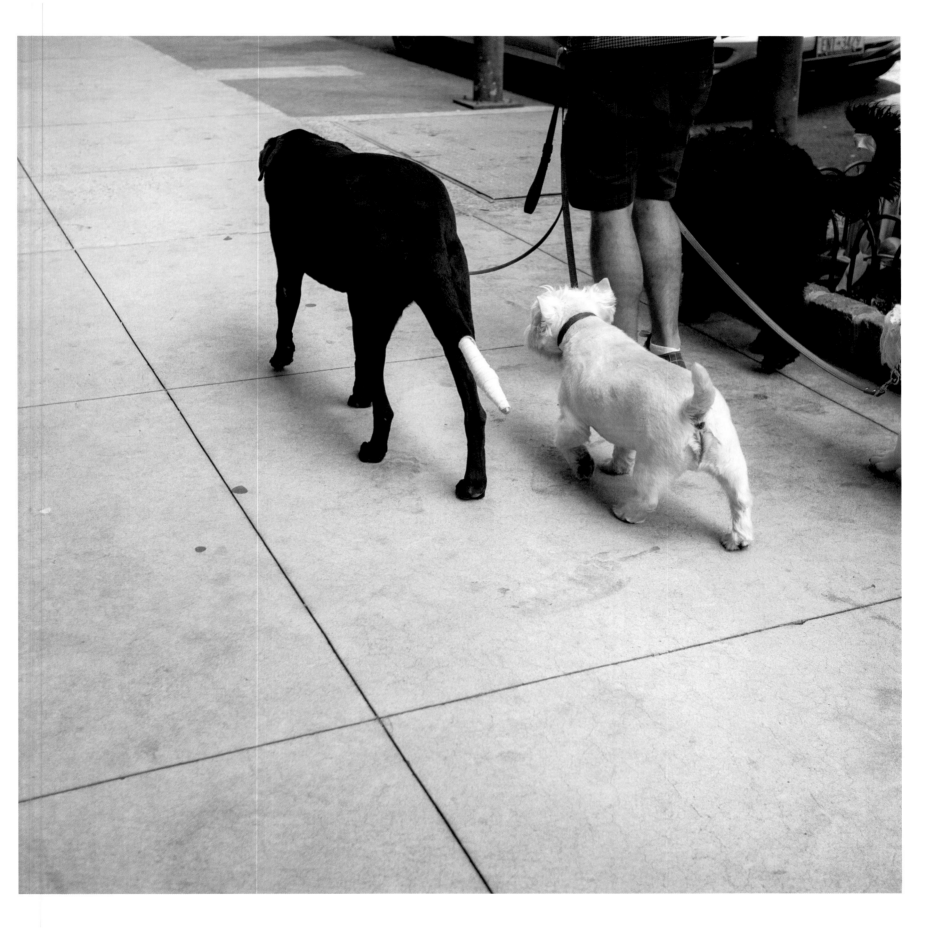

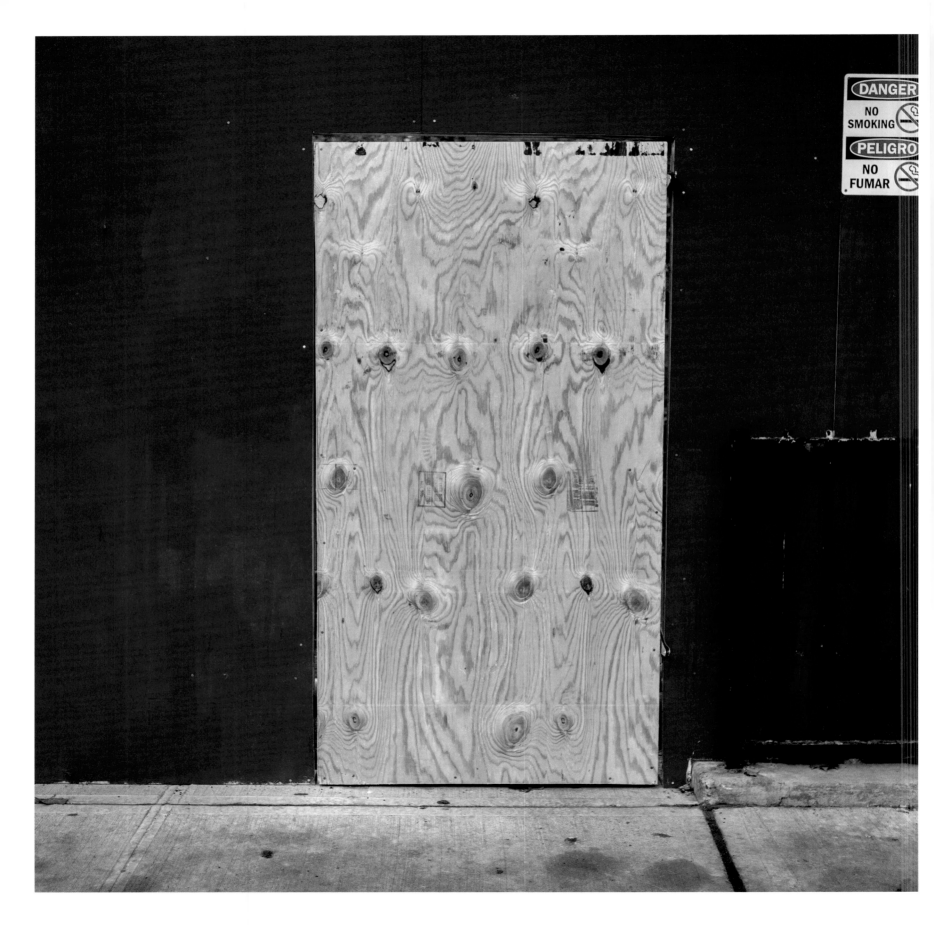

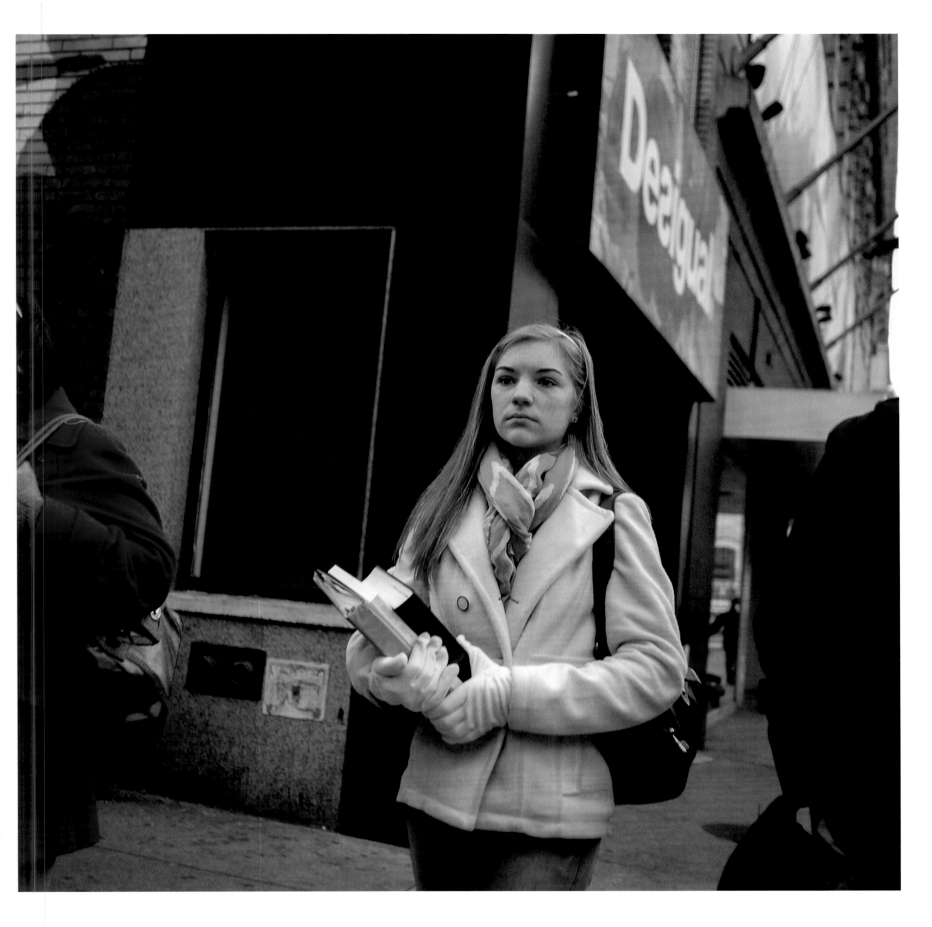

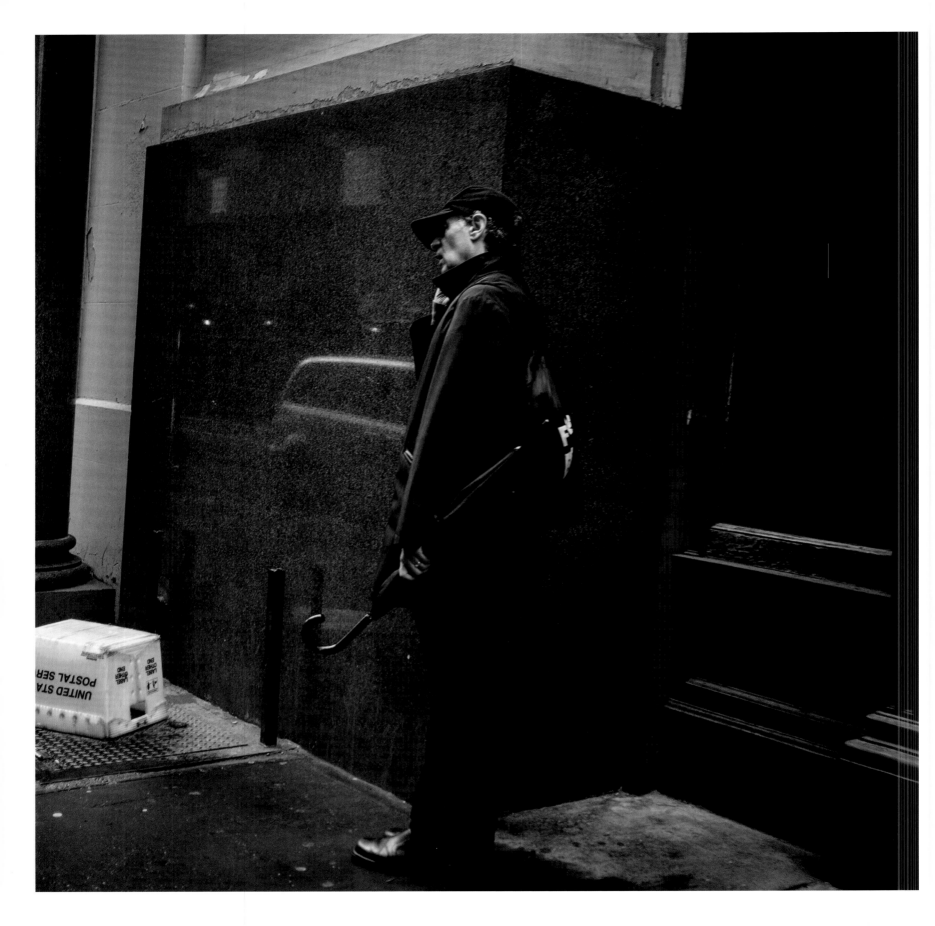

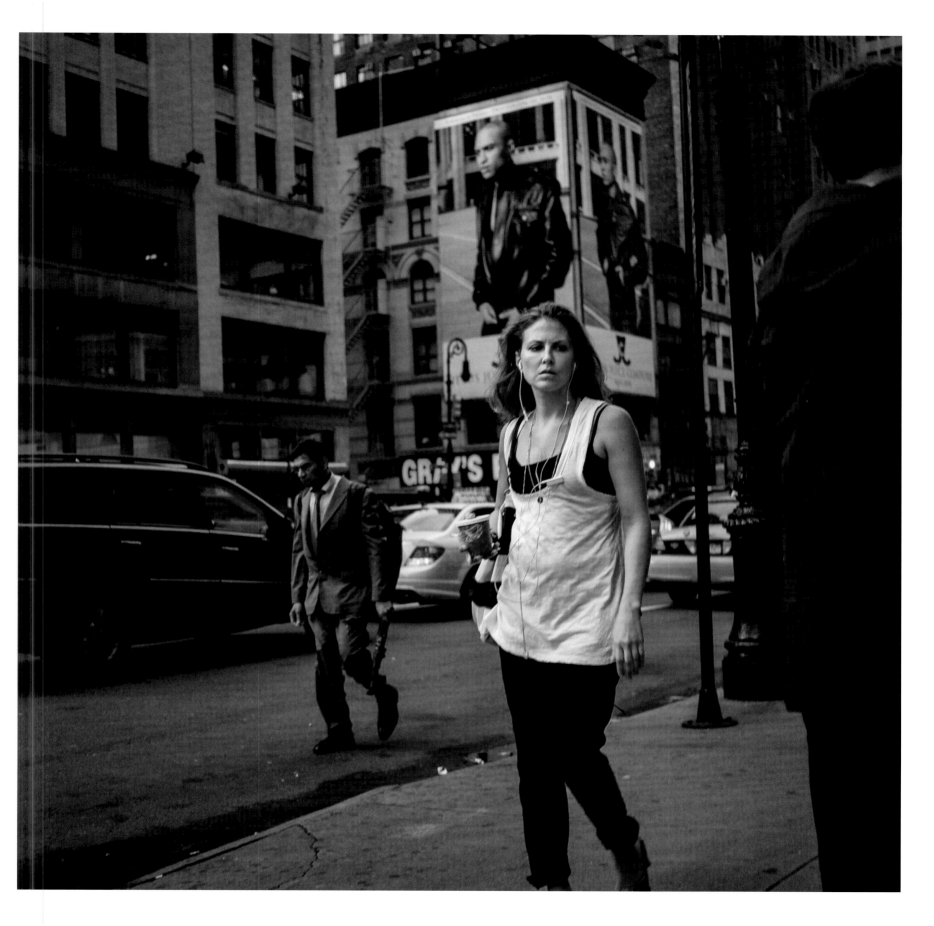

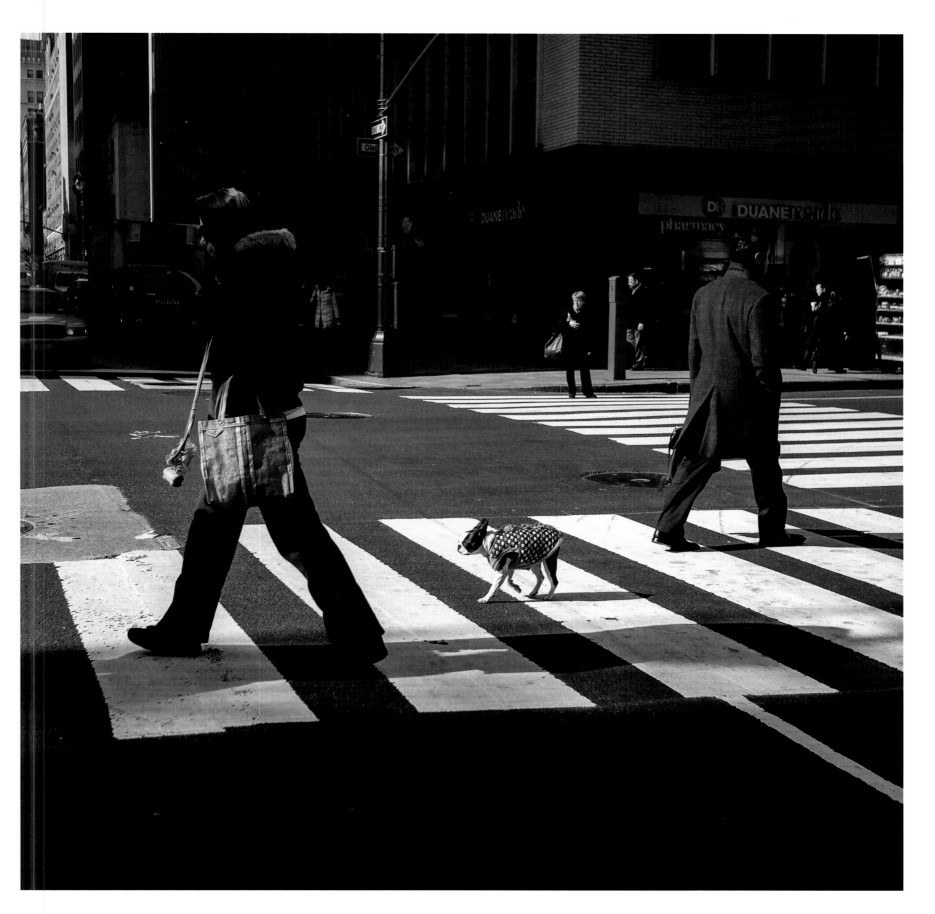

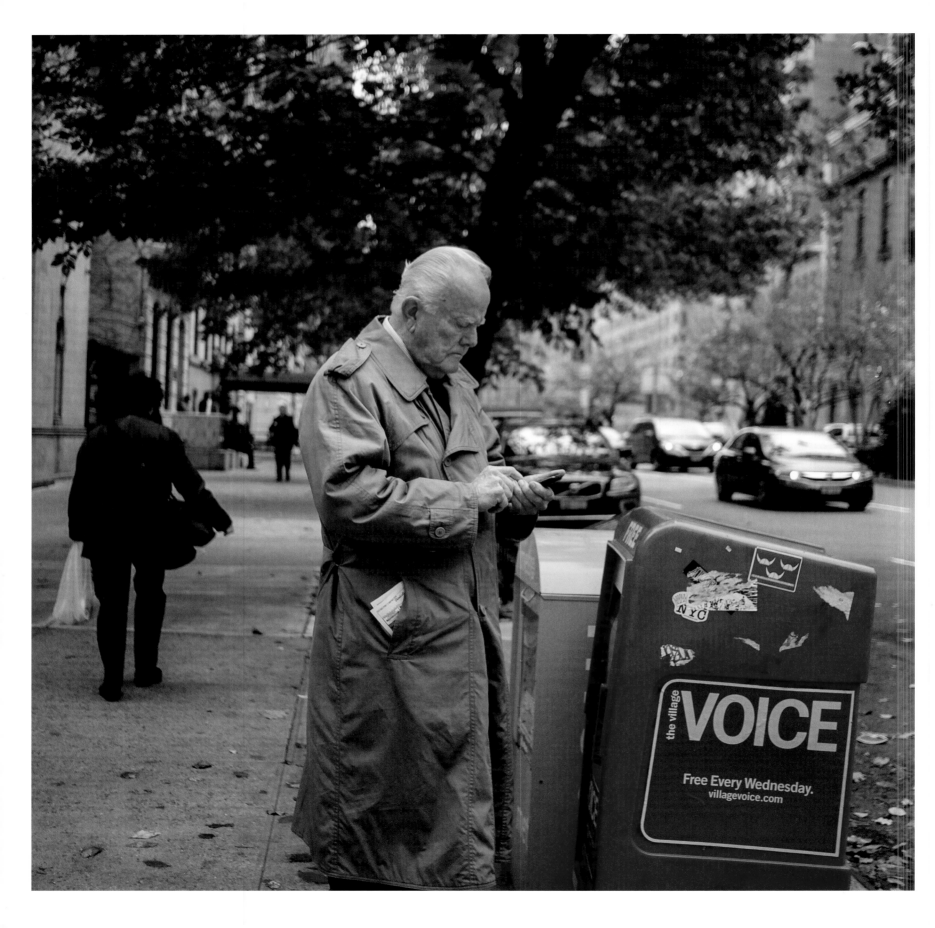

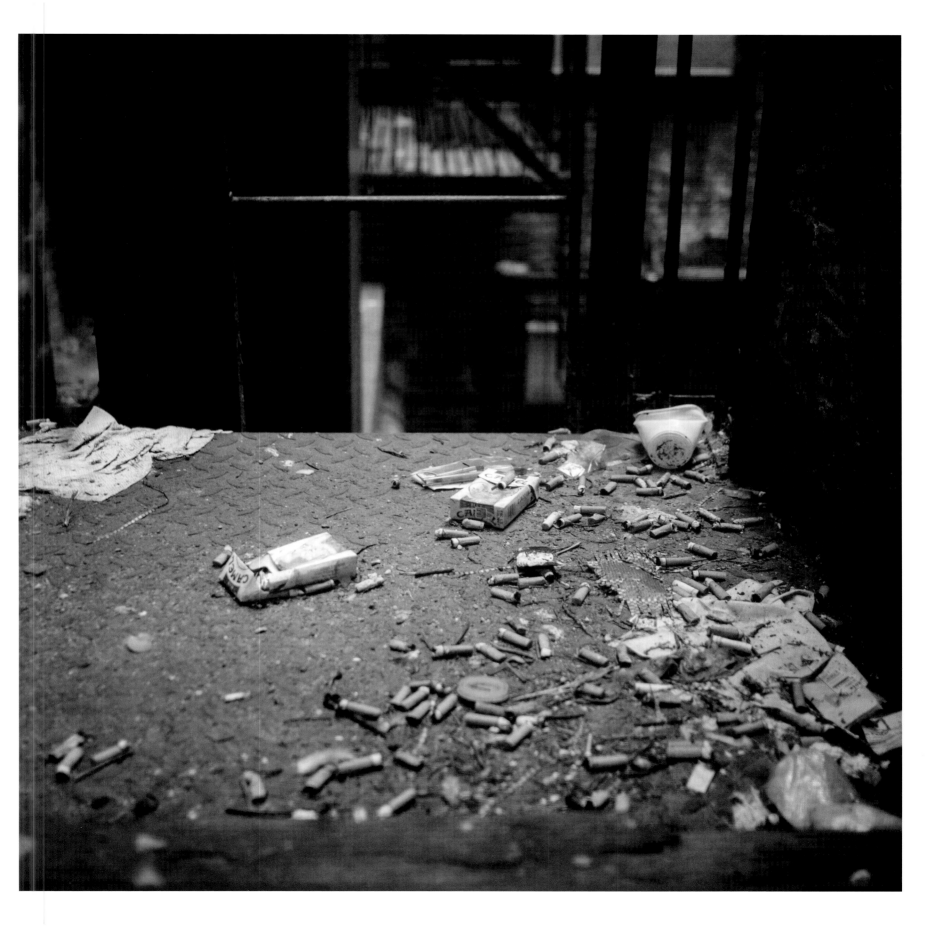

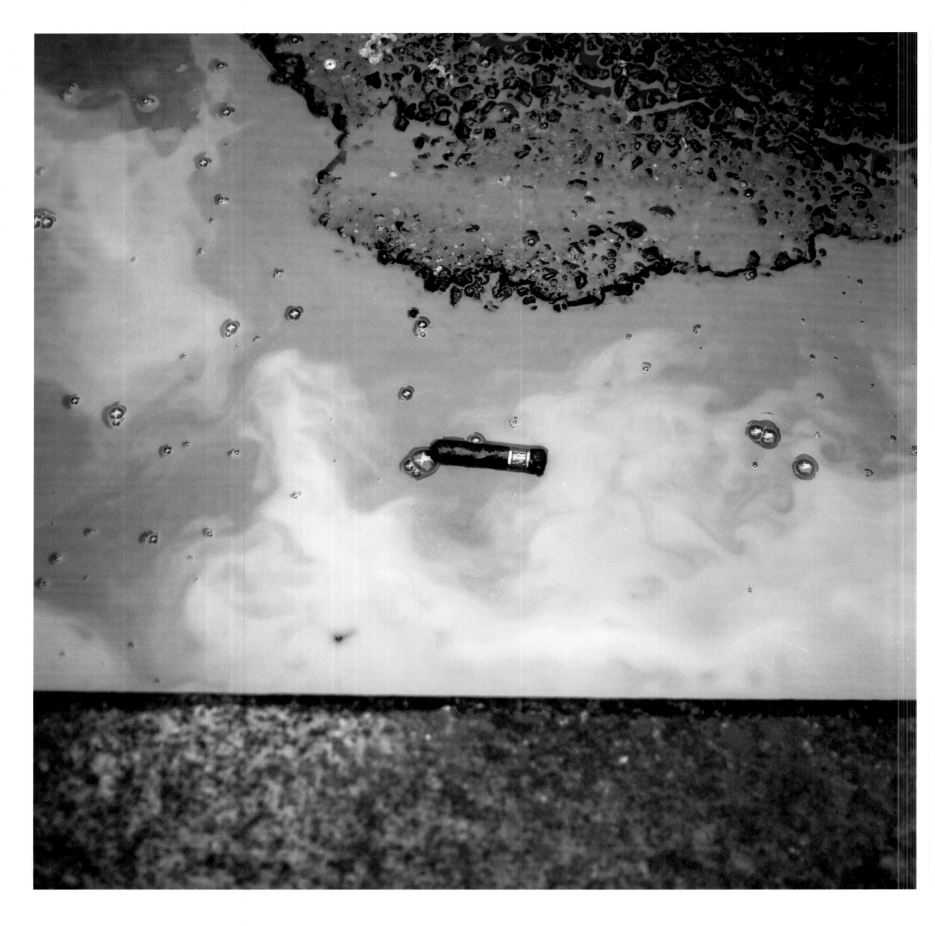

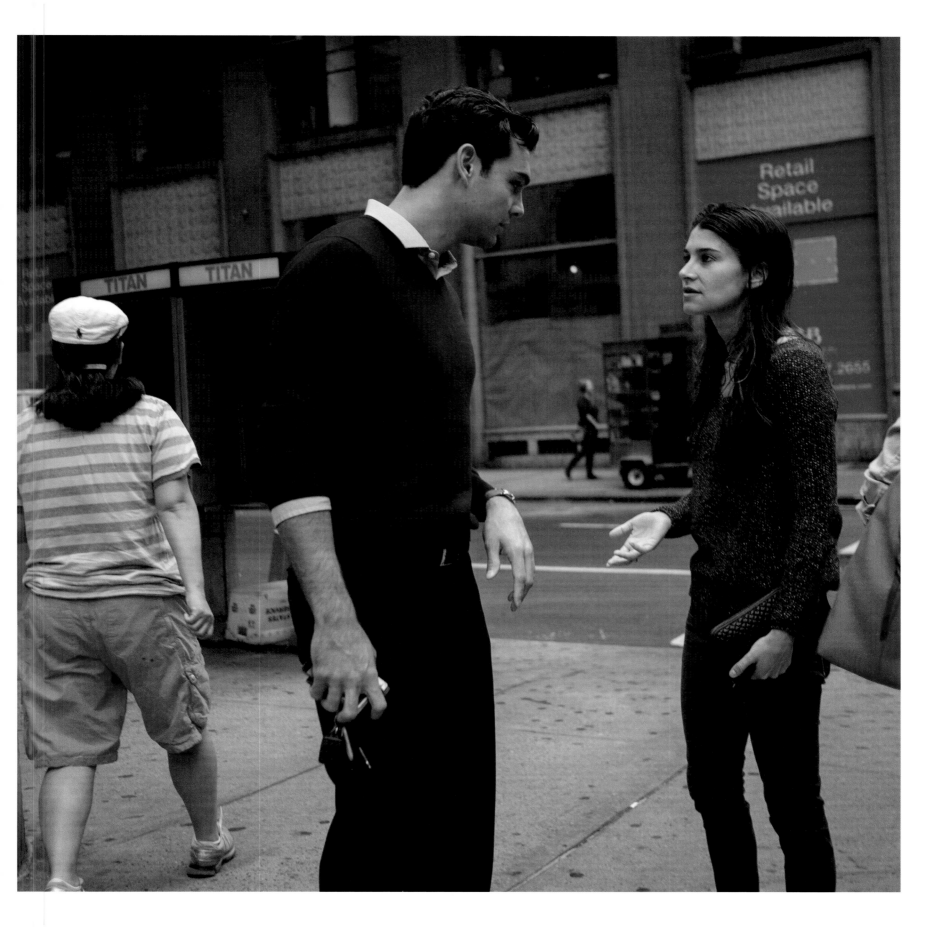

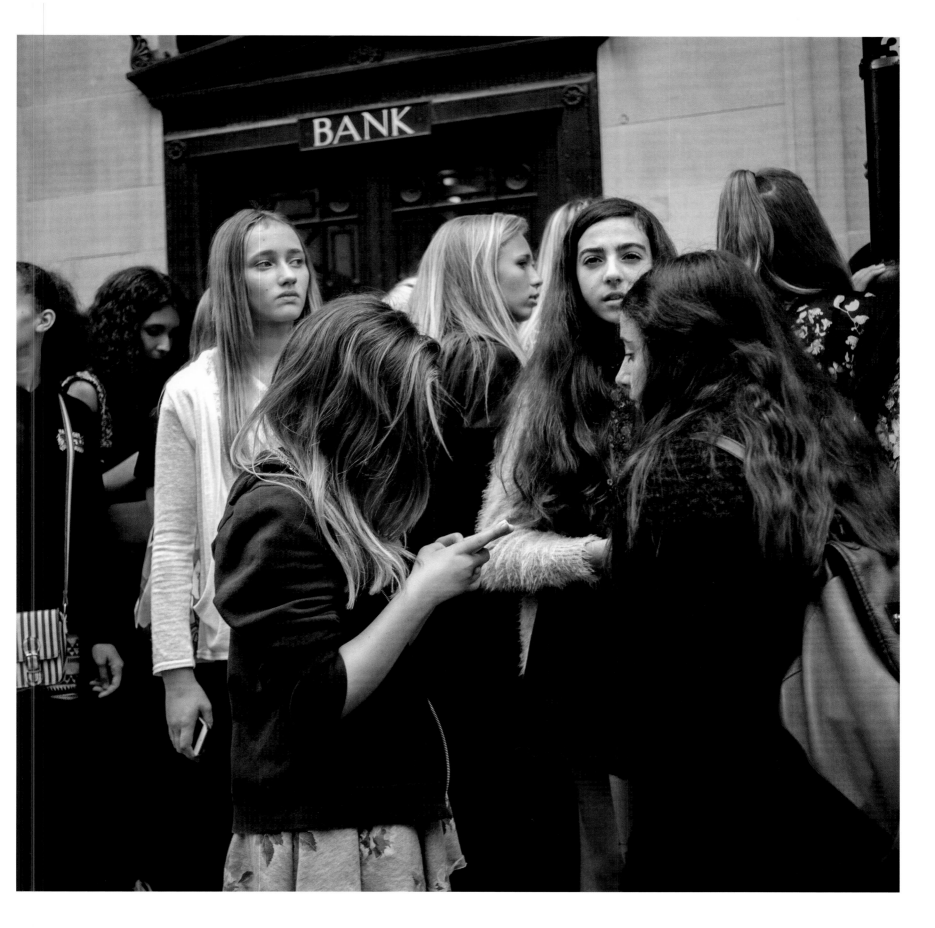

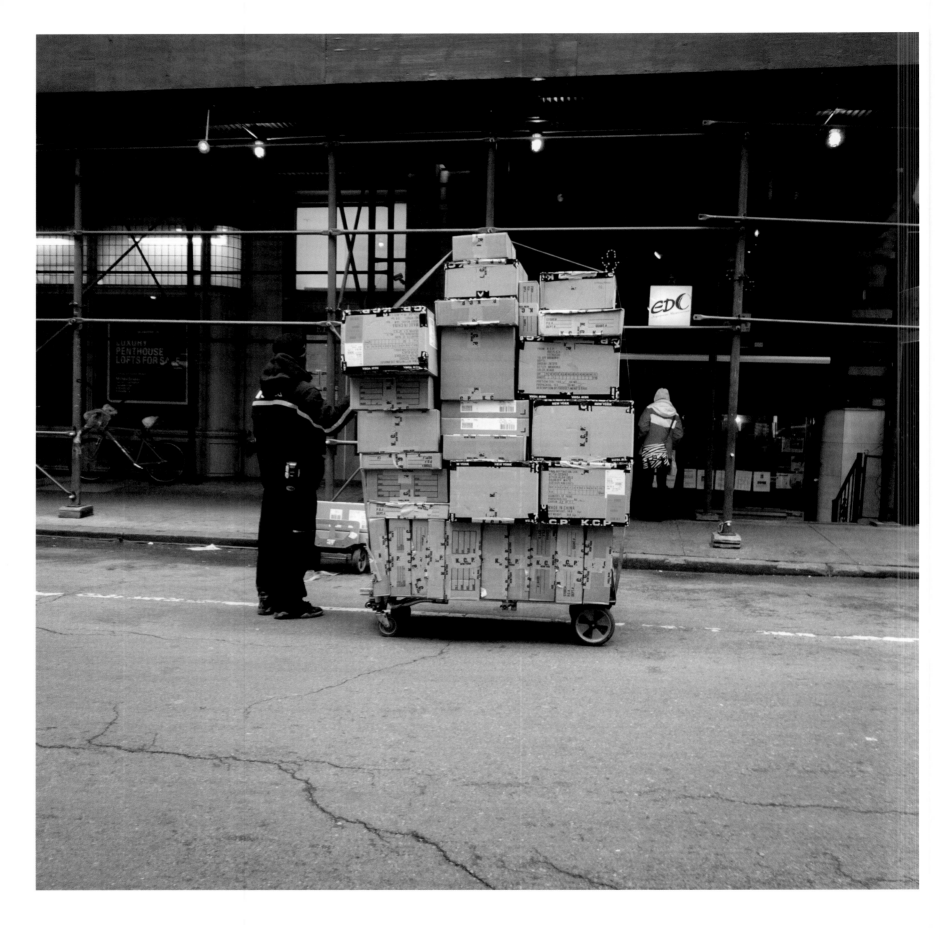

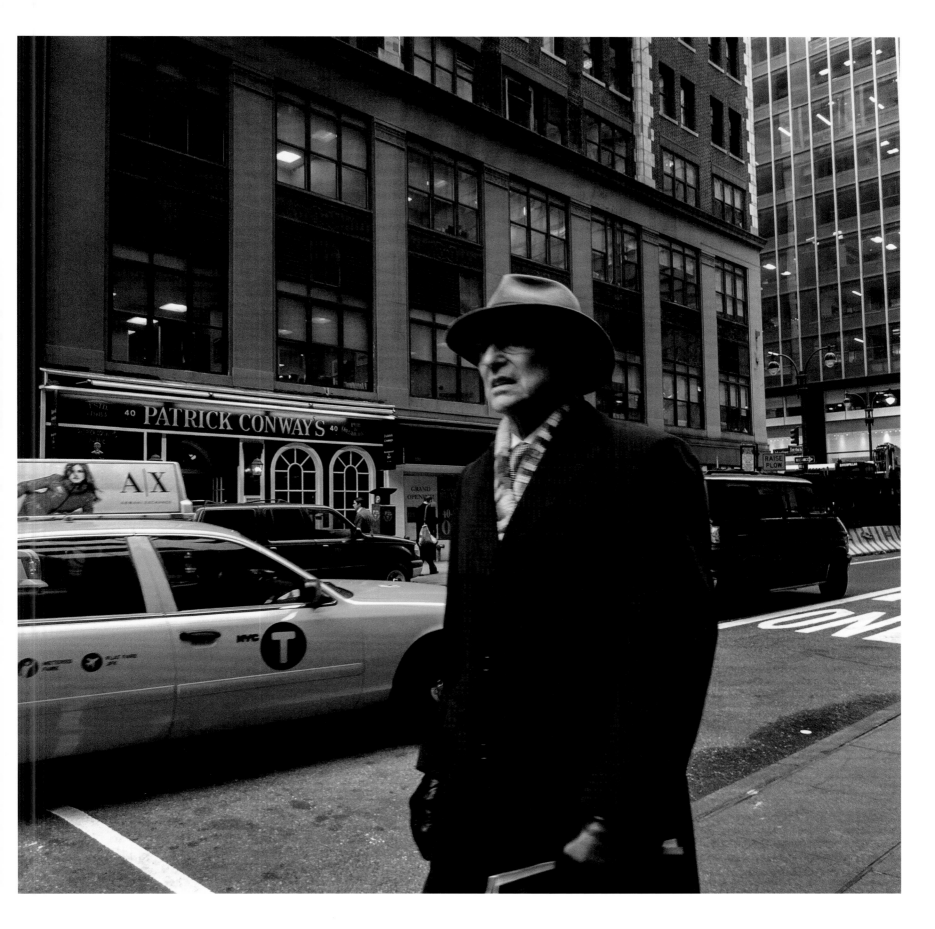

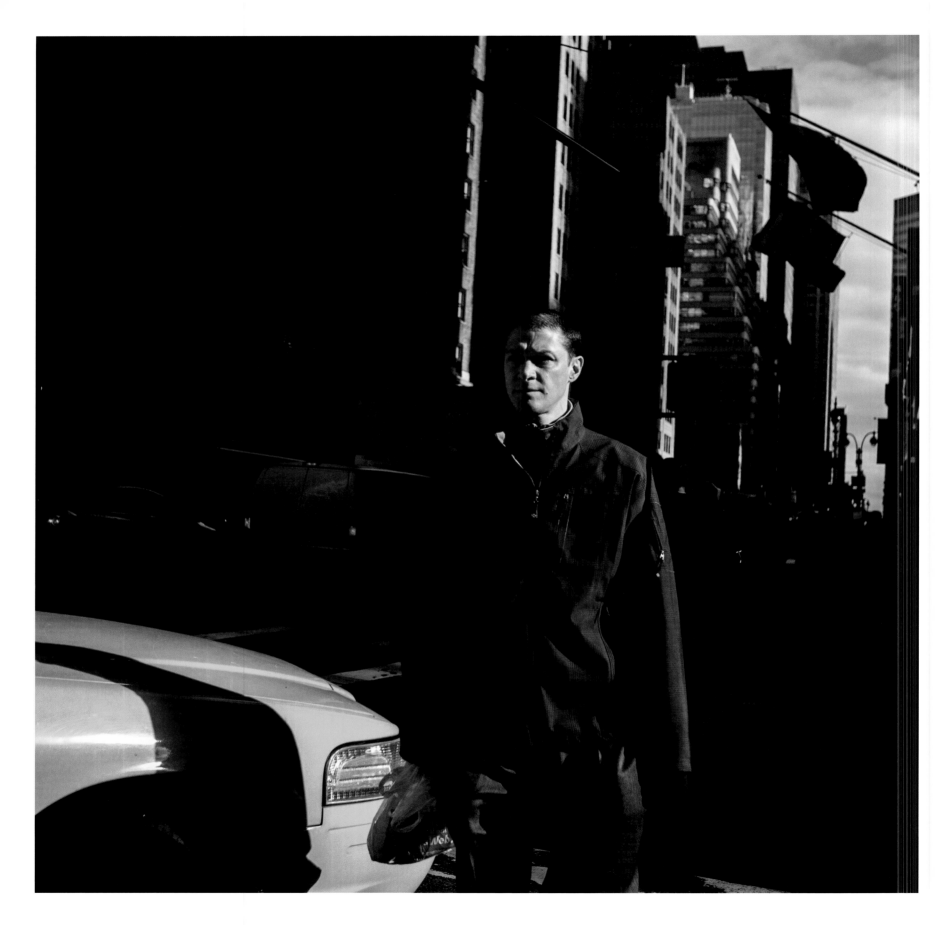

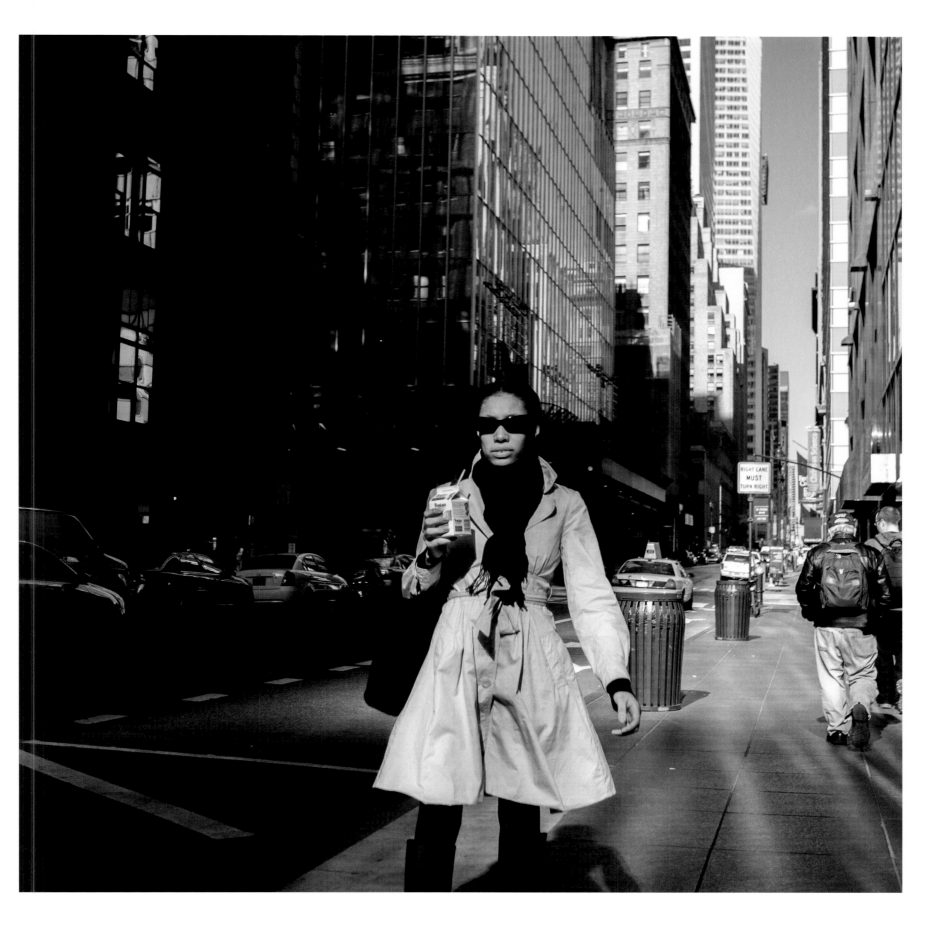

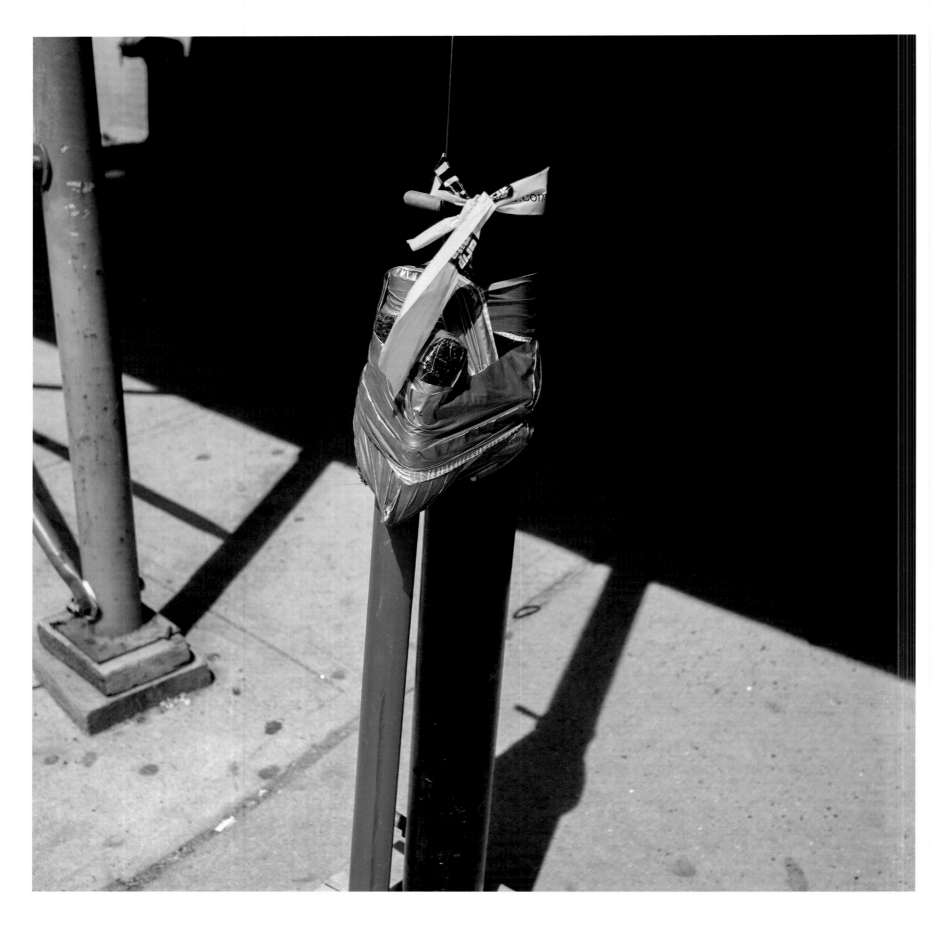

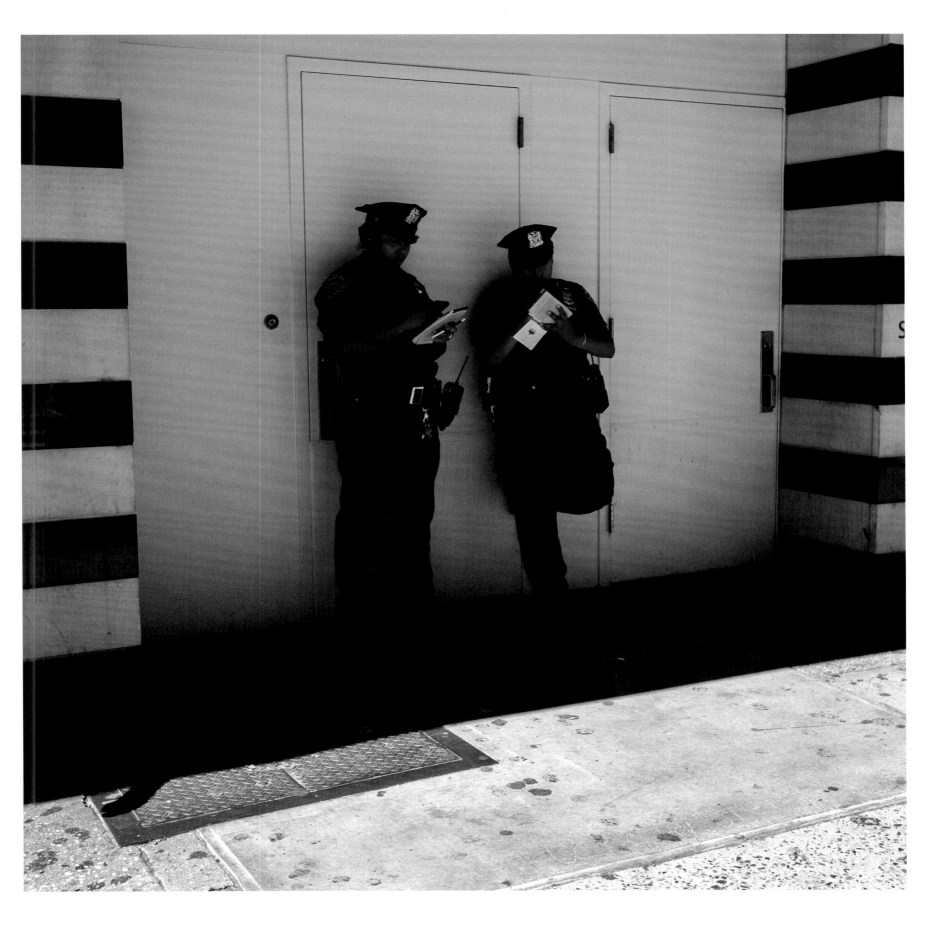

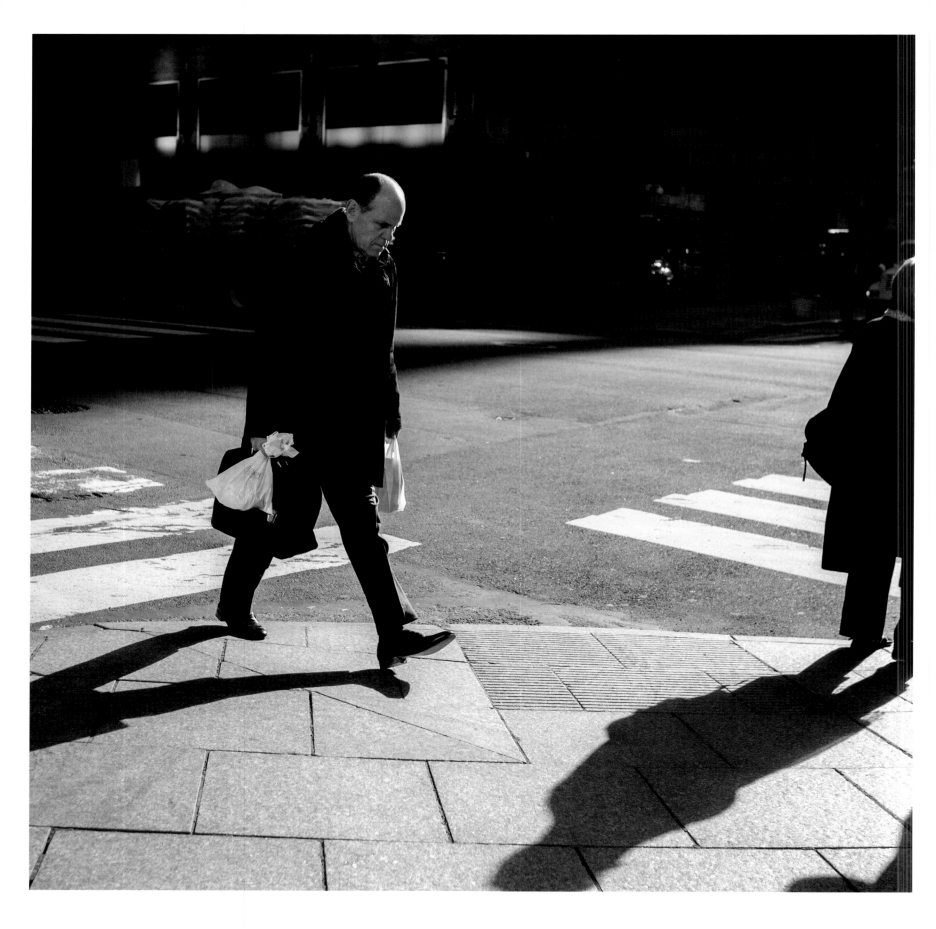

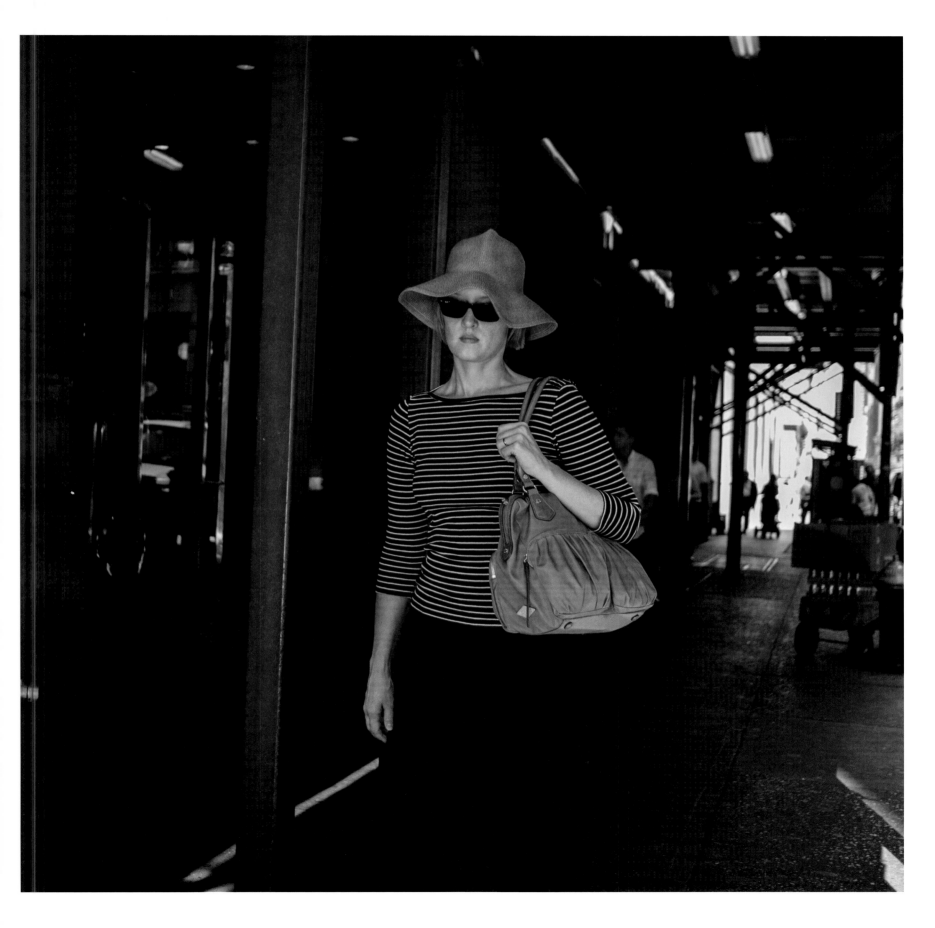

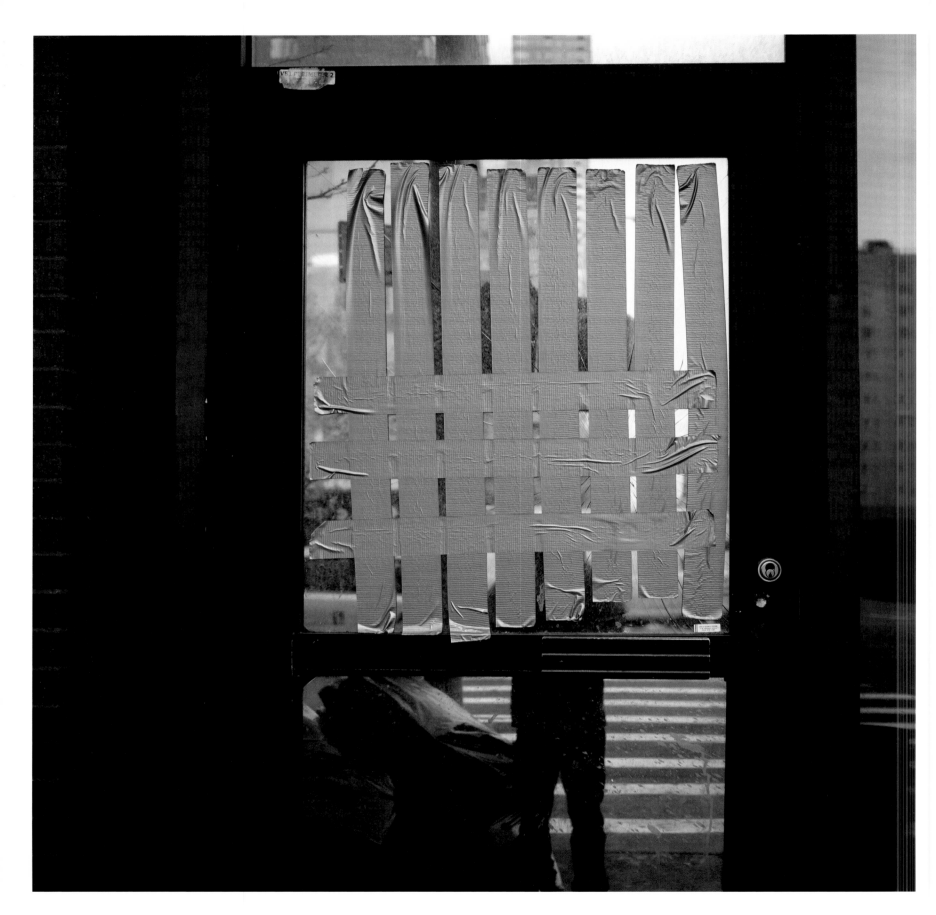

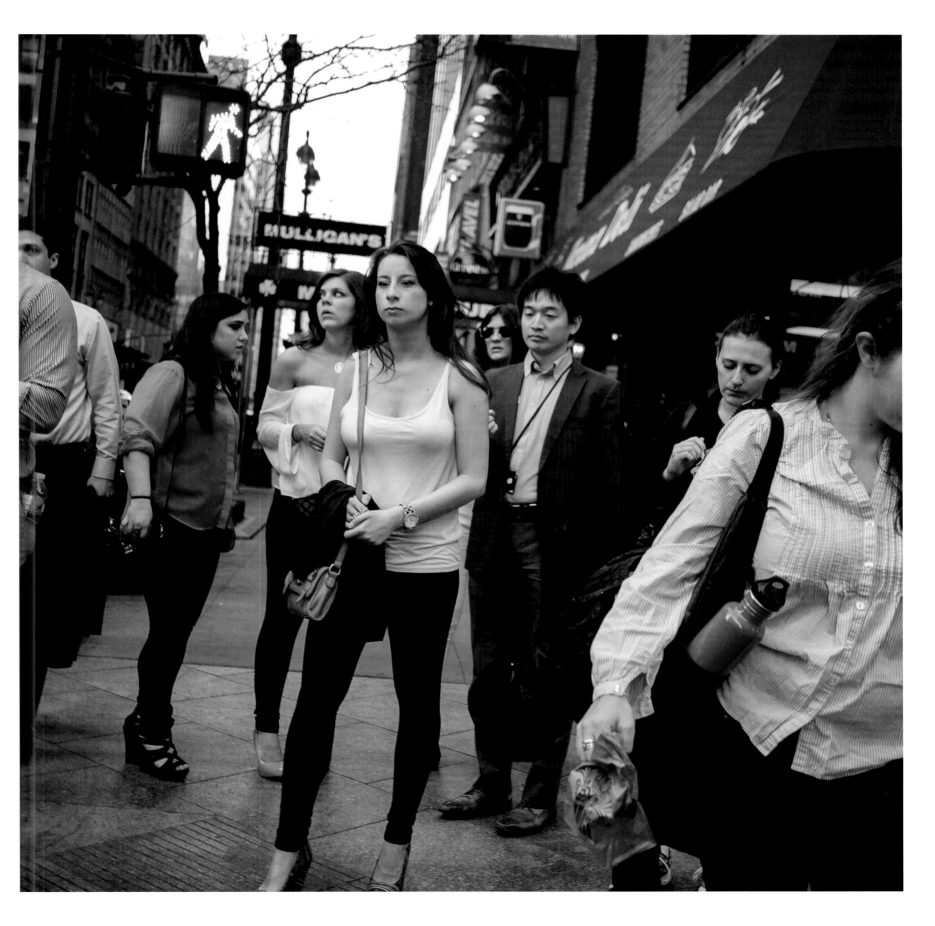

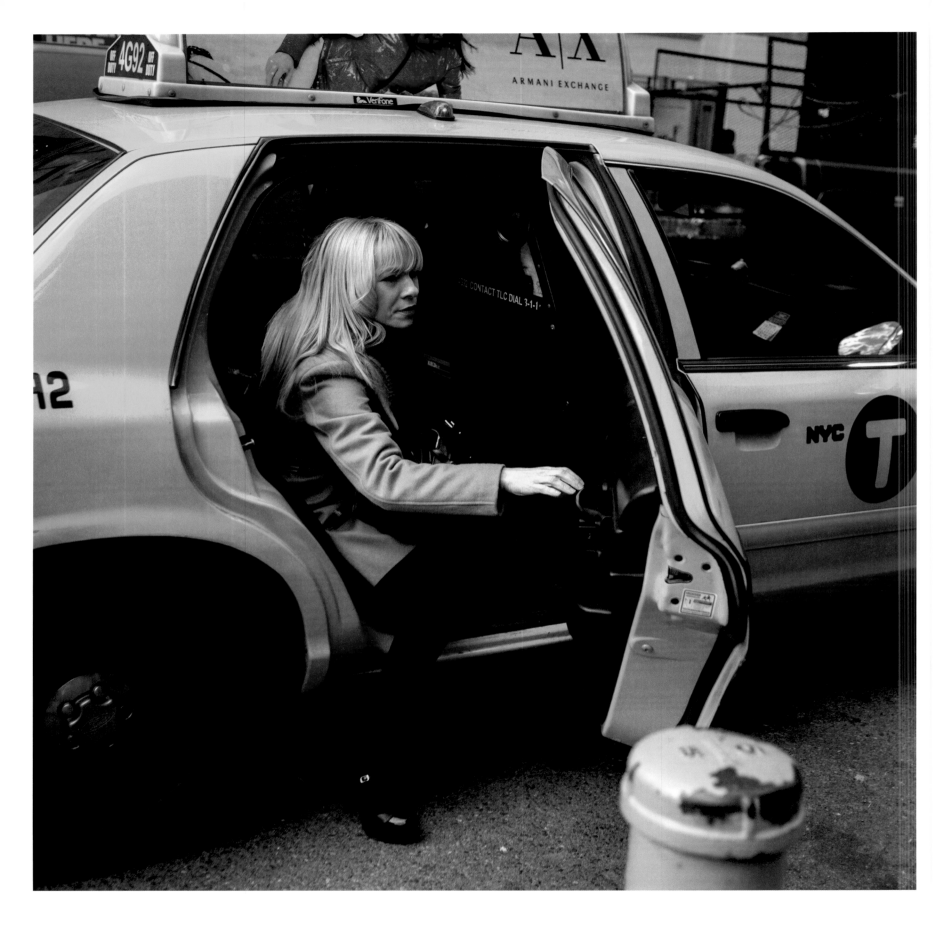

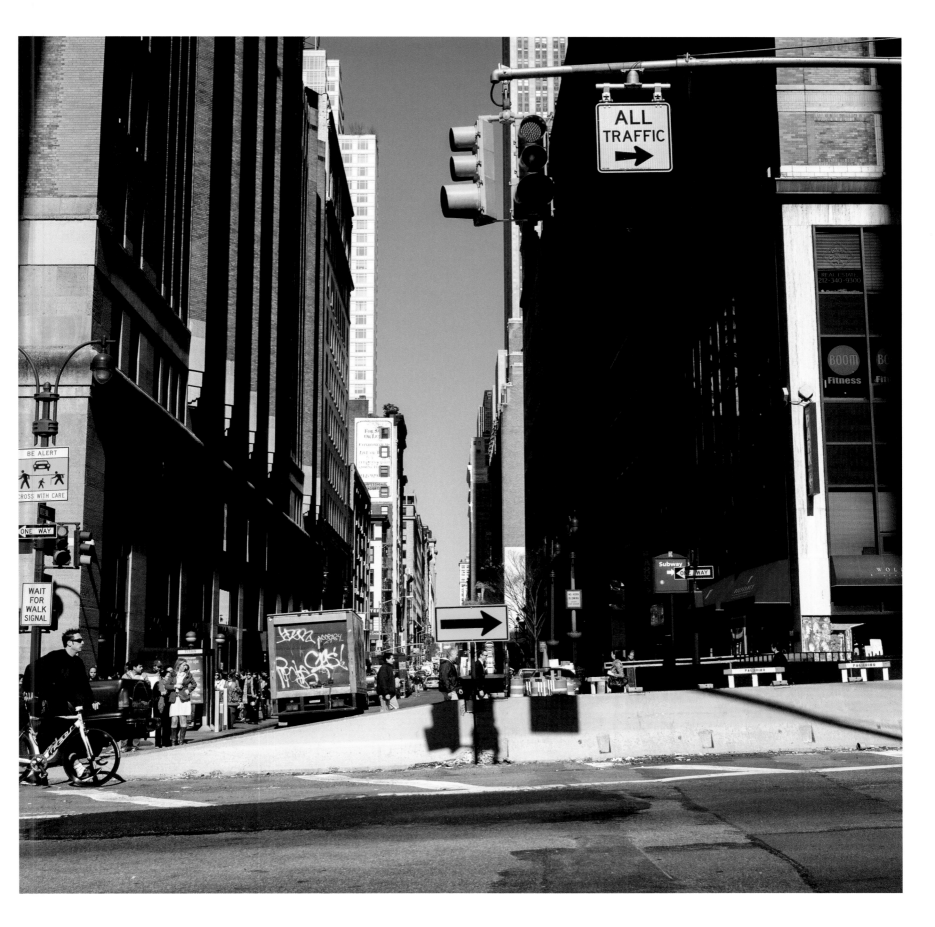

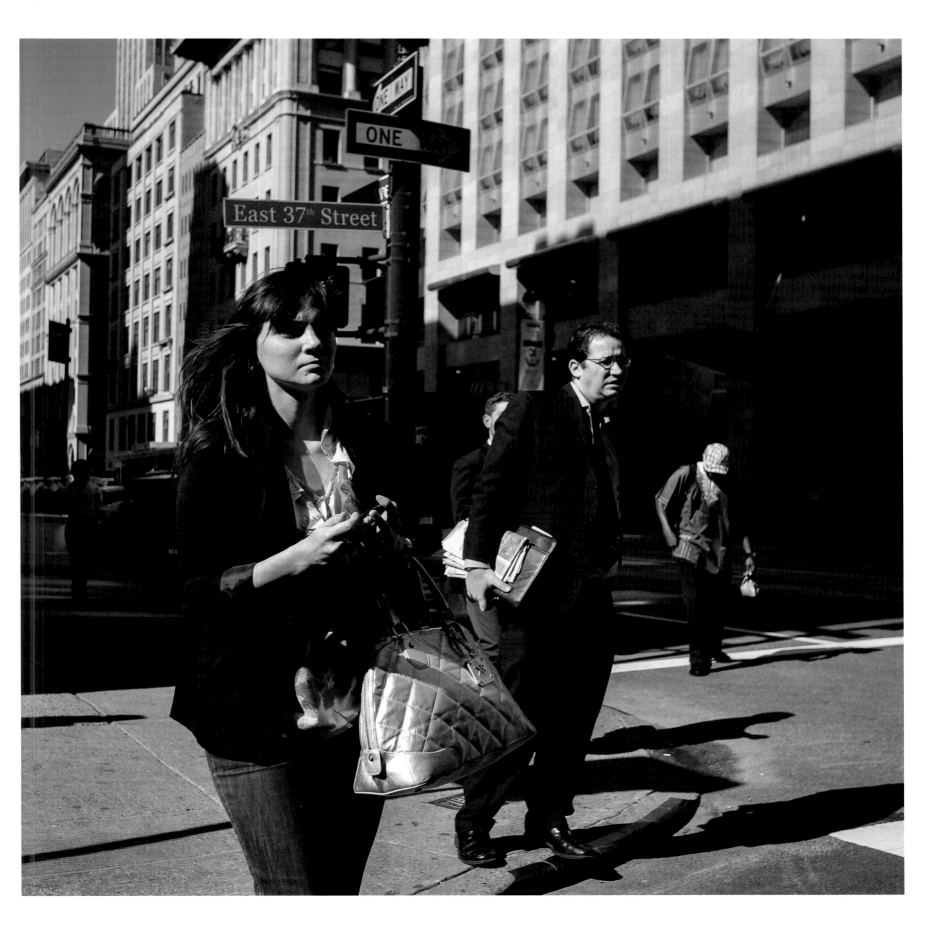

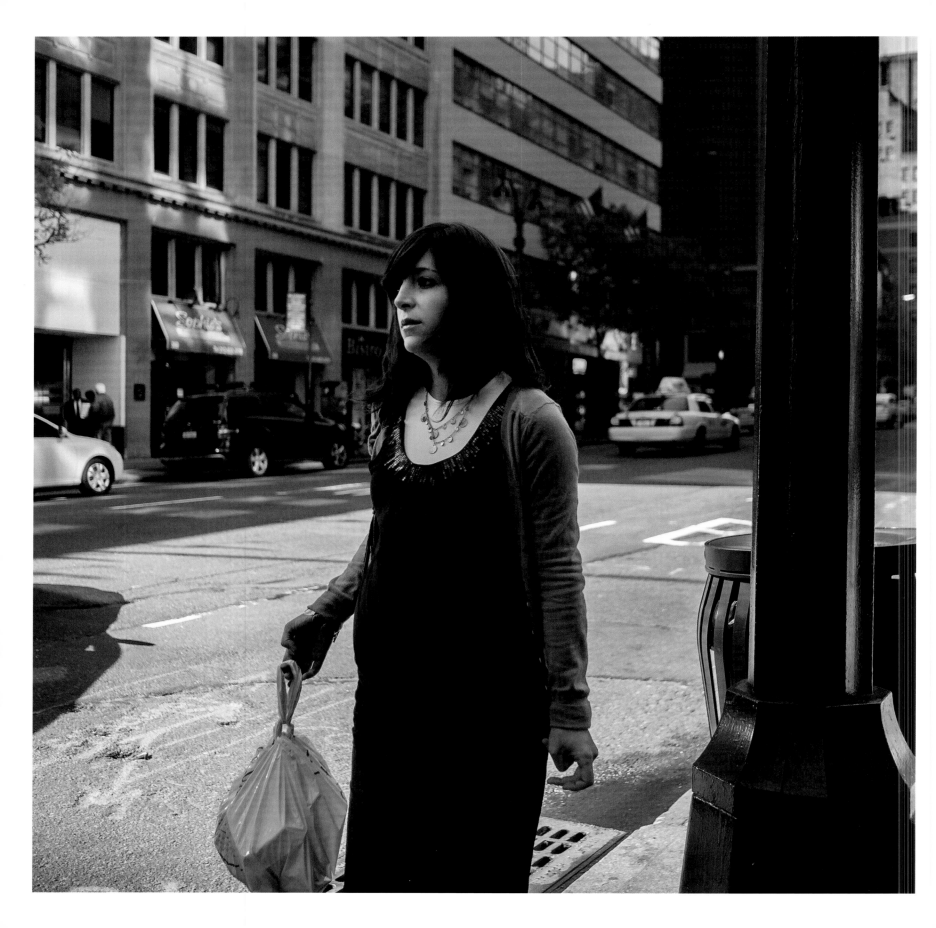

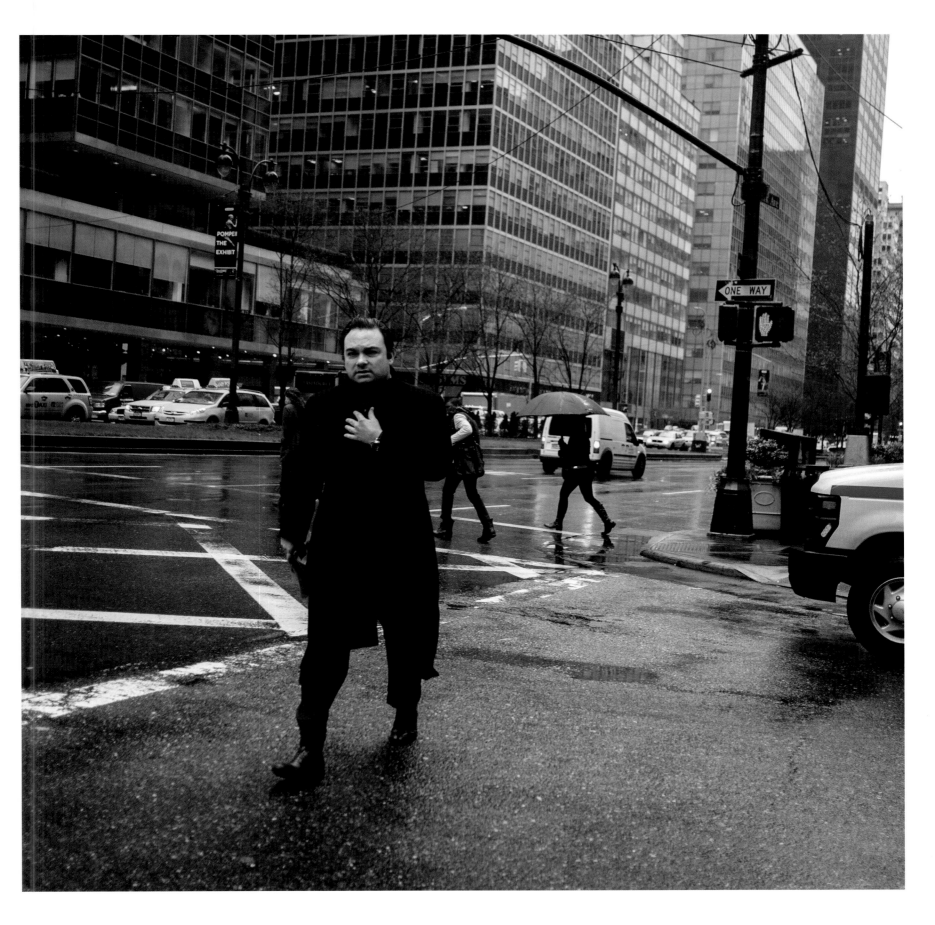

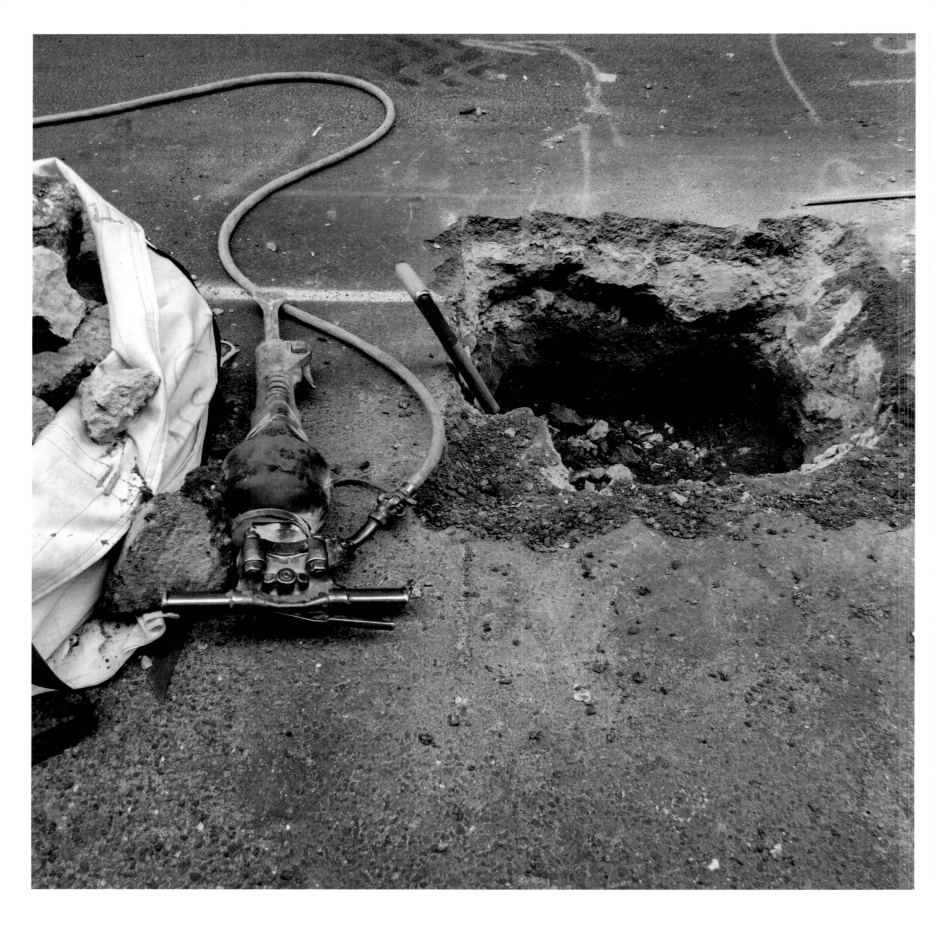

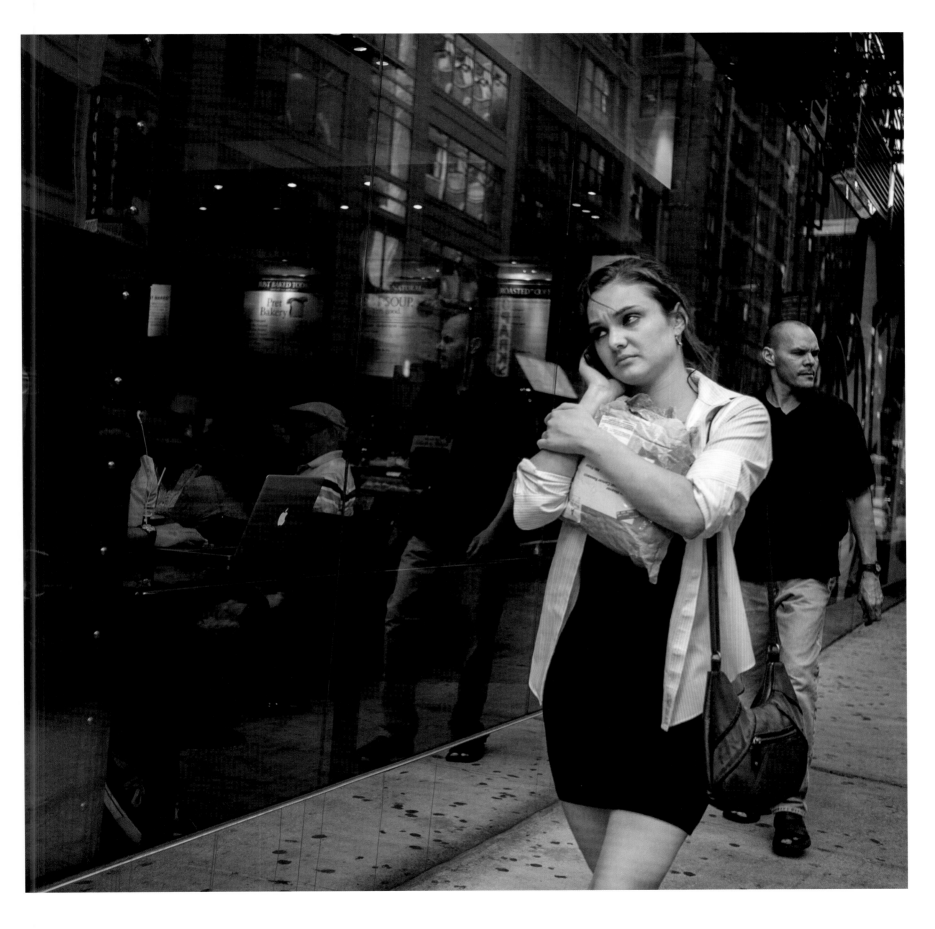

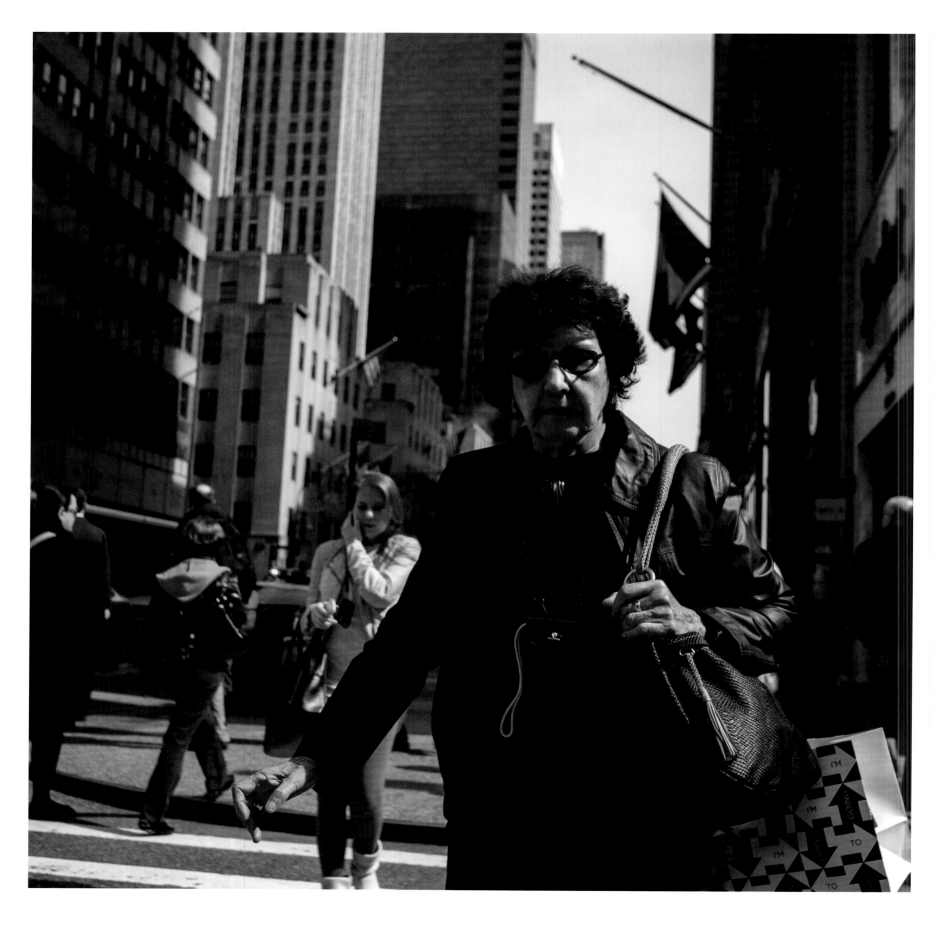

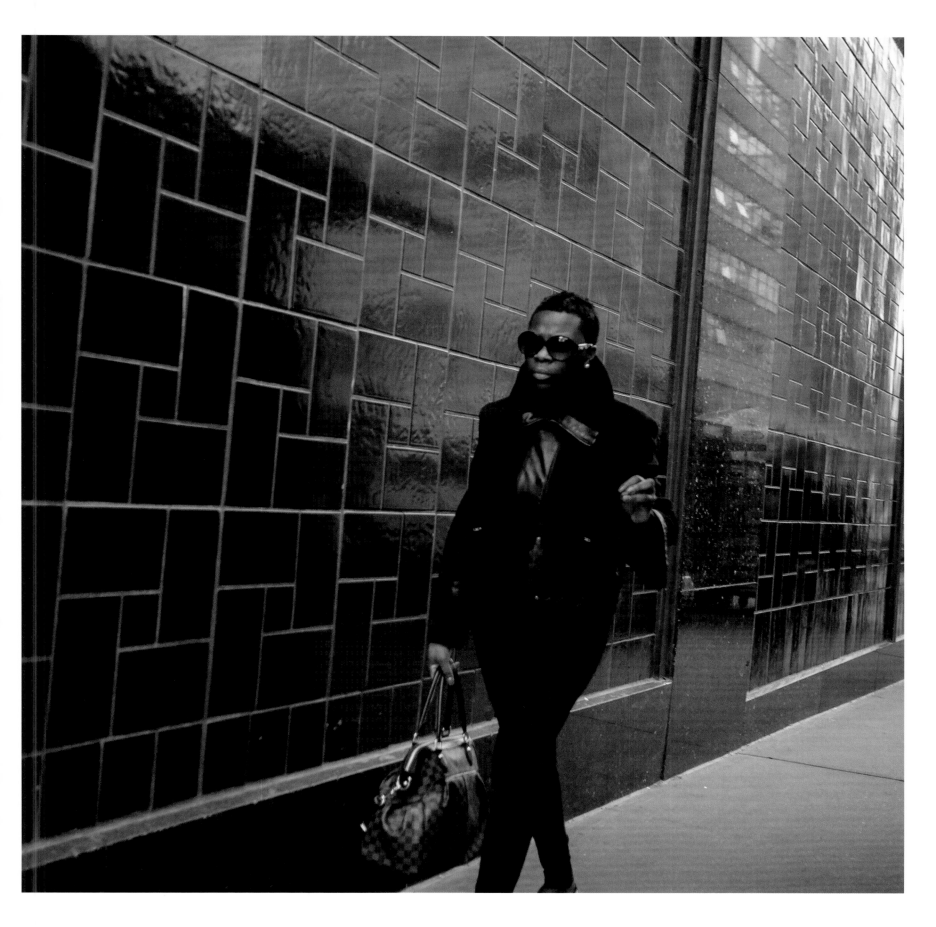

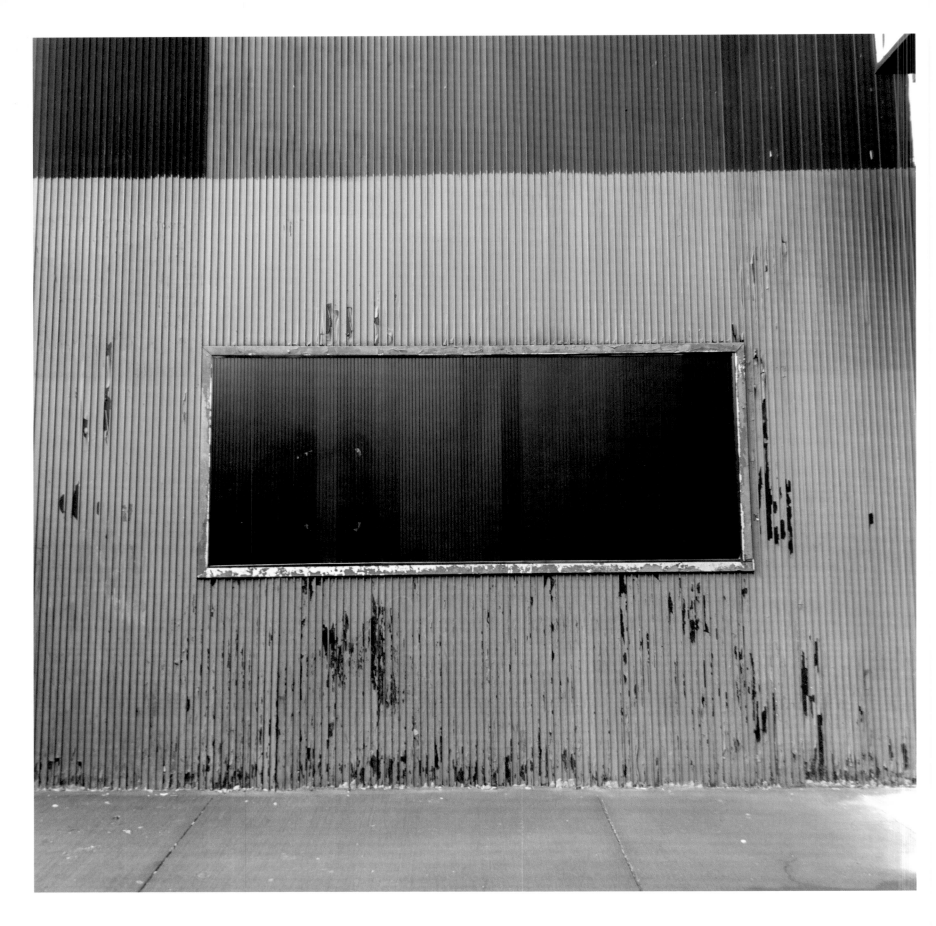

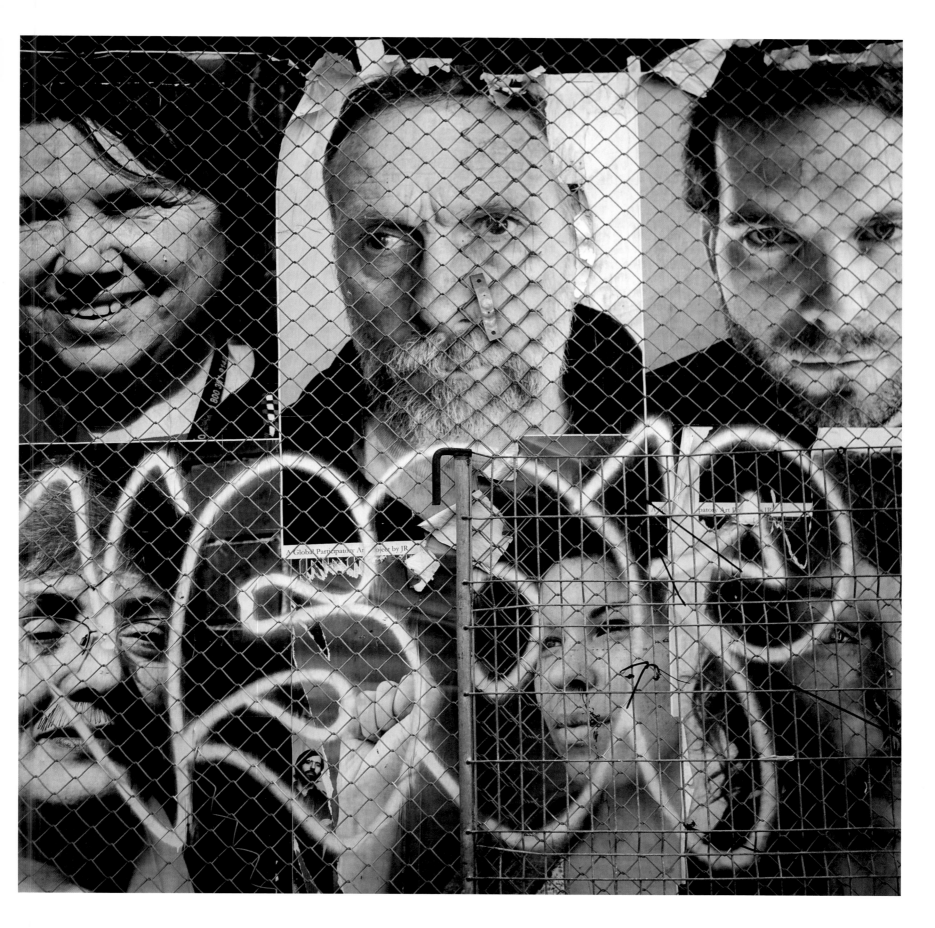

A Global Participatory Art Project by JR

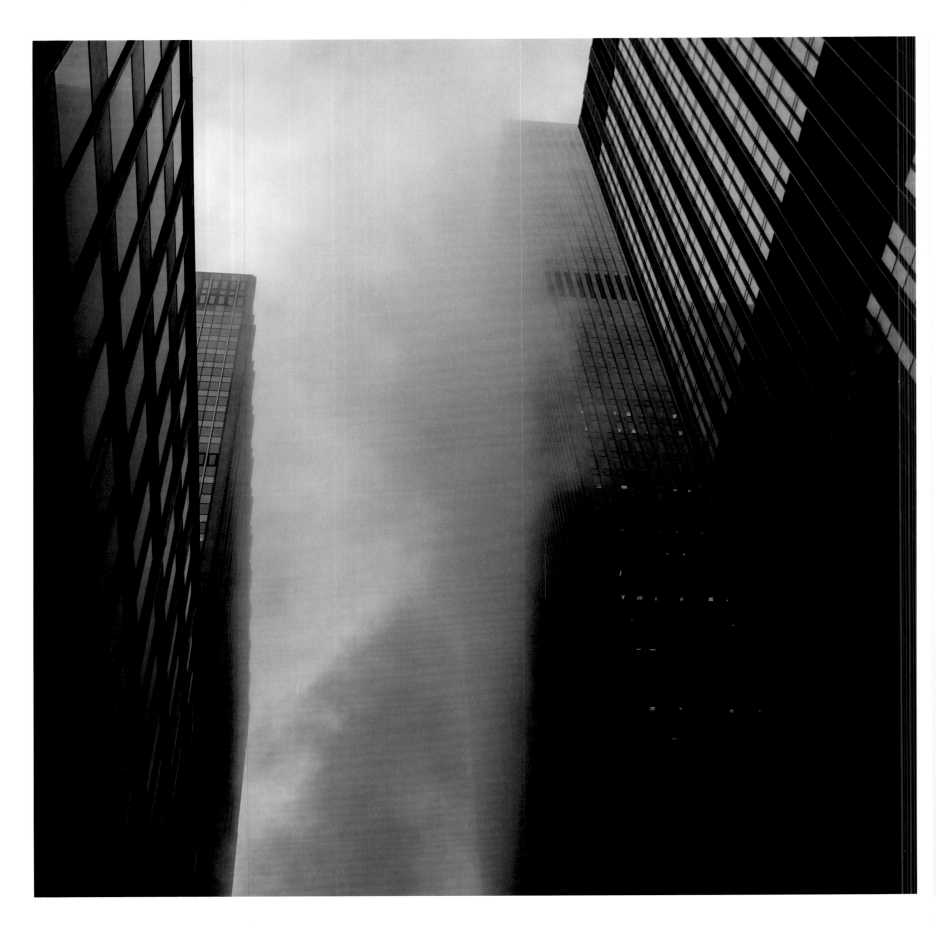

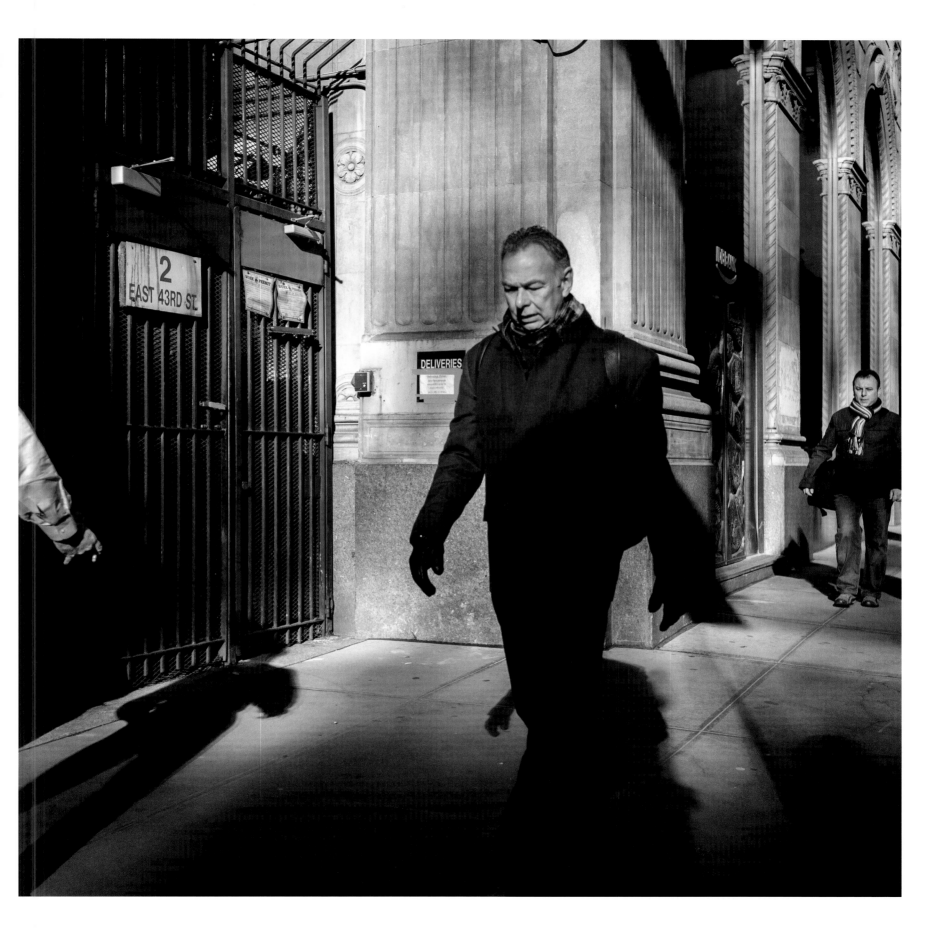

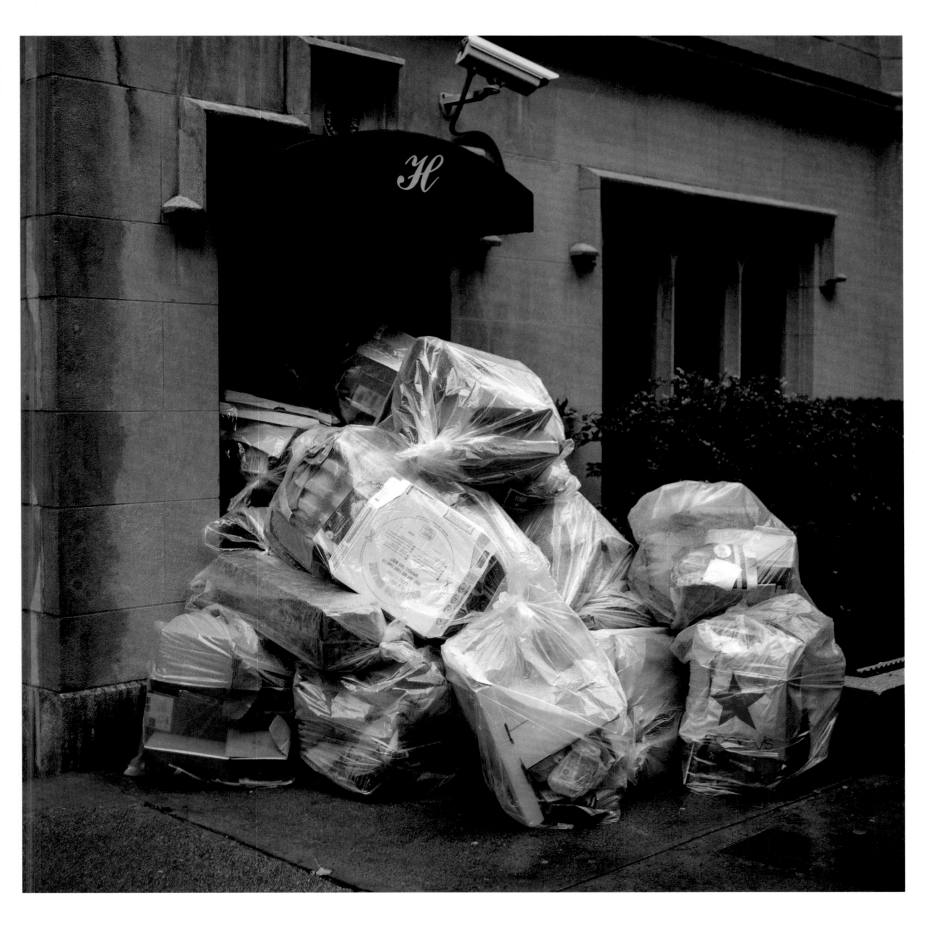

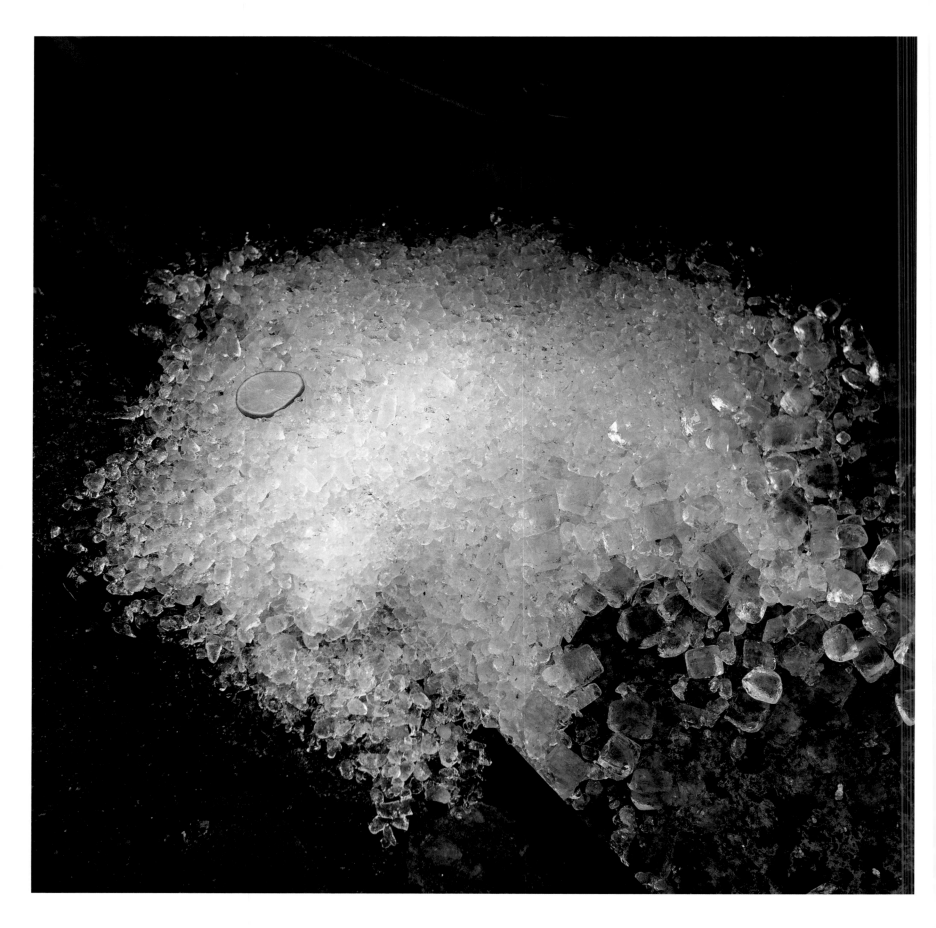

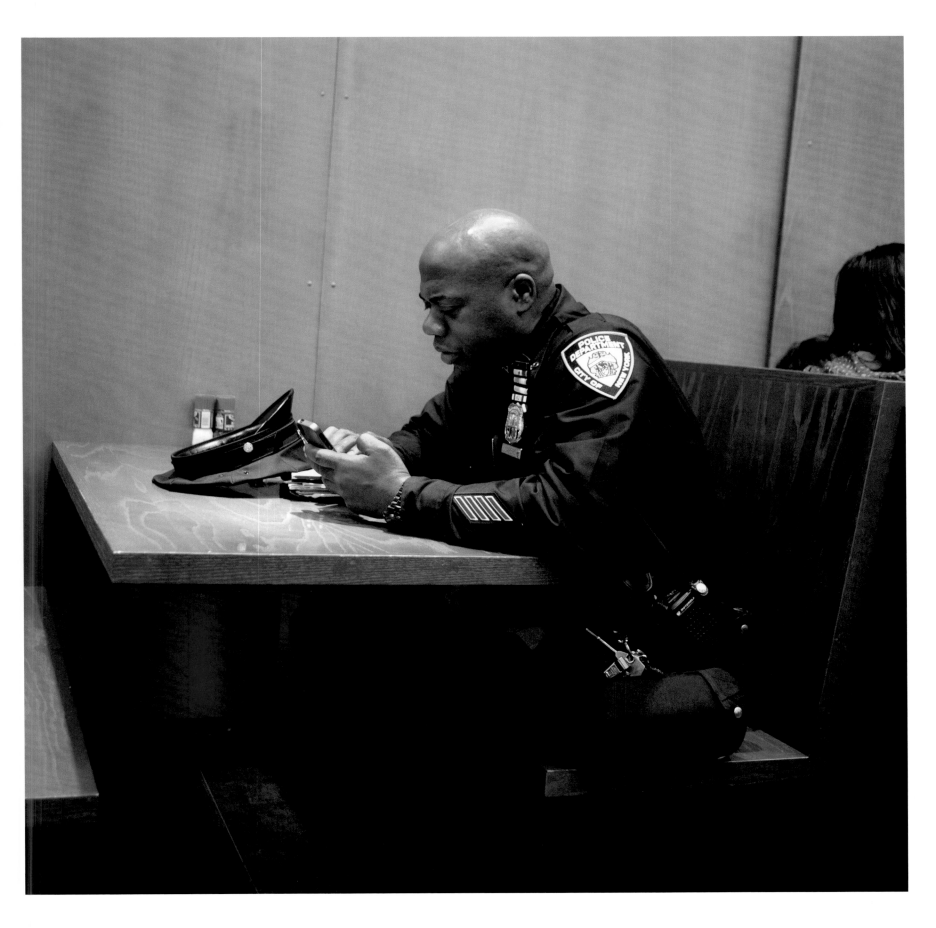

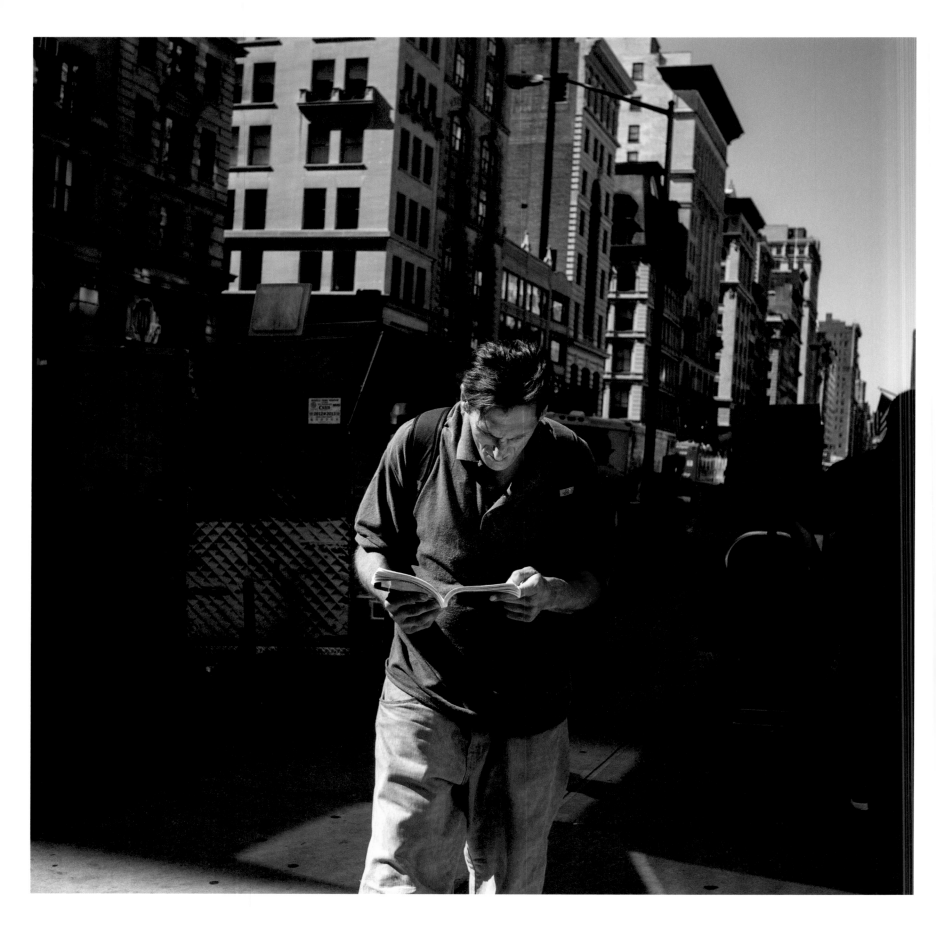

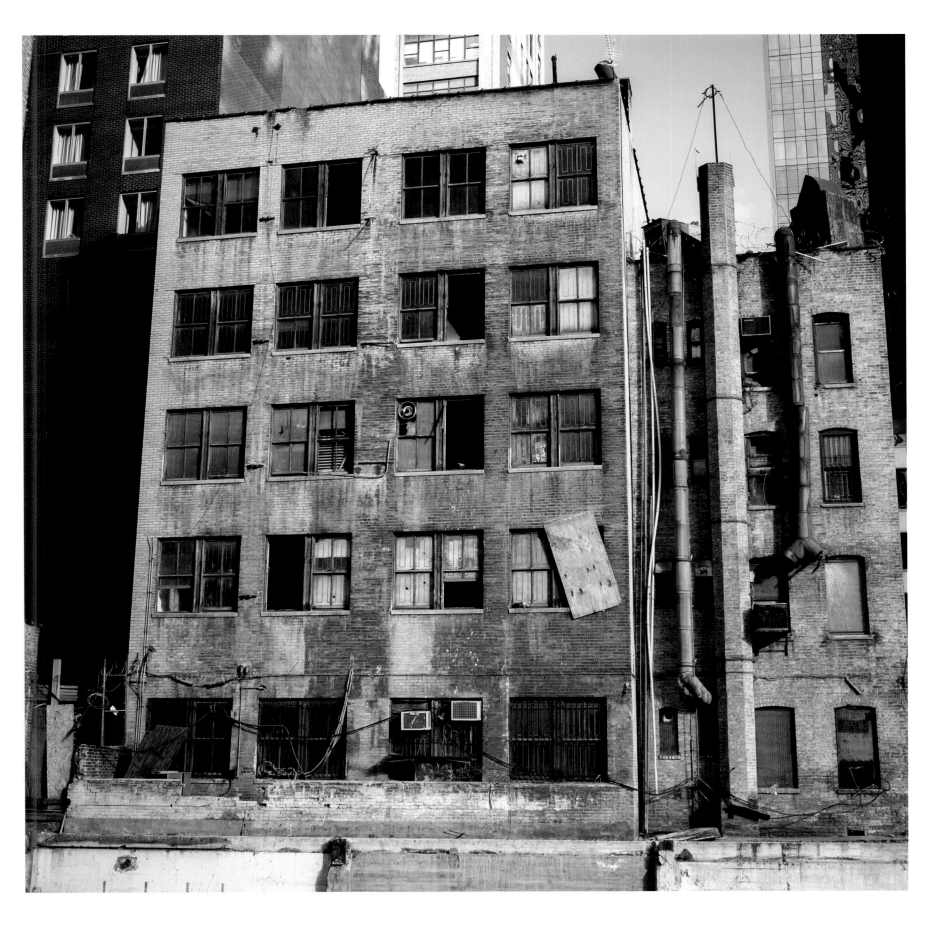

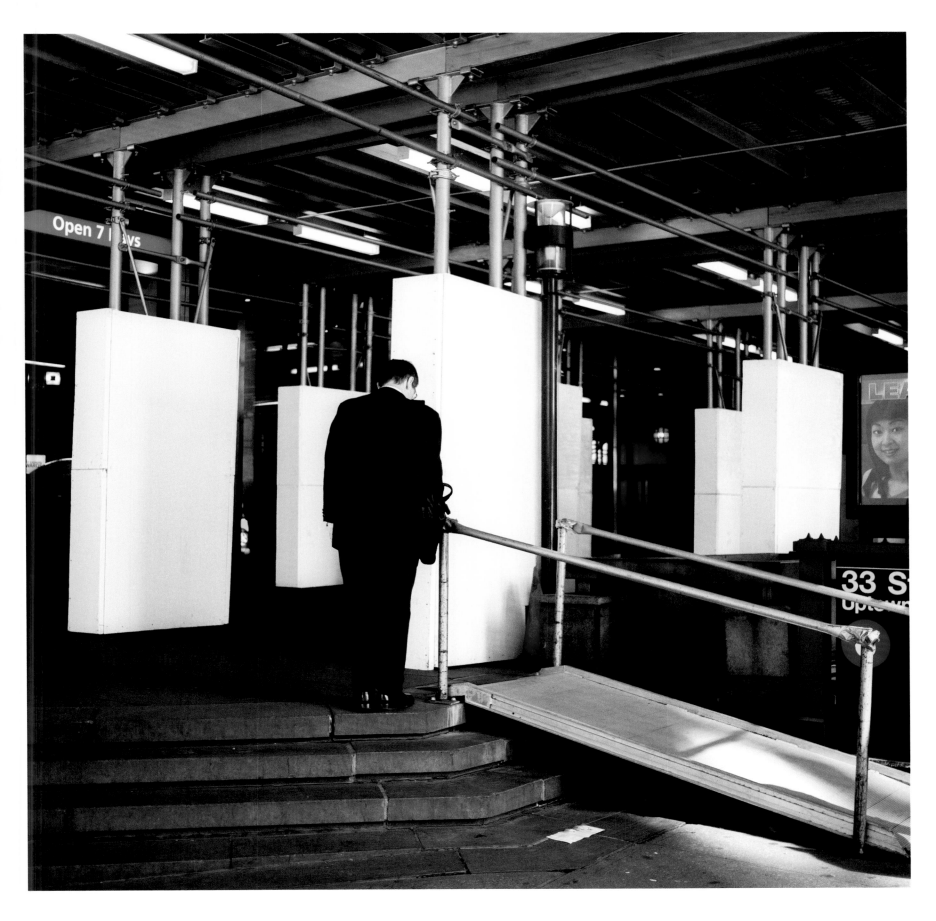

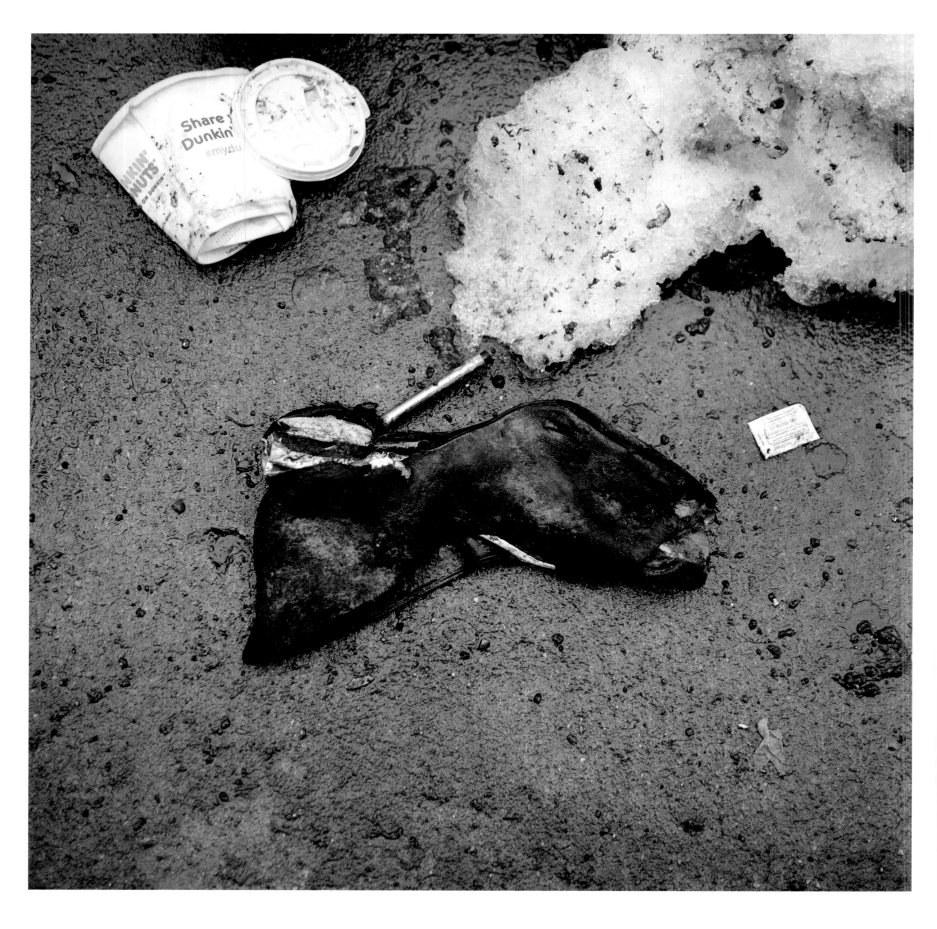

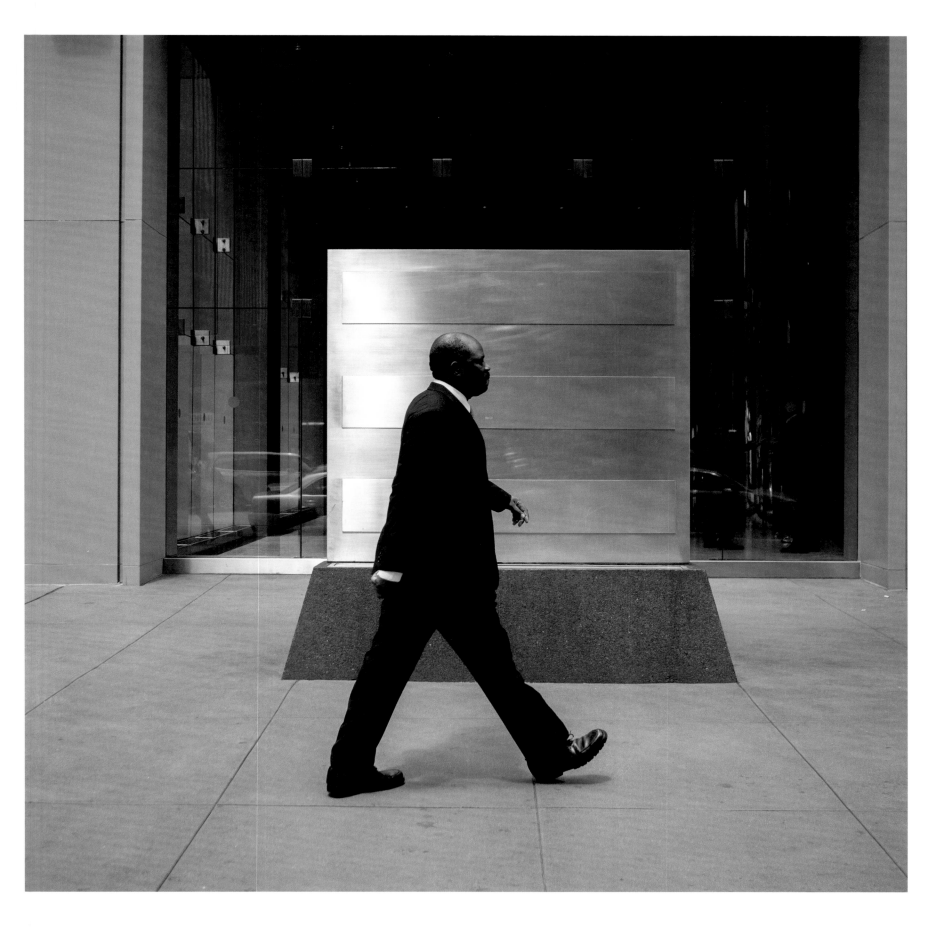

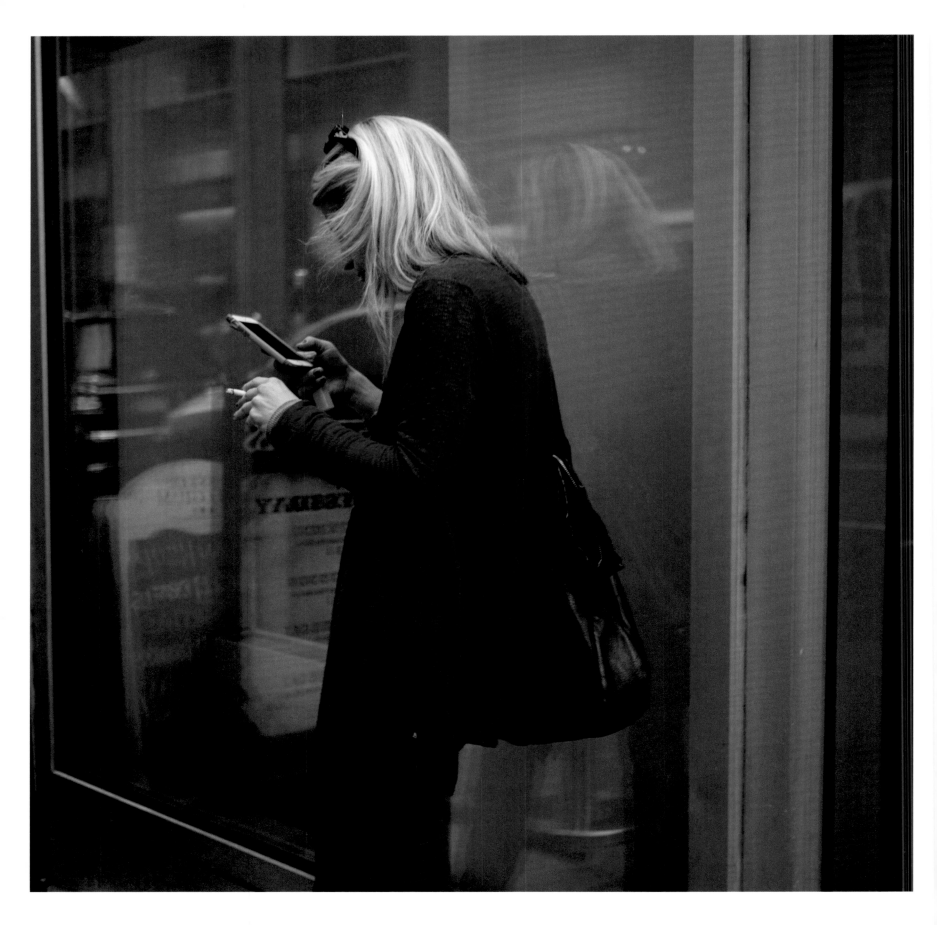

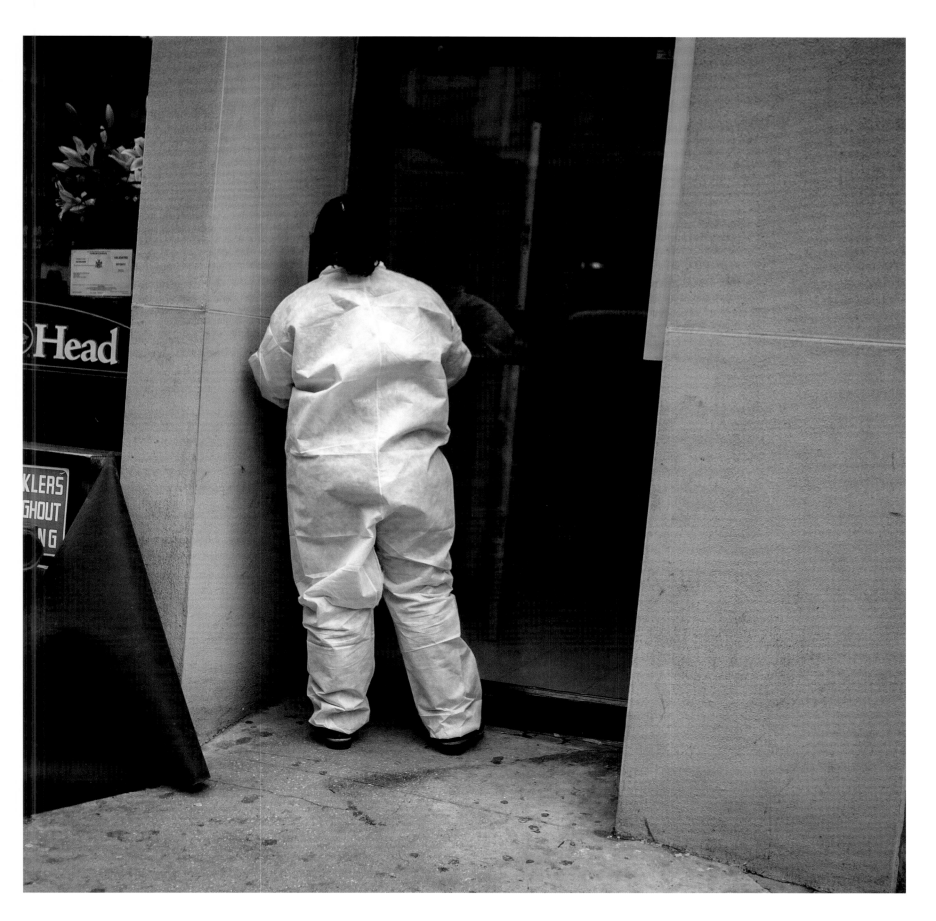

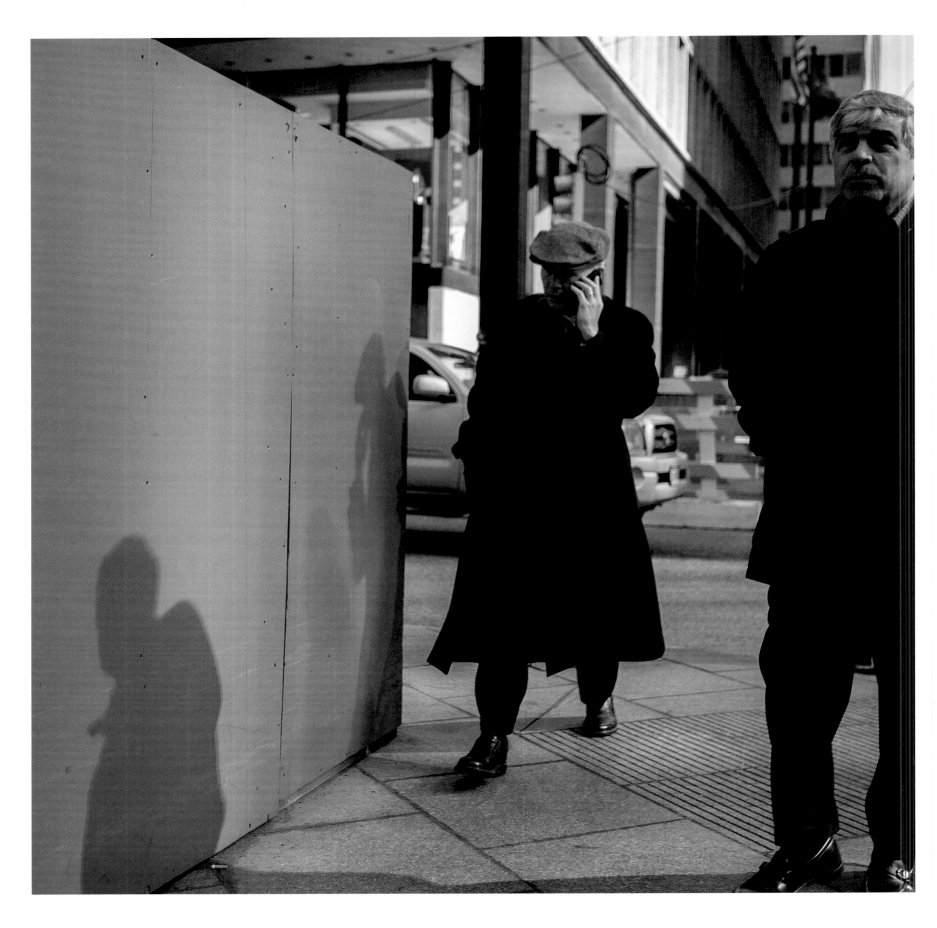

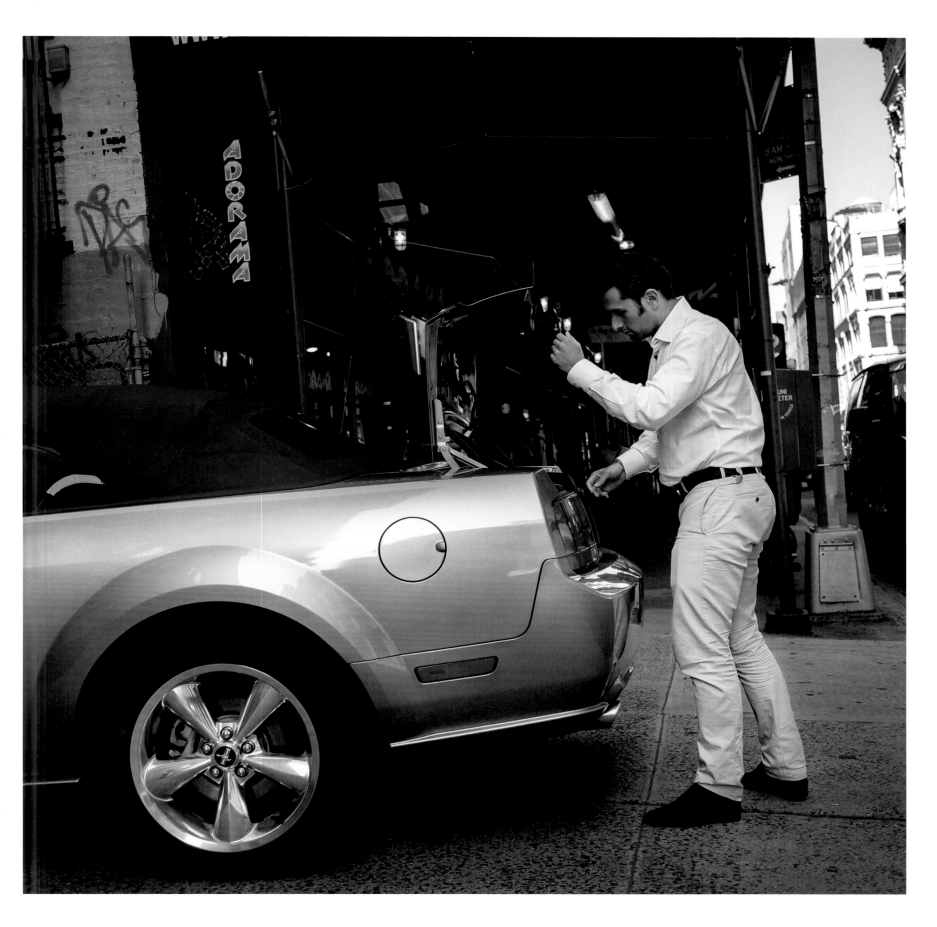

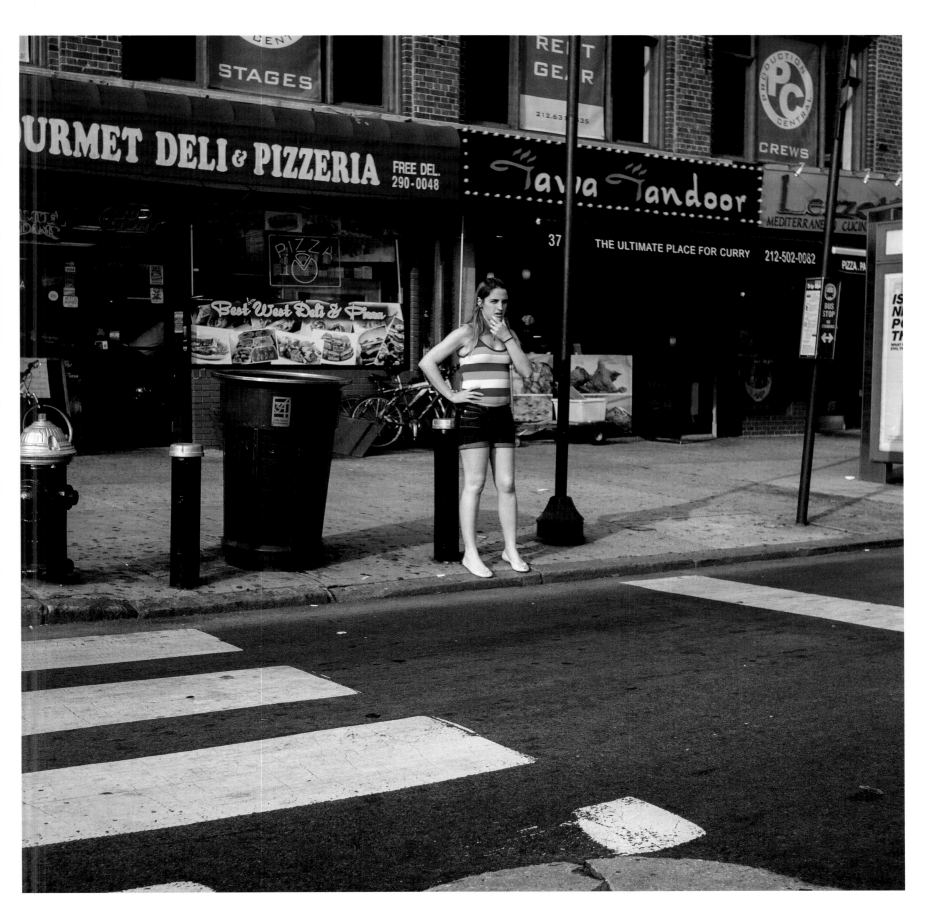

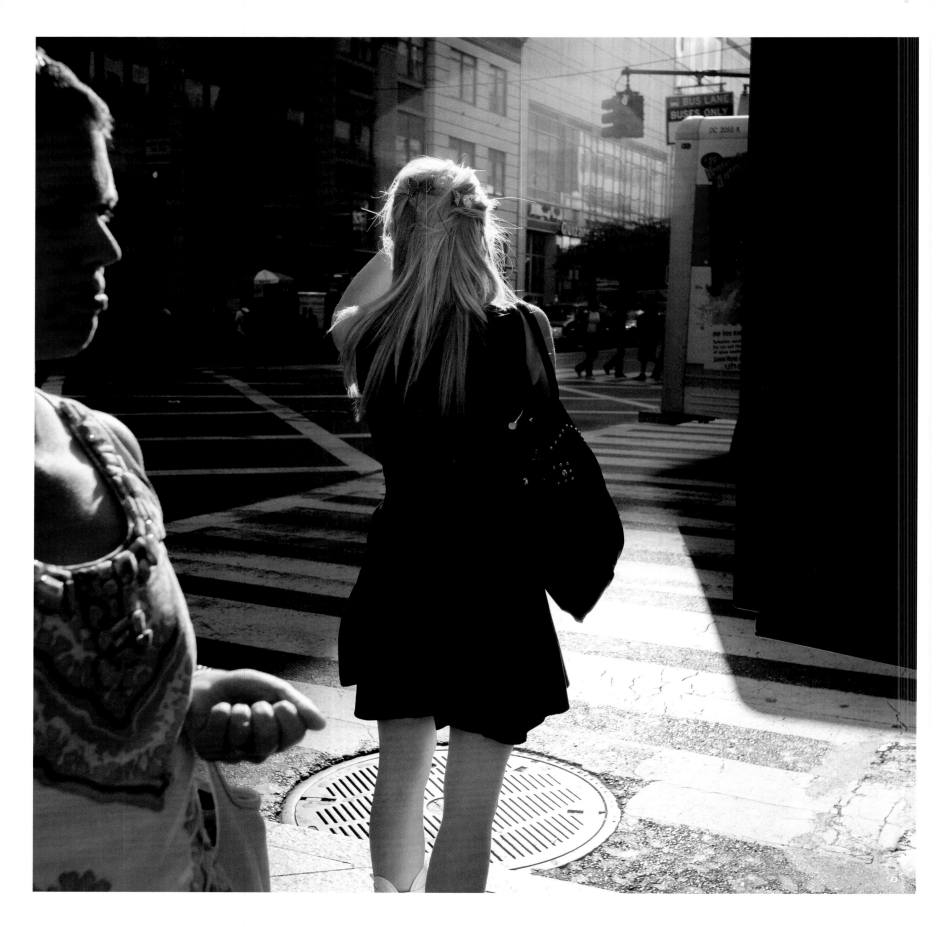

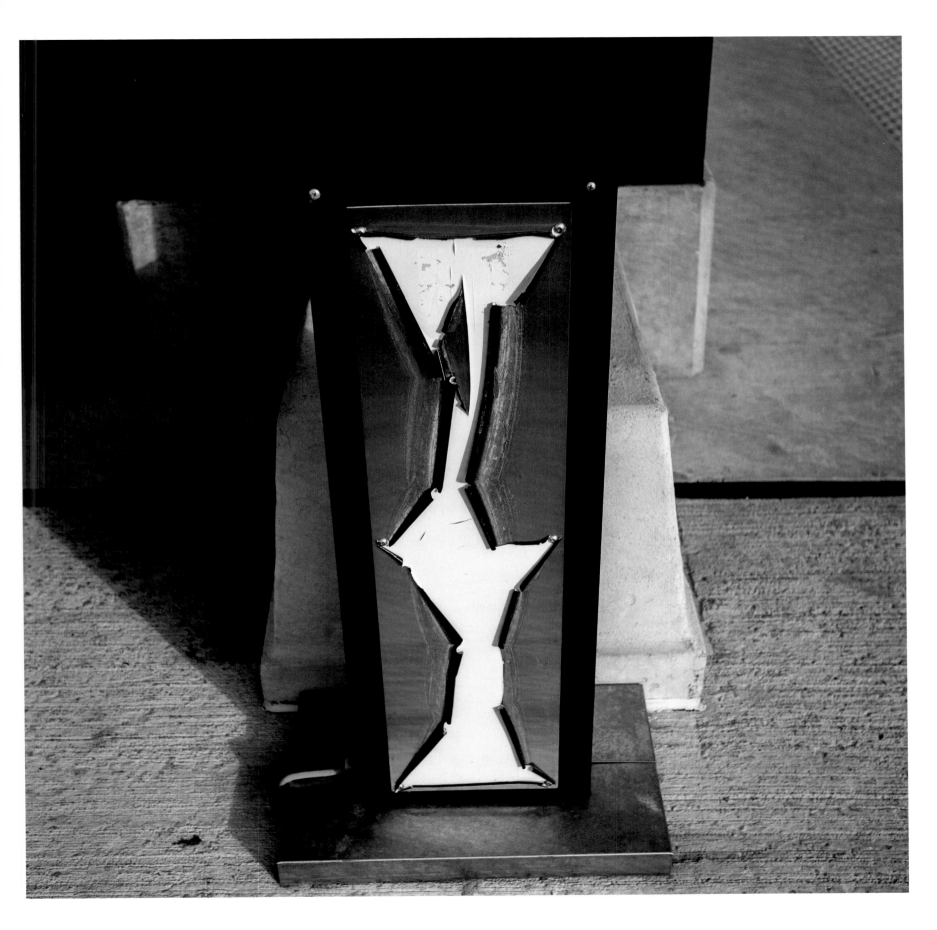

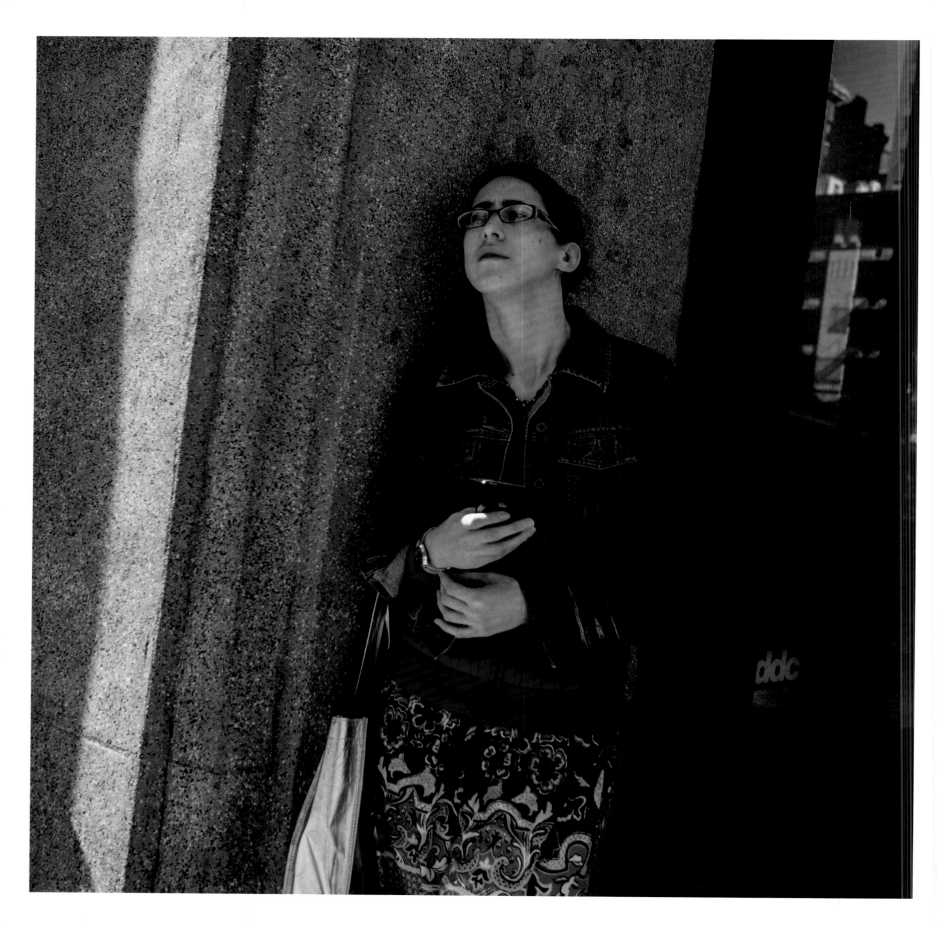

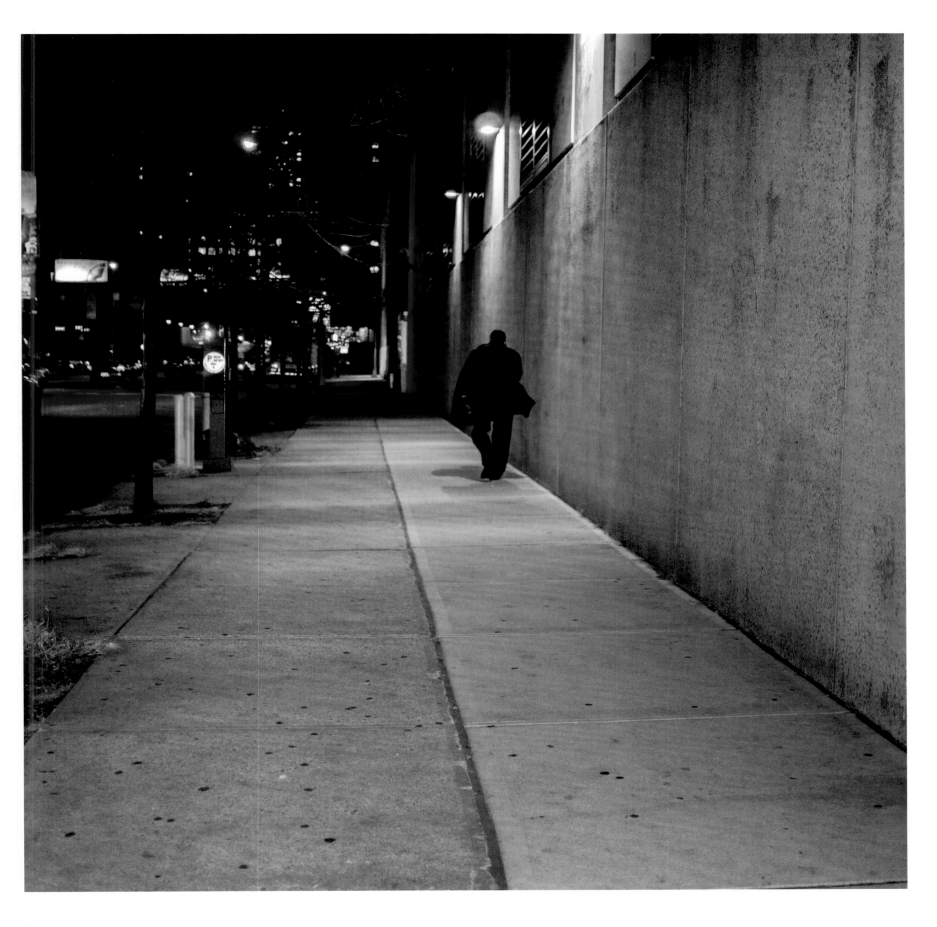

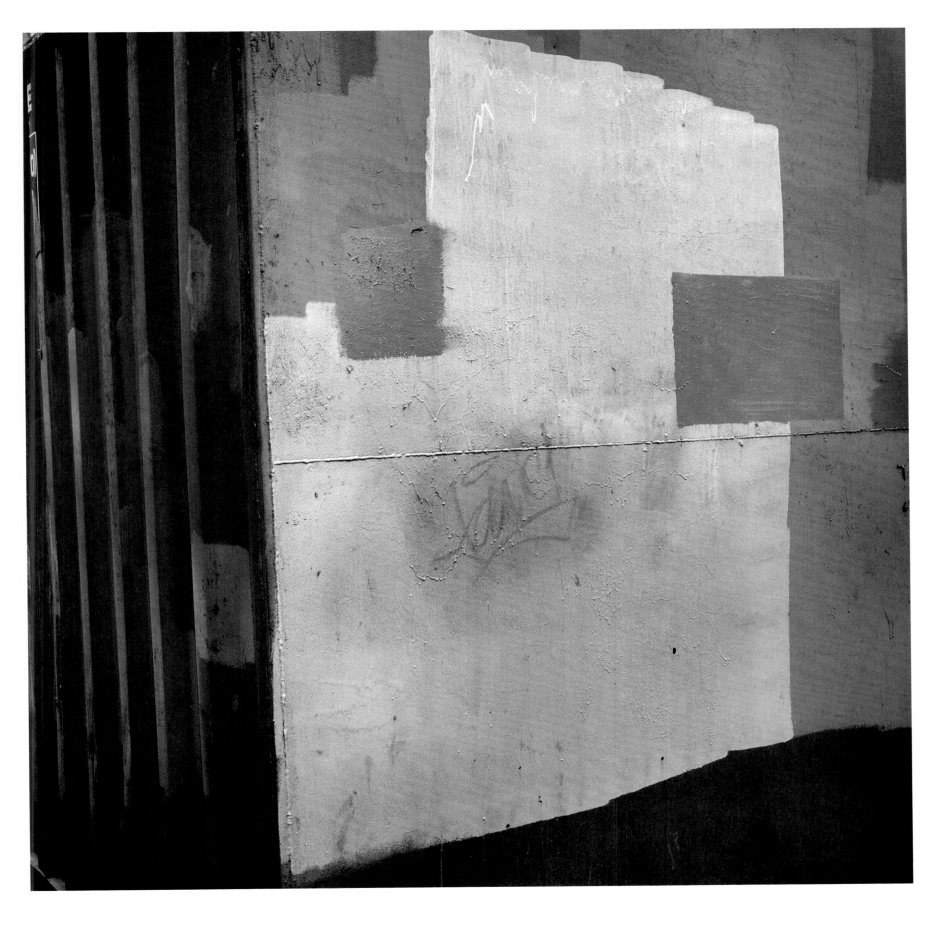

CURRENT

by Robert Sullivan

Say you are the street. Say you are Thirty-Ninth Street, a little off Broadway, toward the west. Say everyone is on their way to work, not just on you but, really, in you—though cutting off of you eventually and heading up, sure, into those taller buildings but also into all those not-as-tall buildings with the little lobbies and the tiny elevators where everybody thinks, No, we're not all going to fit, and then, Wow we fit; or do we?

Say you are Forty-Fifth Street, more toward the east, wherein not everyone is racing but they're moving, though a few are racing, carrying with them that vexing feeling, an itchy sense that if they are late just one more time, it will be a problem, not because it's actually a problem but because their boss is not so cool.

Say you are Twenty-Eighth Street, on the corner of Seventh Avenue, and it's about twenty minutes earlier and that guy with the cart who recognizes everybody has a coffee in that women's hand before she says anything; they smile and speak and do the same the next day and the next.

Say you are Nineteenth Street, not so far from Lexington Avenue, and rush hour has passed. Say you are pavement that was just swept twenty minutes ago, or kind of swept, after which cars quickly choreographed into their parking spots, drivers inspecting bumpers and curbs, offering a few quiet nods before heading into homes and offices, though on this block mostly homes. Imagine it is a cool but sunny winter morning, and things feel just momentarily easy on Nineteenth Street, or even a little secret. It's a reprieve though you know not from what, and you are the street so you don't care. For you, the reason for what happens on the street is not the thing. Everything else is.

At this hour, it's maybe just a little less harried in streets all around, even in midtown, where there are tech workers and advertisers, people in fashion and in finance, people working to feed and assist the aforementioned and more. The street isn't empty but it's not as peopled as it was earlier, during the morning rush. Now, a few hours later, all those then-just-awake people are now just yawning, while minding their own business, or more likely somebody else's, till lunch, which is far away but calling. Lunch marks the moment when they will return to you, the street, and to all your neighbors. And they will return to you at first relaxed, then watch-watching, then moving up in the buildings, till later, when each little tributary flows into each avenue again, each avenue leading to the little holes in the ground, to the doors to the stations or the stairs to the busses in the terminals, terminals marking the end of the day, until, when the sun goes down and up again, they mark the beginning of the next one.

*

As you know. Because you are the street, and you are in the middle of it all. People are honking horns or shouting or whistling on occasion, and you perceive these things in a way that, yes, includes sound but goes beyond sound and yet for a moment maybe still ponders the obvious question: Can't they just wait? No, they can't wait! And you know that too, of course, and because they can't, they are double-parked or triple-parked or just stopped, with blinking hazard lights on their cars or rental vans. The vans are inhaling racks of clothes, and the vans are ejecting people, in plain shirts and worn pants. In between them all, like someone dressed for the wrong party, the giant, shiny SUV is polished as it waits, engine on, AC running, until, at last, doors suddenly open and close. And in that brief time, a tiny blast of chilled air escapes, the little island of cool lingering in the hot summer air, a spill.

People are sometimes far apart, sometimes bunched up—on hot summer days, they're seemingly pickled. A thousand people pass a thousand others, as the person delivering a crisp, white envelope manages to avoid smashing into the back of a commuter who stops suddenly to text a friend. A cascade of human dominos is successfully avoided, a small triumph mildly acknowledged as the receptionist who witnesses the miracle reaches out for a pen offered, to sign, and more powerfully, to accept!

*

If you are the street, then you are not concrete and curbs. If you are the street, you are made of who is in you, who is passing by or standing still, visiting or returning. You are their movements, their thoughts, their past and future histories. And today, like every other day, people are mumbling or singing, or asking and listening, or just listening, or listening but ignoring, and ignoring big time, depending on the particulars of the particular asshole, and yes, as is well known, there are so many assholes in particular. You feel everyone as the street, the assholes and the nonassholes; you feel all of them. You don't feel them one by one. You don't feel them in little bits and pieces. You feel everyone all at once, just as, through you, everyone feels everyone else, whether they know it or not.

As the street, time is different for you. You notice time not as time but as the clicks or beeps or invisible lines that define the movement of crowds through you. These are lines that say before and after, and these lines are everywhere, though all are pointless to you as the street, each moment being not only too fine to split but also too infinite. You feel all-time, which is to say you feel the hug at the corner of Thirty-Eighth and Madison that happened fifteen minutes ago when those two old friends recognized each other, and you feel a fall at the corner of Tenth Avenue and Thirtieth Street that happened in the rain about three years back. As with the hug, you felt the fall in the feeling of all, though in the case of the fall, the feeling felt terrifying, a jolt-like feeling the street so often feels.

As you know, being the street, all interaction and, really, all action is contained in the street's time, which is a kind of time that doesn't see streets or cities or states or nations. To keep things simple—even though, from the street's standpoint, things are never simple at all—let's just say that the street is more than vaguely aware of the street itself as a colonizing tool— the street being, on the one hand, an expression of the grid, a grid that's born of a survey, surveys so frequently being attempts to make the land more productive and thus profitable, to exclude and control. And yet the street at some point in the past or in the future or maybe at this moment (to speak briefly of time in non-street terms) might be controlled not by the surveyors who surveyed it, or the gridmakers who gridded it, but by the people who choose to pass through it, and the people who choose not to—those who, each and every day, perform who they are, as beings, in part by being in the street.

Tourists, notably, have other reasons. They are either trying to see the street, or are moving through it to see somewhere else, and, naturally, they are performing their role too, as emphasizers and underliners. In a general way, tourists are our visiting exclamation marks.

*

But the point (in terms of you being the street) is that you retain all the things that have happened or that will happen as people move along, as people move from their homes and back, or out into the world at large, or as they leave the street, never to return. All the things that happened in the street are like scars or muscle memories for you: the collected movements of bodies, bodies moving quietly and separately but never alone, even when they are. You remember people recognizing one another, small epidemics of surprise. You remember people who didn't hide but looked the other way, or looked distracted, or acted as if they had just gotten a seriously important call. Ex-spouses, bad dates, people you never really knew or never liked, or liked a lot. Emotions coursing past emotions, like highly charged electrons.

Emotional currents, psychological tides, flows of apprehensions or happinesses: the street is a sea of moods, affected by lunar cycles and the ocean's tides. At the same time, the street is made of itself, and in fact, the street may not even be there—the street that you see if you are not a street, anyway. Because the street is everything else.

*

But you know this! You are the street! You see, you feel, you understand, and you feel the pleasure, and yes, the pain that somehow, at some point, becomes a kind of balm, as emotions stream through concrete canyons, flow through asphalt avenues. Just as it is for humans, so it is for the street: in experiencing the pain and dislocation of others, we enrich the world, we deepen it and each other. And it is for this reason that we, like the street, open our ears and everything else, if only so we might help a person cross the street, or to the right address, or up when down. When you open your senses wide, you feel that paroxysm of fear on the corner of Twenty-Third Street as the traffic passes too fast. You see the cloudburst of anxiety that appears after flagging down a cab that doesn't stop, that won't be going to the meeting that, alas, can't be, missed at this point, a desperate time. See the couple holding hands, the distant glance of contentment or perhaps discontent—you can feel all variations, all possibilities. When you see all, you savor the strategic practicality of relaxation, the knack for the perfect respite, a standpipe for sitting. And you notice that so many people are dialing us and dialing us. Can't they leave us alone? Notice too that we are dialing everybody back. Have we forgotten what it is to be alone in the street, or anywhere?

You are the street. You are dreams in stream form. You are worry as little racing rivers. You are freshets of hope and little creeks of lunch-hour joy. You are billboarded and advertised on, and your trash overflows, but there is a balm in you or about you, or something along those lines. Only a very few people are singing on the street like angels, and the last few street preachers left still don't quite preach like Paul. But you are the street and you are good for a reasonably priced coffee, good for a chance meeting with somebody you weren't necessarily looking to meet, and in good times and bad, you're good for the soul no matter how you are and no matter how that soul feels.

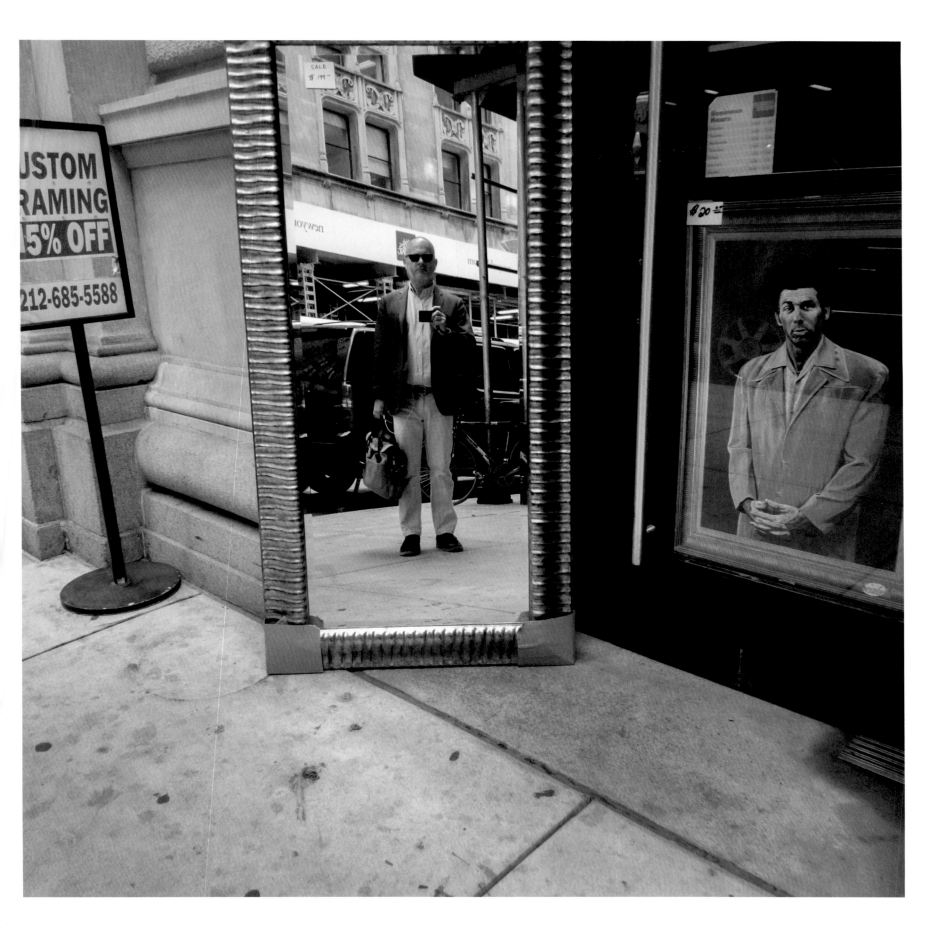

Jeremiah Dine
Daydreams Walking

© Damiani 2019
Photographs © Jeremiah Dine
Current © Robert Sullivan
Frank O'Hara, "Music" from *Lunch Poems*. Copyright © 1964 by Frank O'Hara.,
copyright © 2014 by Maureen O'Hara, Administratrix of the Estate of
Frank O'Hara. Reprinted with the permission of The Permissions Company, LLC,
on behalf of City Lights Books, www.citylights.com.

Edited by Yolanda Cuomo and Jeremiah Dine

BOOK DESIGN BY YOLANDA CUOMO
Associate Designer: Bonnie Briant
Junior Designer: Bobbie Richardson
Files for reproduction: Jonno Rattman
Assistant Designer: Morgan Sloan

Published by Damiani
info@damianieditore.com
www.damianieditore.com

Printed in September 2019 by Grafiche Damiani—Faenza Group SpA, Italy.

ISBN 978-88-6208-697-4

The text of this book is set in Franklin Gothic, designed in 1902 by Morris Fuller
Benton (1872–1948), the chief type designer of American Type Founders.
Gothic was a contemporary term for sans serif. Benton named the font in honor of
the American founding father and noted typesetter Benjamin Franklin.
The book is printed on GardaPat Kiara, 150gsm.